I WAS
INTERRUPTE

Nicholas Ray, 1975. (Photo by Pepe Diniz.)

I WAS INTERRUPTED

NICHOLAS RAY
ON MAKING MOVIES

NICHOLAS RAY

Edited and Introduced by
SUSAN RAY

With a Biographical Outline by
BERNARD EISENSCHITZ

UNIVERSITY OF CALIFORNIA PRESS
Berkeley • Los Angeles • London

University of California Press
Berkeley and Los Angeles, California

University of California Press, Ltd.
London, England

Copyright © 1993 by Susan Ray

First Paperback Printing 1995

Library of Congress Cataloging-in-Publication Data

Ray, Nicholas, 1911–1979
    I was interrupted : Nicholas Ray on making movies / Nicholas Ray ;
edited and introduced by Susan Ray.
        p.   cm.
    Includes bibliographical references and index.
    ISBN 0-520-20169-8
    1. Motion pictures—Production and direction.   I. Ray, Susan.
II. Title.
PN1995.9.P7R37   1993
791.43'023—dc20   92-35003
                                                                 CIP

Printed in the United States of America

1   2   3   4   5   6   7   8   9

The paper used in this publication meets the minimum requirements of
American National Standard for Information Sciences—Permanence of
Paper for Printed Library Materials, ANSI Z39.48-1984 ∞

To Kyozan Joshu, Roshi

. . . [B]eneath *us* the earth is trembling. Where can we place our fulcrum, even assuming that we possess the lever? . . . The thing we all lack is not style, nor the dexterity of finger and bow known as talent . . . Now, what we lack is the intrinsic principle, the soul of the thing, the very idea of the subject . . . Where is the heart, the verve, the sap?

—Gustave Flaubert
to Louis Bouilhet,
February 6, 1850

What is important to a human? To know who or why he is, or not to know, not to be aware. I know who I am. I am the best damn filmmaker in the world, who has never made one entirely good, entirely satisfactory film. Film is a woman you can't turn off and on, except film is a woman, except one day she's gone.

—Nicholas Ray

Only in eras when the world of the spirit is on the decline is teaching, even on its highest level, regarded as a profession. In epochs of flowering, disciples live with their master just as apprentices in a trade lived with theirs, and "learn" by being in his presence, learn many things for their work and their life both because he wills it, or without any willing on his part.

—Martin Buber,
*Tales of the Hasidim:
Early Masters*

CONTENTS

ACKNOWLEDGMENTS

For over a decade Bernard Eisenschitz maintained a belief in the worth of this book and in my capacity to complete it. His wisdom, clarity, love for cinema, and plain goodness guided me at every step of the work.

Jonathan Rosenbaum, generous friend and knower of words and movies, helped me resolve countless questions and doubts.

I owe much to the devoted and painstaking work of James Leahy, whose interviews with Nick were a rich source for this book.

I thank Bill Krohn, Jos Oliver, Gerry Bamman, and Harry Bromley-Davenport for their informed and encouraging interest; my editor, Ed Dimendberg, for his integrity and good faith; Karen Hicinbothem, who tended the manuscript like a mother; Robert Seidenberg, who game me excellent and unstinting counsel; and Arnold Lieber and Elizabeth White, who gave me sanctuary.

I thank Phyllis Stewart, Marilyn Hauser, Sara Miot, Helen Turnbull, Corine de Royer, Leslie Levinson, Rabia Heineman, Diane Cox, Donna Cox, Sheri Nelson, Ellen Nieves, Claudia Handler, Emmanuel, Chet, Ruth and Liam Nelson, John and Caroline Simon, and Andrew Schwartz, who give me heart.

And last, first, and always, I offer loving thanks to my parents, Max and Rosaline Schwartz, who gave me this most interesting lifetime.

S.R.

THE AUTOBIOGRAPHY OF NICHOLAS RAY

Susan Ray

After a screening of *Parallax View* at the 1974 San Sebastian Film Festival I recall Alan Pakula, the film's director, shook Nick's hand, gave a bow of the head, and uttered the word "Maitre." It was a courtly gesture that left Nick both touched and flustered. As witness to such a rich moment I posed to myself some questions: What is a master and what makes Nick one? And what does this mastery of his mean to me?

Mastery to my early mind meant a kind of perfection, a control over craft and circumstance. It was a quality in a work or a life, it seemed to me, that one could not miss or mistake for any other, that would show itself in an orderliness or a harmony and a powerful calm. I found Nick's films unmistakable, but not for their order or calm. As for Nick himself, he was at that time despairing in alcoholic disease and waging battle to support the completion of *We Can't Go Home Again*, not to mention his basic survival. Both his life and work were out of control. I wondered if Mr. Pakula had been too kind or perhaps he had made an error in judgment. Still I held my questions in mind and have continued to do so for years, particularly while working with the materials from which this book has been made.

In September 1969 I took a train west from Connecticut, where I grew up, to enroll at the University of Chicago. I wanted to go to Chicago to study because it was in the heartland, whatever that was, and because the school claimed to care less about teaching right answers than how to ask questions. I also had heard it had the highest student dropout and suicide rates in the country.

I was a curious girl who wanted to know what made things what they were, but I had not learned much by knowing right answers. I could not find the key to my mind, while behind its locked doors stirred vague inklings and the fiercest hunger to contact the world and cut loose from whatever was binding. Pressure was building. I wanted experience, fast. Confused as I was I feared the dense thought forms at school might be just more fog in my way, so before I arrived I was planning to leave, though I had no idea where to go.

Except I did like the idea of a teacher—a private tutor, perhaps, or someone to whom I could apprentice. In what? I could not admit that the skill I wanted to learn was living, so for lack of a better idea I called it writing. And whom did I have in mind to instruct me? To tell you the truth, Norman Mailer. Norman Mailer knew how to write, he often cut loose, and the clincher was he could act. I had not met Norman Mailer, had no plan to meet him, so I kept this idea to myself and signed up for a year at school.

Two months later in a gust of cold wind and the clear morning light I met Nick. We were introduced by Bill Kunstler, attorney for the Chicago 7, at a crosswalk near the Federal Building where we were all headed for the trial. I had seen Nick before in the courtroom press box or stalking the hallways, always with young people around him. He was hard to miss, for his auric field spread out to the walls and crackled with high-voltage charge. Tall and white-maned, the coolest of cats, he came and went as he pleased. Nick, Kunstler told me, was making a movie about the trial and I, he told Nick, was a student at the trial to do research. It was the month of my eighteenth birthday, three months after Nick's fifty-eighth.

"Is that what you do, make movies?" I asked him.

He nodded it was, and held out a cigarette—

"What movies?"—which I took.

He listed some titles, all unknown to me. His movies, I figured, were not very good.

But the man himself looked noble—that was the word I used to myself—like a king who had lost his kingdom or Odysseus after the wars. I was studying myth so archetypes ran loose in my mind, but I did not presume any heroes would have time for me nor did I expect to meet up with this one again. On the other hand, in his gaze, an arctic blue seascape, there was so much room for movement I could have turned cartwheels right down the icy sidewalk I was so grateful. Instead I skipped once to sync my right step with his and on the next beat he skipped back.

The trial went on for another two months and I kept cutting classes to get to the courtroom to watch it. It was the best show in town from several points-of-view, but most compelling to me was the play of three generations of Jews—judge, defense lawyers, and several defendants—turned one against another, each crying betrayal. Although the cause of conflict was clear and in more than one sense familiar to me, the conflict's outcome was not. It was not a casual matter to me to know which generation if any would win.

As the time came for attorneys to present closing arguments, the country's first-string reporters flew into town and I had to surrender my seat in the pressbox. That I would not witness the trial's resolution was a defeat in itself and it left something dangerously dangling in me. I went back to campus a stranger to student life and far behind in my classes, having never really begun them. I did not know what to do with myself.

While the jury was out a reporter I barely knew from the trial sent a cab to my dorm one morning to take me to Nick's house on Orchard Street, I still don't know why. But I got in the car and, as a good story goes, drove over to a new world.

Nick's place was all movement, a dense buzz of people with jobs to do. The living room was the work room with couch, projector, and amassed on the floor, orderly piles of batteries, recorders, cases, lamps, gels, spools, reels, and tins around which feet stepped and heads met to talk. Eyeing the scene with the majesty of a sunning reptile, a black camera poised on a tripod. And groggy but perfectly easy in eyepatch and leopard-spotted bikini, there was Nick. He prowled through the room, mumbling directions through a French cigarette hanging out the side of his mouth. I could not hear the words, but his voice rumbled up from some startling depth like the purr from the belly of a great cat.

Yes it was a wonderful jungle, teeming with exotic life. How would I get myself into this life? Well here one just dove. So I gathered some dirty dishes and carted them off to the kitchen. Soon Nick came in to chat while I washed. He said he would be taking a crew out that afternoon. Would I stay to answer the phones? Yes I would be happy to do that.

When he got back that evening he stacked some court transcript before me and asked me to edit it into a film script. I told him I had not seen a film script before. He told me I would figure it out but offered a hint, like a trick to opening the cap on a jar: I should look for events that advanced the action. Some hours later, as I headed out for a cab, Nick came to the door, folded some cash in my hand, and said, "Here's a week's pay and cab fare. Be back tomorrow at ten."

Once I went to a carnival later on its last night in town. The carnival people had to pack up the works between midnight and four in the morning. I had fallen in love with the ferris wheel, an enormous elegant structure shaped like an infinity sign and built from no more than truck tires, colored lights, ropes, and crude metal bars. All those parts went to bed in a small pickup truck. I watched the wheel's dismantling piece by piece. Under lights strung on trees and telephone poles it looked to be the most gorgeous, perfectly choreographed ballet in the world. Each worker knew just where he had to be when, and how every piece had to fit in the truck. Each had the strength of a weight lifter, the dexterity of a juggler, the balance of a high-wire dancer, and enough true grace that when one man slipped off a bar at a height of some twenty feet, before I could gasp, before he hit ground, there were two men below to catch him. A detail about carnival folk to which I gave little thought at the time: they all carried switchblades in their back pockets.

The people on Nick's film crew were just like that, high-tech carnies except for the knives. They all had the same goal, they worked for the show, so they helped one another, they helped me. Every day was different. Every day demanded a range of skills I had not thought of using before and my skills were useful to others. The day did not stop at darkness but took on more life under lights. There was no fixed schedule, activities just gathered focus and happened. The crew was together from morning until after midnight. We shared meals. The work and our lives became one. We were a family. It seemed to me there were no limits to what such a family could do.

Of course, heading this family and stretching the vistas before me was Nick. If I learned in time how he used Frank Lloyd Wright's inclination for horizontals to expand the frames of his pictures, I experienced that expansion in Nick the first time I met him. In him it was a cellular thing and profoundly hopeful. In such generous space whoever, whatever, however I was at a given moment was fine. In such generous space I felt I could dissolve the knot of myself, let my nature relax, and finally join up with the world.

At the end of the day when his workers, most of them half his age, could barely keep themselves upright, Nick was still going strong and seemed able to do almost every job at least as well if not better than those he had hired to do them. (Of course his techniques were of a peculiar order. To this day I am not convinced he ever learned the mechanics of a camera, but he would kick the damn thing, put his half-blind good eye to the lens, and always get his shot.) He moved from building the set, to writing the script, to shooting a demonstration, to negotiating with lawyers, to discussing the latest government scam, to mending a broken projector, to musing on what would be nice for dinner, to screening dailies, to soothing a ruffled assistant, to viewing the new play in town, and then back to work on the script, all in the span of a day and with full attention and care. But stamina, skill, and concentration were minimal requisites for a director, or so I assumed at the time.

Other ways of Nick's were odd to find in someone accustomed to Hollywood gloss. His place looked like a student's apartment: dissheveled mattress on the floor, bare lightbulbs, an array of cups, ashtrays, magazines, books, and papers spread among film equipment. Nick had chosen a crew of young people, myself among them, many of whom were unknown and unproven, and he spoke to us with respect, curiosity about what he might learn, and the expectation that we would find a way to do whatever he might have to ask.

After only one day at Orchard Street the decision was easy: at the end of the term I would quit school and join the adventure, whatever it was. Whatever it was, it was what I had been waiting for.

Nick was not one for cosmetic disguise to his person, history, or habits so I held no illusions, I knew early on that he was monstrous. One day he aimed an explosive and public display of bad temper at a devoted young man who turned out to be his son Tim. (The outburst was not caused by any lack of affection from either but by Tim in some way having shown disrespect for the celluloid strip, or so Nick insisted.) Nick never opened his mail, seemed not to have to pay bills; he just pitched the unopened letters my way to get rid of. He drank wine for breakfast, "a source of vitamin C" he told me. And then there were the medicaments, a briefcase full that went with him everywhere: needles, ampules of methedrine and B-complex, mysterious pills, bags of grass, blocks of hash, and fresh patches for the right eye whose vision he had lost to a bloodclot. When the moment was right, no matter where he was or with whom, he would drop his trousers to shoot himself in the hip with a mixture extracted from the little glass bottles. He needed this to keep himself going for his doctors had given him only one year to live—he told me this every year of the almost ten that I knew him. His body was built to live to 100 but he had worn it out. He further explained: "The attrition has been tremendous."

I did not know this word *attrition*. I looked it up: "attrition: 1. sorrow for one's own sins that arises from a motive considered lower than that of the love of God; 2. . . . the condition of being worn down or ground down by friction."[1]

That sounded romantic, but to my observation there was nothing at all ground down about Nick. No matter what he put in his system his energy did not quit.

But the money did, overnight. With a shift in political winds the investors in the Chicago film withdrew. Overnight the carnival packed up and left town and the Orchard Street place closed down.

The moment was telling: a life in moving pictures could be cruel, there were knives, and attrition was the word after all. Film families were just as unstable as others and on the other side of bright lights lay shadows equally dark. It was my first intimation that I could not live beyond my own means, of whatever kind. If I had had an idea that in the effusion of his creative juices Nick could slide me past the stoppage of my own, I was in for some jolts. But there were many facets to this understanding that would take me a while to grasp.

As for Nick he kept splashing the paint but his palette got darker. I knew nothing yet of Nick's history and not much about the weight of dismay on the heart when an old well-known ghost starts clanking its chains and slamming doors in one's face. Still, not much was enough so I knew whether he said so or not to Nick the film's shutdown was such a ghost. A great will arose in me to lay the ghost down to its final rest, for myself as much as for Nick. To do so became my purpose. Since purpose was new to my life and most gratefully welcome I did not examine its rightness or roots.

Nick continued to gather numbers of people around him but now only a few stayed to work. Of course I stayed on, I had no thought of doing anything else. Why did I stay?

He had a tender touch for small creatures. He laughed at my jokes. We were dropouts from the same school. He knew how to have adventures. As the Zen master's wife once said about her husband, "Compared to him all the others are fools." If I had once thought he could help solve my problems I now thought we had the same problems, but his were bigger and better, so I would help him with his and mine would get solved in the bargain. He was always interesting to me. I felt at home with him.

---

1. *Webster's Third New International Dictionary* (Massachusetts: G. & C. Merriam Company, 1966), p. 142.

And why did he want me with him? I was new. He needed someone to pick up after him. We had the same problems. I told him his jokes were lousy. I was so lost I had to be looking and above all he honored the search. I caught his drift. He liked my twists. He felt at home with me. I would not go away.

Soon we dropped all politeness between us for a mode of exchange better suited to both our natures. It was harmony based on dissonance or as one observer described it: "You like each other, you understand each other, but you can't speak a civil word to each other." Others took our back-and-forth for a new form of burlesque entertainment. I can see now it must have been droll how Nick coolly poked his way through my sore spots to turn me into a foaming savage, although at the time I did not always catch the punch line.

In retrospect I believe Nick got jealous sometimes, as people can do when they feel themselves aging and faced with someone looking all promise without final loss or failure. I got jealous too, of his commitment, power, and achievement, so I did not see what he had to be irked about, but whatever it was it could make him mean. "Don't enter into battle with inferior weapons," he would taunt any challenge from me, no matter how worthy. I knew my weapons would not hold up, he did not have to tell me, and nothing made me madder than that. But then no one had ever let me cut loose with my rage before and cutting loose in some form was what I was after.

Finally I went with a friend to see one of Nick's movies. When his name flashed onscreen I jabbed my friend in the ribs, but after the first fifteen minutes of story I was slipping down the back of my chair toward the exit. I told Nick frankly I had not been impressed. "Which film did you see?" he wanted to know. *Born To Be Bad.* "It sure was," he giggled.

In April 1970 I joined Nick in New York where he had gone to find backing for the Chicago film. By day we worked in the cutting room preparing presentations or looked at paintings and visited his old friends. At night we went to dinner and theatre. Prospects for the film were poor. Nick was low on cash and wanted to get back to Europe, to the island of Sylt in the North Sea where he had a house and was planning to build a sound stage from driftwood. There I could write, he told me, and work as his apprentice on the films he would shoot on the sound stage. No plan ever had sounded so perfect. I could taste the salt air.

First we planned to fly back to Chicago, but the airlines were striking so we took coach seats on the train. Traveling cross-country with

Nick I felt like a pioneer woman, the frontier stretched before me so vast and near. By the time we arrived at Union Station, sooty and having spent the night at gin rummy, I had learned not to play to an inside straight and it seemed the best thing that we should go on together.

■　■　■

By summer we were settled in New York. Nick deposited me at the apartment of his old friend Alan Lomax.[2] Sometimes he stayed with me at Alan's and sometimes he stayed with Connie Bessie,[3] another old friend, depending on who at the time was less irksome.

Back in New York after ten years away Nick picked up the threads of the life he had lived decades before during the Depression and Second World War. He revived old friendships with Alan and Connie and with Jean Evans, John Houseman, Gadge Kazan, Les Farber,[4] Max Gordon,[5] Will Lee,[6] and Perry Bruskin.[7] With them he was a rough kid, a scapegrace, indulged, prodigious, awkward; but he seemed to me purer that way and gladdened to find his old friends and be seen once again through their eyes. I guessed that the Depression years had been good years for him and he said that was true. Without money people had to help each other and work together, so invention had flowed and values had stayed simple and clear.

Mostly Nick did not like his generation. He thought them betrayers whose acts of betrayal were in his words "like asking your kid to jump into your arms and then pulling your arms away." He was more at ease with my generation, while I was not, and he seemed to know more about them than I did.

That summer he hung out on the streets and like any cat he did his stalking at night. From an office he had been loaned in the Palace Theatre—where Lauren Bacall, widow of one of the men he had most loved, was then starring—he would look out at Times Square and

---

2. Ethnologist and Nick's colleague with whom he collected folksongs for the Library of Congress and produced the CBS radio show of the early forties, "Back Where I Come From."
3. Née Connie Ernst, whom Nick had met while working at the Office of War Information in the forties, and to whom he was briefly engaged.
4. Psychiatrist and author of *The Ways of the Will*, to which Nick refers in his classes.
5. Owner of the Village Vanguard, a center for the New York jazz scene for decades. Max's was the first face Nick saw that he knew when he first came back to town.
6. Who worked with Nick in the Theatre of Action.
7. Also from the Theatre of Action.

wait for the limos to leave and the marquee to go dark. Then he would emerge with the night shades—pimps in zippered zoot suits, whores in pastel boas—as they barreled down Broadway in long white T-birds or strutted the sidewalks, radios at full blast. Nick roamed among them monitoring their moods and comings and goings, trading insults with winos, drinking at local bars, playing cribbage, pool, poker, and endless rounds of bingo at Fascination on 48th Street. (The doors to Fascination were lit like a pinball machine. When I went through them the caller would greet me over his mike, "You looking for Wiley Post?"[8] and point the way to Nick's station. Known or unknown, Nick was never unnoticed.)

The whole Broadway scene absorbed him—its dance, colors, language, con men, and crooks, and the ferociousness of what he saw as "the fight for the watering hole." He began to write a screenplay, *New York After Midnight*, about a man called Eyepatch who returns to New York and Broadway to encounter loose ends from his past among present more savage despairs.

As Nick came and went I wondered why the man would not take for himself those most basic instinctual comforts any animal needs for refreshment: he would not sleep, he would not come in from the cold or the heat or whatever the element of the season, and if someone did not spread a meal before him he'd get by on white wine, tobacco, beer, gin, Mars bars, and those high-octane injections. This behavior I called perverse. It went against nature and enforced my impression that Nick's house was haunted and he was the ghost. He seemed to believe that if he did surrender to sleep, sleep would seduce him and keep him from ever finding his way back to waking. So he more or less ceaselessly roamed, dragging behind him his noiseless invisible chains. Just as a specter floats through walls so Nick seemed to move from night into day into night, from outside to inside, between sleep and waking, between death and life, defying, ignoring, dissolving lines drawn between oppositions.

I did not go on these jaunts even when asked (I needed sleep, I needed to find a job) but waited until he had worn out his companions and even his body refused to go further, when finally at dawn he would come home to refuel. After a meal he would collapse into sleep until noon, when he would want to be roused for a meeting.

His waking was a dreadful event and not just for him. It would

---

8. A craggy character played by John Wayne wearing an eyepatch.

begin with deep moans, a blind reach for tobacco which knocked bedside things to the floor, the strike of a lighter, a lengthy inhale, then hacking coughs and more moans. Then shielding his eyes against light he would mumble "Feet." Nick's feet, I knew because he had warned me, would not support him through the day unless they were rubbed. Once this was done he might sit upright.

And so he would, on the side of the bed leaning elbows on knees, head hanging, with a cigarette in his mouth. Like a stone he would sit for a very long time in silence unbroken except for the sound of his ashes falling to ground. As I had not yet begun to explore silence on my own I found his dense weighty kind hard to take, but I tried to just let it be. Then my first approach was always gentle, cajoling: "What's bothering you?" I'd ask. The silence sank in response. "It couldn't be that bad, could it?" Well it could, it was far too bad to discuss. "Say something, would you?" He'd just draw in smoke, pull the cigarette from his lips—"Nicholas, you're going to be late"—and exhale. "Nick!"

Finally he would turn my way and we'd enter a new and more verbal stage of negotiation. I could usually catch "attrition," "betrayal," or "sonofabitch" in the mumbled part of a sentence he'd offer. I would sit by his side and wait for the rest, but I had no patience for vacuums so I filled up the air with pep talk: this would be a really good day, he had so much to offer, so many loved him, his fortunes were about to improve— Cutting into my sentence at last he'd finish his (the first part of which I'd by then forgotten) and slowly rise to his feet. I describe this routine in such detail because in the almost ten years I woke up with Nick he did nothing else more predictably.[9]

One morning that summer looking up from his feet Nick told me while making *55 Days to Peking* he'd had a nightmare and that when he woke up from the nightmare he knew he would not complete another film in this lifetime.

■ ■ ■

Seasons changed and Nick spread himself like a vast organism over the town: he was at Warhol's Factory and the Electric Circus, Village bars and the Vanguard, Max's Kansas City, off-Broadway theatre, Times Square, East Side embassies and salons, and the hidden lofts of eccentrics dealing in mind expansion. He wanted to know what

9. Apparently such behavior is not uncommon. See Françoise Gilot's *Life With Picasso* (New York: Bantam Doubleday Dell Publishing Group, Inc., pp. 154–156.

was going on but his role was not the observer's; whatever the scene he had to take part and his part could not be small. He made himself at home everywhere (except in some old-blooded circles where he became a rough kid again or assumed British tones which were met with mild disdain). Everywhere there were those who were ready to join him and stay on for life. They gave him their talismans, cash, and time, but when the tide turned many found themselves beached while Nick passed by on a wave. No matter how short-lived the contact had been the ones left behind seemed to grieve it.

Nick wanted a chance for his film—if not the Chicago film then any film that could stir him—and a chance for a film always means money. There were many young and old writers eager to have Nick Ray help develop their screenplays, so on the condition that he would direct he helped them. They gave him meals and get-around money until the projects aborted.

In winter 1970 Nick met Bob Glaudini, Terry Ork, and Sam Shepard, all at work on Sam's *Cowboy Mouth*. Nick sat in and advised at rehearsals. He also sowed seeds for a book about leftist theatre[10] and had his hand in a half-dozen other creative ventures at any one time. (He was always a wellspring of juicy ideas, the fullest, most generous I've encountered to date without exception.)

Meanwhile I set about seeing his pictures. Where I grew up film was still considered a bastard art to enjoy but not recognize. I loved to go to the movies but was no cinephile. Apart from what I'd absorbed in a year with Nick I knew nothing of cinema technique or history. I had no trust in public opinion so all the good things I'd heard about Nick Ray's films meant less than nothing to me. Still I wanted to know what the films would tell me about the man who had made them.

Nick's movies were far too disturbing to be entertaining. They offered no peaceful place. They made me work and I found myself not always eager to see them. Sitting through *Johnny Guitar* from beginning to end I took barely a breath, the tension was relentless. Seeing *Hot Blood* I thanked my stars I'd met Nick only after his engine had run down a bit. Watching *Bigger Than Life* I recalled having seen it years before on TV one lonely weekend, and having been sick at the sight of madness so close to home yet unable to turn it off as it ran on the screen and later in my mind. Sharing with Nick my memory of that time I told him, "This is your story before you lived it." But

---

10. Jay Williams (*Stage Left*, New York: Scribner, 1974).

each film was his story, nakedly so, and each story was different, so I had to marvel at the scope of his life and his willingness to let others see it (I did not at the time think it courage).

I did not want to like *Rebel Without a Cause*—everyone liked *Rebel*, almost a contradiction in terms—but how had Nick known about the claustrophobia of suburban life and what it was like for someone like me growing up? And what was all the fuss about Dean when Dean was so clearly—to me anyway—aping Nick?

How did Nick know about the acid women can hold and sometimes explode with, as does Emma in *Johnny Guitar*? Or about how the air seems to knit itself between two people in love, like Charisse and Taylor in *Party Girl* or Mitchum and Hayward in *Lusty Men*? How had he learned his respect for simple everyday people, for their troubles, dreams, heart, and reflections, while living his complex uncommon life? Whatever it was I expected Nick pushed beyond expectation, tilted, took up or down half a pitch, not for the sake of risk or contortion or in defiance of truth but because expectation can be a thick skin and Nick's truth was raw and skinless. If *Bigger Than Life* was his story, *Savage Innocents* was his soul—the title said it all.

One early morning we watched *They Live By Night* on TV. Bowie looked to me like pictures I'd seen of Nick when he was young and I said so. Nick nodded and rambled on for a while about the first shot ever made from a helicopter, but by the end of the film he was weeping.

That Nick knew more than I had ever imagined did not surprise me, but until seeing his films I had not known how much he felt. For me then, so young and unable to support my own nature, it was simply too much to bear. But the films, I had to admit, were not so bad after all.

We both were at loose although opposite ends. He at least knew his calling and had a wealth of people to see things to do on his nightly jaunts, while I was too unsure of myself to look for my own friends and occupations and was not about to trail in his shadow. One day I drew a faceless self-portrait. Nick wrote on the page: "She is already who she wants to become." Who was that? I longed for but did not know her so it was a deep and warm comfort to have her so coaxed to light.

I could not, however, count on comfort from Nick.

I read Norman Mailer's essay "The Prisoner of Sex" in *Harper's*[11]

---

11. Norman Mailer, "The Prisoner of Sex." *Harper*, March 1971, vol. 242, pp. 41–46.

and passed the magazine meaningfully to Nick. Here was a teacher, I let him know, and maybe if Nick ran into Norman he'd tell him about me? Next morning Nick gave back the magazine, but the essay in question had vanished beneath the collage of cutouts, tape, and commentary he had built over it in the night. When it came to finding Norman I was on my own.

Another morning some time before dawn Nick shook me from sleep to say he'd brought some people for me to meet. I came out from the bedroom sour as a lemon, but when I set eyes on the couple I was not sure I had waked up yet. Before me stood a red-haired Merlin and the goddess Kali in hotpants. I took the woman off to a corner, for I wanted to know why at four in the morning she had come to my house. She put up with my questions and then caught me straight in the eyes: "Don't you see, he wants you to have a friend." Nick had found this woman at a Grateful Dead concert in a full crowd on closing night at the Filmore. (She and I are still close and, as it turns out, are related by blood through our mothers.)

At the same show Nick bumped into Dennis Hopper, who before long offered to fly him down to his ranch in Taos, New Mexico. I was to settle things at my job and then follow.

Nick was unemployed, about to turn sixty, and methamphetamine had just been made illegal. It was a good time for him to get out of town. In Taos Dennis provided shelter, food, drink, entertainment, new faces, wide vistas, guns, horses: a deluxe outlaw's den where Nick could rage freely. When he met me at the airport I could see right away that he'd gotten wilder, gone over an edge he'd held back from before. He was acting a caricature of himself, a limping one-eyed satyr, and for the first time he seemed to think himself old.

He had grown a beard and a surplus of paranoia and had taken to wearing a gun in a holster. I did not like the beard and thought the holster was asking for it given the state of his judgment and eyesight. So he shaved the beard and shot a rattlesnake in a stone wall. There are those who witnessed the shooting and Nick pulling a snakeskin (we never did find the body) from the rocks who claimed the skin was a plant, but either way he had made his point.

When he wasn't at target practice or out god knows where with the boys he tinkered with his script *Mister Mister*, a western about kids who seize control of the town from their parents. He also sat in while Dennis cut *The Last Movie*, a film he liked very much. A salesman came out to the ranch to demonstrate his new products, video-cassettes and a machine on which they could be played in the home, and Nick observed: "In ten years people will have stopped going out to the movies."

Nick was withdrawing from speed, if from nothing else, and at night he suffered terribly, requiring non-stop vigilant care to his feet. One night between moans he asked me to marry him. Since by then I knew I would be with him at least until one of us died I told him we could consider it done. Nick gave me his ring, I gave him a pearl, he went back to moaning, I went back to rubbing his feet. Next day he was up and out and kicking up dust as before while I caught up on my sleep.

The visit to Taos offered daily adventures, great beauty and space—I had not seen tumbleweed or the Rio Grande before—but Nick was knocking around among too many rocky unknowns. He was caught in a change and I had to wonder if he would ever get loose.

■ ■ ■

Nick's history has been well told already;[12] it is enough to say here that in early 1971 he accepted a job to begin teaching film that fall at Harpur College, State University of New York at Binghamton. Nick moved there in late summer. I planned to work four days a week at my job in New York and join Nick upstate for long weekends.

Binghamton was a valley town with dense and damp air that could weigh on one's mind, even if nothing else did. Still Nick went to work perky and full of plans. He bought himself a white truck and red jacket, commandeered some equipment, applied for a government grant, and outlined the structure for his class. The students would rotate jobs—from acting to camera, lights, script, props, and wardrobe—to study the problems of craft, technique, and how to work as a group. They would learn movie making by making a movie. But what was the movie about?

I suggested as subject Nick's ghost, the "premonition" of a decade before that Nick would not finish another film. By addressing the ghost Nick would chase it away, or so I believed and argued. Nick began writing a script called *The Gun Under My Pillow*. One night as he wrote an ambulance drove by our rooms to the infirmary nearby. A body—we never found out whose or its condition—was wheeled out of the truck on a stretcher. Nick threw out his first few pages and began again with the approach of a siren and red flashing lights.

---

12. See the biography by Bernard Eisenschitz, *Roman Americain: Les Vies de Nicholas Ray* (Paris: Christian Bourgois Eidteur 1990), published in English as *Nicholas Ray: An American Life*, Trans. Tom Milne (Wincester, Mass.: Faber and Faber, 1993).

For their first assignment Nick sent his class scurrying off to find film, props, and equipment to start shooting that night in the infirmary driveway. As was his way Nick dove right in and took everyone with him. So as not to disrupt other classes and with an outlaw's preference for darkness he called his class for nightfall. Night after night they shot until dawn fueled on wine and illicit white powders. Secrets were shared, loves and hates erupted to be soothed or abandoned, and everyone got very well acquainted.

Nick observed that an era of social action and conscience was over, young people were pulling back into themselves to "do their own thing." The students brought him their stories and the stories were always about what Nick called "the search for self-image." Soon the stories began overlapping and, as told to a movie director "long discontent with life in the capitol of the dream merchants" but concerned with the nature of image and self, they became the fabric of the film called *We Can't Go Home Again.*

Although he was never not introspective Nick too became more withdrawn, like a Chinese sage who after achieving enough in the world takes up the life of a hermit surrendered to nature and the paradox of his own spirit. Only in Nick's case, again, the transition was not smooth.

I could only watch. Somehow I had slipped from my role as apprentice, king's jester, and sidekick, for which I had felt very well suited, to that of gofer, shrew, and occasional solace, for which I held no respect at all. I still had no focus; this was my greatest problem. There were excuses: Nick was so big and close all else was blocked from the view of my lens; and the great man's wife no matter who she may be is rarely seen in full light except as ornament, obstruction, or big mistake. Still I was stuck, and railed with envy as Nick nursed and prodded his students—who were, after all, my own age—into a film crew and family. He gave them his time, fretted for who they were in themselves, drew out their poisons and poems, and expected I would work things out on my own while tending his papers, ideas, budget, and feet. Which I did, but not always sweetly. At least I held onto my job in the City and kept my visits short.

And the cameras kept rolling. In the two years of his contract at Harpur Nick shot most of a feature film. He also antagonized most of his colleagues and the school's entire administration. This was no surprise: they were inclined to make or maintain rules and Nick was not. "In the land of the blind the one-eyed man is king," he explained. He was sure they were sabotaging his project—I can only guess what they thought he was doing—and his suspicions may not have been so far-fetched. But then I never saw him get along nicely with any authority, not without muttering under his breath minimum.

In 1973 we took an early incomplete version of *We Can't Go Home Again* to the Cannes Festival, where it received a standing ovation. A number of people offered Nick money to complete the work, but the amounts were not enough or the backers wanted too much control. After a brief stay in Amsterdam Nick took the film back to the West Coast for lab refinements, but much of the workprint got lost or damaged in transit and then, according to Nick, the people who were supposed to be helping kept screwing up. When it came to this film things went wrong with uncanny consistency. More than once Nick called in the deep of the night to announce, "I'm throwing the whole goddam thing in the ocean."

For the next two years while I stayed in New York Nick flew back and forth between east and west coasts carting boxes of work print. His stated purpose was to scare up backers so he could finish the film or find some other film to work on. But nothing was working and again I had to wonder. Several editors lamented to me that they would cut a sequence just as Nick had directed and the sequence would look fine, but next day they would find it had been pulled apart in the night. Was this Penelope at the loom? Francis Coppola offered Nick an editing room but then took it back because Nick and his crew kept tripping the Zoetrope burglary alarms on their nights out to the wild side. Nick wore out all his hosts. Reports of his outrages came to me from all over as he cut a wide trail through new friends and old. Those who had scolded me for my bad tempers with him began to call in spent voices to say: "He really is monstrous."

I could have taken some satisfaction in having said so all along or delighted at the range of his exploits—so original, so funny, so perfectly played—but Nick was sinking fast. He no longer could drink without becoming a falling-down drunk. Each time he came east he looked more wracked and fragile. He kept trying to stop the drugs and booze but could not. I would get him to doctors, feed him, and put him to bed but he would not let himself rest. His despair grew denser and denser, like a black hole sucking everything in.

Then just as it seemed he was down for the count he was up again and covering ground like a fire. He went back to work on *We Can't Go Home Again* and made notes for an autobiography. He filmed a country music festival in Turlingua, Texas, spoke at schools, and flew to Spain to head the jury at the Film Festival at San Sebastian—where his translator would not translate his apparently demented speech and Pakula called him master.

Around this time he also wrote me this letter:

[*San Francisco, 1973*]

    FROM: Nicholas Ray
        TO: Ms. Schwartz
            217 East 12th Street
            Manhattan
SUBJECT: Biography of Nicholas Ray

It has seemed to me that ever since the subject of my biography or "autobiography" has become a factor in some of our discussions that you would be the only person of my acquaintance who would be capable, talented and humorous enough to write such a work, unworthy as it may be. . . . But if you are to do it, it should be soon. Externally I am still able to laugh at me and conciliate myself with rage; internally, only you, and on rare occasions, Tim, can make my belly roll, my tears appear and the nakedness of my thoughts become expressable, whether or not they would be comprehensible. . . . Who else knows more about my absurdities than you? Perhaps all people I've encountered have seen the fragments—no one else the entirety. . . .

Right away and in a cooperative spirit I contrived an outline and began to gather some notes. But I had no idea how a life wove itself nor interest in telling a factual history, even if it were Nick's. The job was too big for me; I had trouble enough with the man himself. So I filed his letter away with my notes and watched Nick turn orange with yet one more frustration. The task had been set, however, and if I did not understand it I also could not forget it.

■ ■ ■

In the spring of 1976 in New York Nick began work on a film called *Murphy's Law* about a New York City hooker and storefront lawyer, both down on their luck and lonesome. The project's producer found Nick a fine office and studio space and asked me to join the production staff. The budget once raised would allow for professional actors, equipment, and salaries all around. The word was out about Nick Ray's new film. Rip Torn and, of special interest to me, Norman Mailer[13] were going to take part. Only the major monies were still

---

13. My long awaited meeting with Norman took place at a midsummer costume party. We had been introduced already at the film office, where he had shaken my hand and moved on. Upon eyeing me in my costume, however (I came as a fool and he wore the dark velvet robes of a medieval scholar), he told me I had surprised him and invited me to a "dialogue." I could barely speak for spasms of shyness, so said something rude and skittered away to find Nick, who came as a white knight.

outstanding. With the tax shelter laws then in effect we were sure we
would have what we needed.

With some change in his pocket Nick easily found all the herbs,
liquids, and powders he claimed he wanted to quit and he went for
them all; but he stayed on the job rewriting the script in three days,
scouting locations, talking with actors, abounding with visions and
plans.

In the course of things the blonde who was to play the lead confided
to Nick that she only looked good in blue. Blue, he told me, could
cause trouble on film as even a tiny Delft teacup would tend to bleed
through the frame. He nursed this dilemma until at lunch with the
costume designer he awoke from a doze over his soup and announced,
"We'll shoot the whole thing in blue and call it *City Blues.*" A simple
solution, but to find it he had had to embrace a breadth of given
conditions, from the sorrowful moan of the City that summer to the
ache in the story's hero to his star's demands for her wardrobe. It
struck me then that the man's thoughts did not follow in lines but
exploded in spheres, whole worlds at a time, and that his technique
of multiple image was not cinematic invention but really the way
that he saw things and some form of the way things were meant to
be seen.

I also observed that beneath Nick's acceptance of so many givens
and his willingness to allow their essential connections to bubble
up and find their own unity, there had to be faith. This man who
manipulated so boldly, told preposterous lies, and suffered and suffered had the deepest respect for earthy, raw, foolish life as it was.

The first day of shooting on *City Blues* was postponed and postponed again. We still had no deal and then the tax shelter laws were
repealed. Every night I told Nick, "I still think it will happen all
right"; then asked him, "Do you?" The producer kept proffering
promises but summer was nearly over and Nick shook his head:
"There's a familiar stink in the air." We had no money nor home and
were living off the kindness of strangers. Nick drank day and night.
Victor Perkins,[14] in town for a week, nursed Nick through the first
draft of a script for a horror film. But the horror was not just on paper
and finally I had to leave.

A week later, in September 1976, after falling down a flight of stairs,
Nick checked into the detox unit at Roosevelt Hospital.

---

14. British film critic.

I went there to see him. A social worker pulled me aside. She said, "You know he's very sick."

I told her I knew that. I told her he had been very unhappy for a very long time and that was why he drank and took drugs.

She said, "If he doesn't quit the drugs and booze now he'll either die or turn into a vegetable, guaranteed."

The brightness of Nick's gifts, like the proverbial lotus flower, grew roots in the mud of his rage and despair; it could not have shone had he not met eyes open with darkness. But a crucial balance in Nick's growth had gone askew; what had been rich soil was now quicksand. That Nick made the choice not to go under, to quit drugs and booze and begin a recovery program, was as far as I know the most difficult act of his life. He pulled up short in his tracks, turned one-eighty degrees, and locked eyes with the ghost that had chased him for sixty-five years. He was scared, hurting, and in need of help and he said so out loud and to others. Such honesty had come to look foolish to me, too naked and risky, but when I saw it in Nick it was revelation, heroic, a quality for me to strive for. And I knew it had something important to do with the cutting loose (cutting through) I had always believed could make life fresh and free.

In November Nick was released from treatment and back to the world. We found a new home, finally a place big enough for us both. We looked for jobs and joined other couples for bridge and quiet evenings at home. Nick worked to get well with a trust that was so conscientious it could not help but rub off on me. I began to learn ways of calming my mind, and this helped the days pass more smoothly. Nick said, "I wish I'd learned that stuff at your age."

Nick went every day to Alcoholics Anonymous meetings. Sometimes I went with him. He liked meetings to which the hard cases would go, maybe because he was a hard case himself or because the hard cases were women and men who had lost their lives and found them again, so they knew a thing about value. Also they had good stories to tell and no time at all for jive. The truth blew through those meetings like a high mountain wind, sharp, clear, and chill, and we both felt enlivened by it.

Nick knew he had been given a rare second chance and his gratitude for it made him gentle and patient in ways he had not been before. A "vulnerability that one could not but be moved by . . . even frightened," which he had described in James Dean, was Nick's vulnerability too.

That winter, supported by Elia Kazan and John Houseman who

three decades before had started him in the movies, Nick began teaching at New York University and the Lee Strasberg Institute.

I believe Nick loved teaching, especially at this time. Teaching provided a laboratory in which he could research his craft and fellow humans. Teaching helped him to clarify his thinking and draw some conclusions. Teaching allowed him to guide and nurture young people as he himself had been guided and nurtured and had missed being guided and nurtured. Nick wholly gave himself to his students as mostly they gave themselves to him. I believe he felt a new peace at this time. This time had the tenderness of a seedling just before the first frost.

One early morning in November 1977 I had a dream. This was the dream: Nick was packing his bags. Talking over his shoulder he told me, "I'm leaving now, you don't need me anymore." I woke up as my fist hit Nick's face. Pouring hot tears, I saw he was already awake, watching TV and nursing a bag of chocolates. The blow did not seem to startle him much. He just gathered me up while I sobbed.

Two weeks after that Nick checked into hospital for tests. The X-rays and scans showed a tumor on his right lung.

No young woman joins her life to that of a man forty years older without considering death. I had thought about death a lot in my time—my parents' deaths, Nick's death, death by Nazis, death by atomic bomb. Dying as far as I knew meant only pain, terror, decay, and the deprivation of life for whomever was dying. Dying concerned me a lot—my own death did not—but I thought nothing worse than the limitless hard cement landscape of grief I would be left alone in by the death of someone I loved. I had never seen death close up and I knew I would have to before I could understand anything, but if given the choice I would let understanding wait.

If understanding would wait death would not. Surgery followed diagnosis by days and the scalpels cut nothing but hope. The cancer had grown around Nick's aorta and had probably entered his bloodstream. The doctors sewed him back up with his tumor intact. In their fondness for numbers they told me they gave him two years and those years would be hard.

Nick had met with so many close calls I had lost count of the total, I could not recall if this were the cat's eighth or ninth and last life. For a while I believed if we both willed it hard enough Nick would get well.

No one told me nor could I have imagined what terrible beauty is loosed when someone like Nick is dying. Our culture, of course, has no place for dying so we have no tradition of study about that fifty percent of existence. Why get a guidebook to a country one wants to avoid? Which just goes to show how ignorant wanting can be for Nick's dying was an adventure, and since dying would not be avoided a guide to its ways could only have helped. So much for spilt milk. Nick's dying opened new lands for everyone who came near him, as for Nick himself I have to assume, for his wonder and alertness to the shifts in his world became only more acute.

I dreaded watching his mane fall out and his body shrink down to bone, but he did lose his hair and his body shrank down and everything extra burned away with disease. What was left was essence of life which in Nick's face took on a look of such pure sweet sadness it was transfixing. In his pain and exhaustion he could digest only what was most simple, basic, direct, and true. To offer him anything less seemed cheap and a threat to his vitalness, and yet I was young, undisciplined, and still an unknown to myself. Whether he had planned to or not Nick once again had set a hard task. When for moments I could meet it—meet him—fully and clearly nothing else mattered, all was complete. Such moments became the goldmine of his legacy to me. The fact is the way Nick was dying brought me to my life.

For the first time I asked Nick my real questions, only one or two every couple of weeks for I felt inexplicably shy:

Q: When you're gambling and on a roll how do you know your numbers?

A: Sometimes I hear the music of the spheres and I just know what the next note will be. But then I get cocky.

Q: If you could give me just one piece of advice what would it be?

A: Don't care so much what others think about you.

Q: One more piece?

A: Examine your fear of violence.

Q: Why wouldn't you help me get started the way you did all the others?

To this last he kept silent.

One day he turned from the cop show on TV to observe with some pride in us both: "You've become an experienced woman."

Of course a man only changes so much in a lifetime and his pain was horrific, so Nick did much moaning and with his best ploys and invention kept a crowd scurrying after his needs. He took to wearing a heating pad under his shirt on his back while pacing the long length of our loft. As we had few electrical outlets and mostly relied on extension chords, a friend spent his visit from London following Nick to and fro, frantically sorting wires and unplugging and plugging before the heating pad cooled or the TV was yanked off its table.

While in hospital Nick insisted on smoking in rooms where oxygen was in use, so to avoid explosions the nurses trained me to care for him at home and begged me to keep him there unless his condition became very bad.

Tim Ray and a medley of friends came for visits. Tim taught Nick meditations to relax the pain and to rally his psyche's fighting forces against the cancer cells. All joined hands to keep the house going, cooking and shopping, taking Nick to his radiation appointments, rubbing his feet, copying his notes, bullying him into taking his pills—whatever he needed. From the great bed at the end of the loft through moans and groans Nick directed this comic and bustling scene that with no decision on anyone's part had turned into a celebration.

Then in early spring of 1979 and for the last time the carnival came back to town: Wim Wenders arrived at the door with film, crew, and equipment. Several people, including Nick, had ideas for Nick Ray's last film but Wim made the strongest bid for getting the show underway.

Tripping on lights and cables trying to get to Nick's bedside I was not convinced that making the movie was such a good plan. That was like wondering if the tornado should have struck. Still, debating the point in my mind raised some questions not unrelated to the themes of this book and Nick's life.

Nick thought the film should concern a man sick with cancer who wanted "to bring himself altogether" before he died. Since that was what Nick himself wanted to do and since he had chosen to give his remaining time to the movie and that time was scant, it made sense to combine his two intents into one. Beyond that we had no script or plotline.

With such skilled improvisers as Nick Ray and Wim Wenders one would think no script would be no problem. But problems arose right away, perhaps because the laws of creation allow only one visionary per vision or more likely because fear broke loose. Fear took us over—not violently as it can do but by spinning sticky invisible webs. I cannot say for sure what stirred up the fear but I had not felt it so strong around Nick's dying before. As is its way fear not only made us all desperate, it distorted perception and instinct, and the film soon ran off like a terrorized child all alone in the dark night.

Did Nick want to make *Nick's Movie (Lightning Over Water)*? He never said so, even when I asked him directly. He did not want to disappoint Wim and his backers, he did not like what he saw of the dailies—that much he did say. He was too weak to work as he would have wanted to work and he saw for the time that Wim Wenders was lost, both behind and before the camera.

For myself I knew Nick would not live much longer, the time left with him was dear, but I could not get close for director, crew, and equipment kept blocking the way. It seemed Nick would not have the chance to "bring things altogether"; in fact things were flying apart. I felt the rite of the most sacred time in a life had been raped while Nick's and my need for each other was dismissed as inconsequential. Who was to blame? Were I to point a finger it would be at fear.

There were not so many good reasons to want to keep shooting that film, yet I could not find the strength in me to try to stop it. I had to conclude that given the chance to film his own dying Nick could not pass it up, no matter the whos, whys, and hows. There was not one juncture of his life as I knew it that he had not tried to process through film. Film was his way to digest and release what he lived on, as essential to him as the functioning of his kidneys and liver. If the film did not turn out to be pleasing, well, that was the risk, so be it.

At the same time it dawned on me ("Like the jitterbug," said Lenny Bruce, "so simple it nearly eluded me") that Nick dreaded making films. To make a film as he wanted, "as a living, continuously breathing thing," was for him, perhaps, an act of creation too close to God's. In this cruel confusion Nick's gifts and successes turned into agents of torment and guilt. I believe, although he never said so, at heart Nick agreed with Welles: "Maybe there's some rightness in the difficulty."

True to his premonition Nick did not live to finish the film.

■ ■ ■

The courses in acting and directing for film that Nick taught in his last years were in all ways the culmination of his life work. He knew it and had the good sense to record the class sessions and to want their content made known. I knew I would do what he asked, although back then this assignment like that of the "autobiography" seemed more chore than opportunity.

I began work shortly after Nick's death for a bad mix of motives, none of them clear, and quit work dejected just weeks after that. Of course I had not grieved my loss yet, nor had I fought free from Nick's too big although friendly ghost—not to mention my own—to a ground on which I could stand firm alone. These were personal tasks both scary and inconvenient and they would not settle for less than my full attention. At the time I did not understand that grieving and fighting, fighting and grieving, were the stuff of what Nick called "the search for self," the stuff of his life and his movies and classes; so the grieving and fighting I saw before me I fiercely resented as a far too long nasty detour. But I followed my nose, or it dragged me along, until I learned at least two or three times that when it comes to how a life weaves itself there are no extra threads or loose ends—so detours need not be a problem. Of course it only made sense: I could not piece together Nick's search until I had started off on my own—but this I can say only now that the piecing is done. Anyway, it came to pass that I knew without doubt it was time to get back to work on Nick's teaching book or life story, whichever.

As I transcribed some one hundred-plus hours of often unlabeled and poorly recorded tapes and tried to read what he had written by hand in letters and notebooks, on cards and cocktail napkins, I had to mutter at Nick's carelessness with his records, at his obscurations and incompletions. "Never leave a trail of words," he had warned me the writer-to-be, while he himself left many trails all ending abruptly in one wilderness or another. The problem remained: How could so many fragments form a sensible whole? In his words: "But what shall I do about all the transitional phrases or pages necessary to make what follows comprehensible to you?"

I had seen Nick solve such a problem before and always the solution homed in how he felt for the integrity of his subject, for the subject is intrinsically whole without extra threads or loose ends—the same theme again. The burden falls on the observer to catch the pattern of the weave. So I gathered all the pieces I knew of Nick's life together and once more posed my old questions: Was Nick a master? What was a master? How could Nick's life be told to satisfy both him and me? What was Nick teaching? What was Nick really teaching?

History and facts still did not impel me, not on their own, but true emotion did impel, nurture, and free me as did the landscape in which it arose and dissolved and the wisdom it could leave behind. Finally I knew that much of myself and I knew it in a new way about Nick. Tracing what moved me about him I trusted the shape of his life to emerge of itself, a phoenix from the fragments, for I had been well taught: content determines form; form conditions the content.

The class transcripts form the skeleton of this book. They have been pieced into a composite combining three series of classes and three groups of students into one series, one group. The emphasis of each class session falls on the exploration of terms and/or techniques (action, monologue, backstory, sense memory, making an entrance). The sessions are linked by developing themes (the character party, "The Forger" scenario) and the evolution of the students' understanding.

But what Nick taught was not so much terms and techniques: Nick taught experience. He taught from experience, through experience, about the nature of experience, about analysing, integrating, and synthesizing experience into a gift of experience for others. Because this is so the class transcripts do not make a whole teaching text without reference to the experience—Nick's—from which their lessons are drawn. The work in class on "stripping . . . down to the essential" and on the scenario of "The Forger," a man who "must steal another's identity," is the same work Nick did at home as he wrote about drink, love, and dying. The work at home fed the work in class and vice-versa. To extract one from the other would be a theft of dimension and so perspective as dire as believing our world is flat.

Nick taught as he lived: he dove into chaos and found his way out and expected his students would do same. A good many did and have become respected directors, producers, editors, writers, and actors in theatre and film. For an impatient man Nick became a most patient teacher. What he taught was simple but not easy and he knew to repeat it in different contexts with different shadings until it was fully absorbed. He asked more questions than he gave answers for, as he said, he taught to learn and to awaken his students' intrinsic knowing, not bludgeon them with his own.

And what about my old questions? Almost two decades have passed since I first asked them. Since then I've met many people who spent time with Nick, if only an hour or two, and it's curious to me how many claim that he changed the course of their lives. I do not believe that was his intention, it just happened that way as he went about his own business. But then his business was acting. Whether before or behind or away from the camera Nick was an actor, one who "in . . . three hours travels the whole course of the dead-end path that the man in the audience takes a lifetime to cover."[15] As an actor he could not help but take whomever was with him to the edge where he lived and then push—and surprise, they did not fall off and the world was not flat and who could forget the view. Nick acted all the time. Nick taught all the time. He taught through his actions, whether

---

15. Albert Camus. *The Myth of Sisyphus and Other Essays* (Random House, Inc., Vintage International, 1991).

he meant to or not, whether his actions looked smart or insane. A hasidic tale tells of the student who goes to the master not to learn scripture but to watch how he ties his shoelaces. In that light maybe Nick was a master, for he did things so boldly and with such heart it was impossible not to watch him. It was impossible not to watch him because what he did was *new* and because as I watched I felt my own being grow brighter—not by reflection but by generation of light.

Really I'm not in a position to judge if Nick was a master or not, the question is not so interesting now. I know surely he was a seeker. He knew what questions to ask, he knew what it was he was after, whatever its name, however far he was from it. And I know I will not need more than the toes on one foot to count the true seekers I'm likely to meet in this lifetime. That I knew even one is a rare unaccountable boon.

However this book is read I offer it first as the telling of a journey. Not everyone makes movies or works in the theatre but everyone takes a journey, and it seems that no matter the style of the journey the landmarks are the same. That being the case, even the roughest map may prove a good guide and comfort.

NICHOLAS RAY:
A BIOGRAPHICAL OUTLINE
Bernard Eisenschitz

Raymond Nicholas Kienzle Jr. was born on August 7, 1911, in Galesville, Wisconsin, population 1500. His father, Raymond Nicholas Kienzle, a contractor and a builder and the son of German immigrants, had divorced his first wife and married Lena Toppen, of Norwegian stock, eleven years his junior. Raymond Nicholas Kienzle Jr. was his father's last born and only boy after daughters Alice, Ruth, and Helen. The family grew up in a town surrounded by farmlands cultivated by European immigrants and still inhabited by Indians.

After World War I, Raymond Sr. decided to retire and to move back to the bigger city of La Crosse, twenty miles down the Mississippi. There Raymond Nicholas Jr. spent the years of prohibition and witnessed his father's early death in November 1926. While attending high school, he wrote and produced for local radio, and won a tri-state radio competition, which he later recalled as "a scholarship to any university in the world."

In the summer of 1931, Nick Ray, as he had by then decided to call himself, left home for the University of Chicago. His academic career was short. Soon he moved to New York, where he met Jean Evans, a young writer just arrived from California. They lived together and eventually married. Meanwhile, Ray was invited by architect Frank Lloyd Wright to join Wright's newly created Taliesin Fellowship, less an educational center than a microcosm of Wright's utopian society. Nick Ray spent a few months with Wright, participating in the Playhouse's activities. After a sudden falling out with the architect, Ray went to Mexico, then returned to New York and Jean Evans.

Back in New York, in 1934, he joined a left-wing theatre group, the Workers Lab, soon to be renamed Theatre of Action. Influenced by European forerunners, the troupe presented pieces and skits in the agit-prop style, moving scenery by subway, putting up shows before picket lines, at factories or in union halls. Several of the troupe's members became lifelong friends. Its musical director was Earl Robinson (better known as the composer of "Ballad for Americans" and the "Ballad of Joe Hill"). The troupe practiced communal living and strong discipline and training: every morning, before the afternoon and evening performances, classes were given by acknowledged professionals—performers, choreographers, and members of the Group Theatre.

During its first five years, the Theatre of Action performed before an estimated audience of 100,000. By then the group felt the need to graduate to "legitimate" productions. They commissioned a play, *The Young Go First*, whose treatment of a timely subject, the CCC camps, sharply criticized Roosevelt's "militaristic" policy. The play was jointly directed by the Theatre of Action's founder, Alfred Saxe, and Elia Kazan, fresh from the Group on his first professional production. *The Young Go First* premiered at the Park Theatre in May 1935, with a cast including "Nik" Ray as the camp barber. A year later, Ray appeared in the cast of the Theatre of Action's next and last production before the troupe disbanded, *The Crime*, a play of contemporary unionism directed by Saxe and Kazan (March 1936).

Ray would never forget the enthusiasm of his days with the Theatre of Action, nor Kazan's work with actors and the large amount of attention devoted to improvisation. Throughout his life, he kept in touch and worked with Will Lee, Perry Bruskin, Earl Robinson, Curt Conway, as well as with Kazan, Norman Lloyd, John Garfield, and Clifford Odets (who was to help him on a couple of screenplays). When he returned to the United States in the radical days of the late sixties and early seventies, he conceived the idea for a book (*Stage Left!*) about the theatrical "movement" of the thirties.

The Federal Theatre Project of the Works Progress Administration had been created in 1935. As the financial situation of the Theatre of Action had become impossible, several of its members individually joined the FTP in order to become equity members and to receive a basic salary. Ray, as stage manager and sometimes as actor, worked on one of the first "Living Newspaper" productions, *Injunction Granted* (with Norman Lloyd and "a cast of hundreds"; premiere: July 1936), directed by Joseph Losey, also from La Crosse. After the play's three-month run, Ray accepted an offer to take over theatrical activities at Brookwood Labor College, a Socialist-oriented workers' university run by unions. Bringing with him Earl Robinson as music director, he trained union activists in drama and acting.

Early in 1937, Ray was hired by the Resettlement Administration, headed by Rexford Tugwell, Secretary of Agriculture, and moved to Washington, D.C. Tugwell initiated a renaissance of grass-roots American culture. Nick Ray was put in charge of theatre art. His job was to get people to sit down and talk about their lives, to help them develop their awareness, create documentary plays, and express their problems and needs in theatrical terms. Ray also organized improvisation groups and worked with community theatres. By himself, sometimes with Jean Evans (who was pregnant), and once with Kazan, Ray went to mining camps, lumber camps, and the backwoods of the South. He brought one group from the mountains of Alabama to perform on the White House lawn for the Roosevelts and their guests. He enjoyed the company of the group in charge of the Archive of American Folk Song at the Library of Congress, Charles Seeger, his son, Peter, and Alan Lomax. The Rays (their son Anthony was born in November 1937) shared a house with the Lomaxes in a Washington suburb and lived and worked with folk singers like Josh White, Aunt Molly Jackson, Leadbelly, and Woody Guthrie. The WPA programs fell under severe political harassment, and Ray was discharged in July 1940, about the time he separated from Jean Evans.

Back in New York, Ray mixed with Café Society and the jazz scene. Together with Alan Lomax, he produced a weekly folk music program for CBS Radio: *Back Where I Come From* (August 1940–February 1941), featuring Burl Ives, Earl Robinson, Woody Guthrie, Pete Seeger, Leadbelly, Josh White, and the Golden Gate Quartet. He brought Leadbelly and Josh White to Max Gordon's Village Vanguard (November 1941).

After Pearl Harbor, Ray was rejected by the Army because of a congenital rheumatic heart condition. He was hired by John Houseman for the OWI (Office of War Information) *Voice of America* radio programs. Houseman put him in charge of folk music, and Ray reunited "Nick's Barefoot Boys," as the group of performers from *Back Where I Come From* was called. He also directed and supervised propaganda records and news programs in many languages and enjoyed working with the famous Czech comedians and political satirists Voskovec and Werich. The venture was soon brought to a close under pressure from anti-Roosevelt forces and a congressional investigation of OWI. Houseman resigned and was followed by the rest of his team.

Ray went to Hollywood in 1944, having been sent for by Elia Kazan, who was directing *A Tree Grows in Brooklyn* for 20th Century-Fox. Ray followed the whole production, without working in any specific capacity. Then he worked as a dialogue director for Fox and tried unsuccessfully to sell film ideas and break into the industry. Together with Joseph Losey, he staged a civic tribute to Franklin D. Roosevelt at the Academy Awards ceremony of 1945.

Ray was Houseman's general assistant on a short film for the Overseas Branch of the OWI, *Tuesday in November* (1945), designed to explain the American process of democratic elections to the world. The film combined documentary footage, staged scenes (directed by John Berry) and animated sequences (by John Hubley), and had a full-length score by Virgil Thomson. Ray was responsible for post-production, including picture and sound editing. Back in New York in the summer of 1945, Houseman produced and Ray directed a pioneering TV drama, a half-hour program adapted from Lucille Fletcher's radio play, *Sorry, Wrong Number*, starring Mildred Natwick (in the role later played by Barbara Stanwyck in the film adaptation). Houseman next directed, assisted by Ray, a Broadway musical starring Mary Martin and Yul Brynner, *Lute Song*, premiered in February 1946. That same year, he and Houseman embarked on another musical inspired by *The Beggar's Opera*. It was to be the first integrated Broadway show, with a score by Duke Ellington and a libretto by John Latouche. *Beggar's Holiday* turned out to be expensive and disastrous: Houseman (as well as the star, Libby Holman) was fired and replaced, and Ray was the only director credited (for "staging the book") when the show reached New York (premiered in December 1946).

In 1946, Houseman had Nick hired as his assistant at RKO, and put him to work on a Depression-era novel, *Thieves Like Us*, by Edward Anderson. Ray wrote several drafts of a screenplay, hoping to direct it. In February 1947, when Dore Schary was appointed head of production at the studio and initiated a "new directors" policy, the studio agreed to let Ray direct the film. *Thieves Like Us*, retitled *Your Red Wagon*, then *They Live By Night* for release, was shot in 47 days during the summer of 1947. Its scheduled release was postponed when Howard Hughes bought the controlling shares of the studio (May 1948). Although Hughes had guaranteed Dore Schary unlimited freedom, the tycoon canceled three productions and put several completed films on the shelf: Schary promptly resigned. *They Live By Night* had only a minute release in October 1949.

In the meantime, Ray had directed a second feature for RKO, *A Woman's Secret*, written and produced by his friend Herman J. Mankiewicz. It was during this film that he met Gloria Grahame, whom he married in June 1948, in Las Vegas. Their son, Tim, was born at the end of the year. On loan from the studio, Ray worked on Humphrey Bogart's first production. *Knock on Any Door* (1948, released 1949), adapted from a novel by black writer Willard Motley, was notable for its cast of young unknown actors. Next year, in 1949, Ray again directed Bogart, and Gloria Grahame, in a more personal film, *In a Lonely Place* (released in 1950), a film noir about the making and desintegration of a couple, reflecting Ray's own relationship with Grahame.

For the next few years, Nicholas Ray served under a long-term contract at Howard Hughes' RKO. In all, he directed six features (a third of his Hollywood output) for this studio: *They Live By Night, A Woman's Secret* (released in 1949), *Born To Be Bad* (1950), *On Dangerous Ground* (1952), *Flying Leathernecks* (1951), and *The Lusty Men* (1952): an even balance between personal, independent, and intense works and anonymous studio productions. As a Howard Hughes protégé, Ray was spared the agonies of blacklisting during the witchhunt, despite his leftist associations. He was able to wriggle his way out of directing *I Married a Communist*, without damage to his career. But he had to accomplish several chores for the studio or the eccentric billionaire, such as the "doctoring" (reshooting and supervising of editing and postproduction) of four films: *Roseanna McCoy* (1949, on loan to Samuel Goldwyn), *The Racket* (1951), *Macao* (1952, originally directed by Josef von Sternberg), and *Androcles and the Lion* (adding the notorious "Vestal Virgin Bath" sequence, which was much publicized but never made it to the screen; released in 1953). When Hughes sold his shares in RKO, Ray used a clause in his renewed contract to leave the studio, where he had spent seven years of his professional life (February 1953).

His ambition was to achieve independence by becoming his own producer. "Brilliant but unreliable," as he was considered by the industry, he was never to achieve this aim. Under the guidance of his agent, MCA, and the personal protection of the powerful Lew Wasserman, he was able to work uninterruptedly, going from one studio to another, but never as his own master. On his first film after RKO, *Johnny Guitar* (1953, released in 1954), he did serve as a producer, but the credit was denied him. After this tempestuous production, marked by clashes with the star, Joan Crawford, and day-to-day rewriting (all of which made for its greatness in the end), Ray directed James Cagney in another western, *Run for Cover* (1954, released in 1955). A short and brilliant TV episode, *High Green Wall* (1954, with Joseph Cotten) followed. By the end of 1954, he was at Warner Bros.

working on a project about youth, for which he had written the original story idea. Through different script drafts by Leon Uris, Irving Shulman, Stewart Stern, with notable contributions by Ray himself and producer David Weisbart, as well as extensive rehearsals and improvisational work with the young cast headed by James Dean, *Rebel Without a Cause*, produced in April-May 1955, became Ray's definitive, and certainly most celebrated, statement on youth when it was released in September, only a few days after Dean's tragic car crash.

Immediately after *Rebel*, Ray started *Tambourine* (released as *Hot Blood* in 1956), an old project of his, whose realization was marred by Jane Russell's and his own fatigue, but which François Truffaut hailed as "Nicholas Ray's *joie de vivre*" (as opposed to the French title of *Rebel Without a Cause, La Fureur de vivre*). On completion of the shooting, Ray went to Europe, both to promote *Rebel* and to try and set up independent production deals. On the news of Dean's death, he remained in Germany, and did not work on *Hot Blood*'s post-production. He returned to the states for a two-film deal with 20th Century-Fox: *Bigger Than Life* and *The True Story of Jesse James* were both produced in 1956. At the beginning of 1957 he directed *Bitter Victory*, a European Columbia production, in Libya and in French studios, under arduous circumstances. Although Eric Rohmer described it as "the only intelligent film shown at the Venice Mostra," no other film project materialized in Europe at the time. Instead, Ray joined an American production by Budd and Stuart Schulberg, *Wind Across the Everglades*, shot in Florida from November 1957 to January 1958. An ill-prepared and ill-managed shooting, it suffered from the weather, writer Budd Schulberg's intent to be sole master on board and, last but not least, Ray's heavy drinking, eccentricities, and illness. He was barred from the last stages of shooting and from the editing, and was only able to see the film at a preview in July 1958. In the meantime, he had taken on an assignment at MGM, *Party Girl* (1958), which was to be his last Hollywood film.

In October 1958, Nick Ray married Betty Utey, a dancer and choreographer born in 1935. They had two daughters, Julie (born in January 1960) and Nikka (born in October 1961).

Ray next went to Britain and Italy to direct his own script of *The Savage Innocents* (released in 1960), an international coproduction backed by Paramount. He settled in Europe, intending to open an international film school, among other plans and projects. Those plans were postponed when he accepted an offer from Samuel Bronston, a producer of epics who was using Du Pont money and frozen assets to try setting up a new Hollywood in Spain. Ray brought to the Bronston "organization" two partners who subsequently became his producers: Philip Yordan (writer of *Johnny Guitar*) and Mikhail Wazsynski (a veteran director and jack-of-all-trades in European-American ventures). The first film he directed in Spain, *King of Kings* (released in 1961), was taken over by MGM and edited by the studio without his control. On the filming of his second Bronston picture, *55 Days at Peking* (released in 1963), he suffered a heart attack and was replaced. Nicholas Ray's career within the legitimate film industry had come to an end in September 1962, on a set near Madrid.

Years of wandering across Europe followed. Ray opened a restaurant-night club in Madrid, served as a jury member at festivals, anonymously "doctored" scripts and films, and generally "kept his suitcases packed," living in turn in Rome, Madrid, London, Zagreb, Munich, Paris, and on the island of Sylt off Northern Germany. His most advanced project, based on Dylan Thomas's screenplay *The Doctor and the Devils*, fell through a few days before shooting was to begin in Yugoslavia (autumn 1965). A production with the Rolling Stones, like many others, never came to life.

Ray was finally brought back to the States by a group of young filmmakers who wanted him to direct a project about American justice. Seeing an opportunity to sum up his feelings about the revolt of youth (a wave of which he had witnessed in Paris, in May 1968), he first shot one of the largest of the anti-war rallies in Washington (*March on Washington, Nov. 15, 1969*, a short, was edited from the material), then flew to Chicago to follow the Chicago 7 trial. His involvement with the defendants and their lawyers led him to film the apartment of Fred Hampton immediately after the young Black Panther Party leader had been murdered by the Chicago police. Various sponsors supported the project, then backed off, as Ray kept shooting, by any means available, and began to edit his material. Director Marcel Ophuls recorded one stage of his effort in the documentary *America Revisited* (aired 1970). Under the strain, Ray suffered the loss of his sight in one eye.

A year later, Ray was hired as a film teacher by Harpur College at Binghamton, New York (September 1971). Believing "the only way to learn about film is to make films," he immediately started to shoot with his students. The "work in progress," called *We Can't Go Home Again*, made use of all possible formats and processes, including Nam June Paik's video synthesizer, to produce a new form of split screen. A first, hastily assembled version was shown at the end of the 1973 Cannes Film Festival. Ray remained in Europe for several months, still trying to complete the film. In Holland, he directed and acted in an episode of *Wet Dreams*, a soft-core feature designed to put the erotic dreams of various artists on screen.

Ray moved from Amsterdam to New York to San Francisco to Houston and back to New York, working away on *We Can't Go Home Again*, of which a shorter version, with his own narration, was prepared in April 1976. A documentary about him, *A Stranger Here Myself*, was premiered in 1975. Conceived by critic Myron Meisel and directed by David C. Helpern Jr. and James C. Gutman, the film was a sympathetic attempt to hide his physical deterioration. Finally, in 1976, Ray joined the Alcoholics Anonymous fellowship.

In November 1976, Nick moved into a SoHo loft with Susan Schwartz, whom he had met in Chicago in 1969 and who had been living and working with him since. A few months later, he acted in Wim Wenders's *The American Friend* (1977). He taught courses in film direction and film acting at the Lee Strasberg Institute and at New York University. Several video recordings and a short 16mm. film, *Marco*, were made in those classes. In fall 1977, Ray discovered he had cancer. He continued to teach between lengthy and painful medical treatments.

Early in 1978, his illness already apparent, Ray took a small part in Milos Forman's *Hair* (released in 1979). In March 1979, Nick Ray and Wim Wenders started shooting a joint project with the tentative title of *Nick's Movie*, eventually known as *Lightning Over Water* (released in 1980), from a line Ray improvised. The production came to a stop early in May. Ray died on June 16, 1979.

INTRODUCTION AND GROUND RULES

My name is Nicholas Ray and I am contracted to teach you within the time and space available whatever I can about the art and craft of acting and directing in the media of film and television. You are encouraged to reject anything I say that you consider useless or inapplicable.

Nonetheless, I ask that you kindly regard these next words as basic, fundamental, grass roots, key to your ability to live, develop, and perform with increasing effectiveness in the world of art: Your tools are physical, mental, and spiritual. Are you hesitant about acknowledging the word spiritual? If that word makes you uncomfortable, you would do well to find understanding that *religious* and *spiritual* are different words with separate roots and meanings. That we have a common vocabulary will become increasingly important. You are here to discern and exercise your physical, mental, and spiritual muscles.

In a current issue of *The New Yorker*[16] Kenneth Tynan relates the opening of a luncheon conversation between Sir Ralph Richardson and Sir John Gielgud, who were appearing together eight times a week in the play *No Man's Land*:

SIR RALPH: You're looking very well.
SIR JOHN: Thank you.
SIR RALPH: I haven't seen much of you lately.

---

16. "Profile: Ralph Richardson," *The New Yorker*, 21 February 1977, pp. 45–46 +.

SIR JOHN: We meet in costume.
SIR RALPH: We meet as other people.

A pleasant inside joke. But think for a moment. What were they really saying? Although the conversation took place in obvious good humor and lightness, it is germane to the subject I wish to develop now for our later discussion, and I do not care to leave it hanging as another one of those opening handles to a speech without asking you to reflect on it. What were they really saying? It's a question you need to pose each time you break down a part, and sometimes even in conversation. Of course, you usually don't stop and ask yourself as you are talking or listening, "Who am I? What am I? Why am I?" But aren't those questions the undercarriage of the Gielgud-Richardson exchange? Aren't those the questions you want to be asking?

At this moment in preparing my notes I stopped and asked myself, "What am I really saying?" Quick answers: I am saying that we are meeting together for the first time; that your attitudes and sensibilities are mysteries to your neighbors, yourselves and to me; that you are perhaps hoping to learn something, to share what you learn or question in your learning, and to size me up; that it would be nice if you were aware of your neighbor's breathing, warmth, and reactions; and that by the end of the evening you may decide that coming here was a nonsensical thing to do. But now your group attitude is attentive, and we are as we are.

But what am I really saying to you? At this point, I'm going to interrupt and detour the flow of what I intended for the rest of the evening. I want to give sounds to what I am really saying, now, to let you know where I'm at. Perhaps that is my real action in being here—but is it the only one?

I am here to discuss a subject I think important to the worker in the theatre, and I want that subject to become clear to you, not by what I say, but by what we all say. So I want to find out what you think about what I am saying. That is another action and reason for my being here.

I said, "What you think about what I am saying." Isn't that presumptuous and vain? Why do I use the word vain? Because if I use it first, self-critically, you will think I am not vain. If it is important to me to have you think I am not vain, then I must want you to like me. Yes, I want you to like me.

Some day you may hear me scream at an aspiring or even semisuccessful director, "You want your cast to like you? You're in the wrong profession!" Don't take it for granted that that is what I am really saying. I may be saying, "Why do you want to be liked? To get more authority quickly, so you can manipulate with more facility, so you can have more power, which will bring you more money? What's wrong with your sex life?" If you want people to like you and pay you for it, try prostitution, it walks both sides of the street in different clothing. Permit people to love you or hate you. It's like speaking a line in a play: say it as if for the first time or the last time, but never in between.

Oh, and by the way and *et cetera*, if you do decide to become a whore, become engaged with the role, play it to the hilt. Perhaps you'll experience enough of love and hate and detestable compliance to put you back on the road to becoming a better, more complete director.

On the other hand, a few weeks ago Lee Strasberg and I were sounding each other out, and I mentioned that my first orientation to the theatre was more toward Meyerholdt, and then Vakhtangov, than Stanislavsky. Lee said so was his, and then said: "You know, the middle road is a road in itself." As Vakhtangov was the road between Stanislavsky and Meyerholdt, I thought back to his essay, "The Agitation from the Essence," which has been a principal guideline for me in my directing career, although not so fruitful in personal relationships. End of detour.

I want to state the ground rules for our work together:

1) Those of you who are taking the course for credit will not be graded according to your talent. I do not presume to be able to judge talent working under the kind of pressure we'll have here. C. Day Lewis, an Englishman who wrote good poetry, said: "The greatest enemies of poetry are talk and alcohol." Proclaim and scream out that you are talented and a poet of the celluloid strip, but not among us. I caution you against acting out the hoped for result before you have done the work. And confine your worries about it, as you do other acts of masturbation, to your private quarters.

2) There will be tools here with which you will work according to your capacity, and the principal tool is yourself. Then come the others in the group to whom you are only another, no matter how special another you may wish to become, and temporarily may become.

I advise that your eyes, ears, and other sensitive organs and emotions will serve you best through alertness, objectivity, and an absence of self-deceit. I want you to draw on the pure stuff of you. I'm not a moralizer, I don't believe an artist should moralize in any form of the word, but I do not want any use of alcohol or mood changers in our working situation. If you want to discuss the advantages of drugs, I could filibuster all of you with great and glorious highs. If you need a fix to face the day, I empathize. Just don't participate in class, because if you're high, your judgment is not quite right. Some clouds appear, the mood changes, you can't trust yourself.

Or come to our sessions spaced out if you wish—no blame. You may even serve as a helpful reminder to others, and thus find a noble negative purpose for yourself as the premature martyr. The penalty, however, is devastating. You will not be able to recover your balance without the help of others, anymore than you will be able to learn in this class without the help of others. Even the blessed sanctuary of aloneness you can learn how to manage only with the help and examples of others. Those others may have the inclination to help you recover, but they will not have the time.

We're all dependent on each other. If you want to work here, you've got to have a spine. Where I have not been clear about the function and relation of the individual to the group and the group to the individual, I expect you to use your memory, curiosity, observation, and intelligence to sift it through for yourselves.

3) It's easy to fall into sloppy habits in class, indulging in criticizing others, using too many words. Sometimes it may make you feel good, but your first and healthier instinct probably is to try to find out or express something about yourself. I want you to get away from the habit of making comparisons. I want you to deal with immediate experience. Film is an immediate experience, so go to the root right away by using the other person's work as a source of personal experience, a means of exploring how you identify with what you have seen, what you would do. That way you'll be involved in the class all the time. In this case the use of the first person pronoun is much to your advantage.

4) I come to you with this concept or aphorism, which my wife calls a euphemism: Peter Lorre, exasperated, once said to a director, "But I have only five expressions." Bogart overheard him and, with some cause, repeated to me, "Goddam it, Nick, I've only got five expressions." I once worked with an architect named Frank Lloyd Wright, and he said, "Learn your limitations and take advantage of them." I don't mean learn to live with them. Take advantage of them and stretch them out.

5) Finally, do your "thinking" on your own time. Do your doing here.

I want to get us on our feet as fast as possible, and let the theory come along with accomplishment. And I'd like to start out doing—

All of you have done some theatre work, right? I'd like you to find a monologue or a duologue and do it as if you were presenting an audition for the theatre. And then I'd like to take that and immediately transpose it onto film—or in this case video—so we can begin to tackle the question of what happens on film that is different than in theatre, or different than in life. Shyness towards approaching the camera is usually an obstacle that has to be overcome. If you can come prepared with some material tomorrow, we'll start by diving right in.

Now I'd like to take an hour for lunch. I'd like it very much if you'd break into small groups and get to know each other a little bit, discuss some ideas, and see if there's anything we can do this afternoon, anything you'd like to try.

I'm going to go get a camera. The rest of the equipment will be here tomorrow.

Learning and Teaching

Riding down an elevator I observed two young fellows, both with guitars in identical cases. One fellow was about 21 and in a hog helmet; the other was slightly balding, about 31, with blond hair and beard, and obviously the teacher. I couldn't make out whether he was the teacher of the intricacies of the motorbike they had parked outside, or of the guitar. At any rate, he said to his companion: "I'll teach you how to play it."

The other boy said, "No. Nuh-uh."

The older one said, "Why don't you want me to teach you? You're going to have to learn it. Why don't you let me teach it to you? It'll take fifteen minutes."

The younger boy said, "No, look, well, maybe—" And he stalled and stalled and stalled until the elevator got to the ground floor and the door opened.

It struck me that maybe those in the upper five to ten percent of their classes are there because they enjoy the exhibition of themselves learning something, while the majority are embarrassed at showing that they have learned something in front of other people. The volunteer in the classroom is probably an exhibitionist. Why is it that so many of the men of brilliant scientific or scholarly achievement were so often last in their classes, so seldom one of the top five?

I think the group system of learning is perhaps no longer an acceptable or functioning method.

6

■ ■ ■

Learning is finding out what you already know.

Doing is demonstrating that you know it.

Teaching is reminding others that they know it just as well as you. We are all learners, doers, teachers.

Your only obligation in any lifetime is to be true to yourself.

You teach best what you most need to learn.

Live never to be ashamed when something you do or say is published around the world—even if what is published is not true.

"There is no problem so big that it cannot be run away from." —Snoopy the Dog

Open any book and read what's there: you'll find your problems. Hold a problem in your mind. Open a book.

Don't turn away from possible futures before you're quite certain you have nothing to learn from them. You're free to choose another (different) future, another past.

There is no such thing as a problem without a gift for you in its hands. You seek problems because you need their gifts.

You will find a helping hand at the end of your arm.

Anyone worth knowing is also a little odd.

1971

I am concerned with the state . . .

[8/10/77]

I am concerned with the state of my household.

The center of the stage is a towering mass of second-hand furniture. The oldest piece, a seventy-five-year-old leather armchair, has been moved, year after year, level after level, to the top of a heap (or pyre) of beds, chairs, desks, lamps: Tiffany, fringed, crystal, parchment, multi-switched, rheostated, focused, neoned, tubular, petite, and in-direct—every mode of light but the sun (O Ibsen, where is the sun?). The lamps alone, if formally arranged, could mark off eighty years in as many seconds—not a bad idea to consider for the final staging. Rugs, tapestries, whatnots, paintings and photographs, books, pa-pers, newspapers, wallpapers, handouts and throwaways, petitions and posters. The entire heap revolves slowly, like the prism chandelier of a '90s ballroom. Or a steamboat ballroom. On each new level and at each full turn of the heap, another form or two or three appears briefly, for one revolution. An old man makes his way upwards through the debris. Behind him a blue light, a gentle blue, outlines a naked female body. She pulls a quilt over her head.

I can't find my writing materials. She steals my writing papers. I like to write on library cards. They help me believe I have an ability to keep things in order. I don't, because I rebel against categories, but I like to write on them just the same. Continuity seems more

8

easily kept in such a way. She has to keep her continuities too (he pauses and rattles through a rolltop desk), doesn't she? It seems to me that if she has to write on library cards she could steal them from the office supplies where she works, same as I do from the university (he slams the rolltop) where I work. In the summers. She's forty years younger than I am. She should be at least as enterprising. Maybe she's in competition. (He nears the top.) I came home two nights ago and found her in intimate conversation with a *former* mentor of mine. I grabbed him, rushed him to an open window—this is the fourth floor we live on—and threw him out.

–Nick! He's seventy-five years old!

–If he can fuck he can fly!

He continues to the top, and settles into the old leather easy chair.

I am concerned with my family's sanity—and with my own as well. As well I might be.

—Or—

Begin with the false armistice, mother and sisters, before arriving at the top.

–I never questioned your sanity, father. Perhaps I don't know what sanity is—or is made of. What is sanity made of?

A woman's voice (a quiet, unquestioning, rather than authoritative, voice, and the words are spoken with a Norwegian accent):

—There is some jello and an egg sandwich. Do you want anything, son?

—Jello, please.

■ ■ ■

It seems to me my most vivid recollections of my life reflect efforts to call attention to myself. While I was preparing the script for the filming of *Rebel*, a schoolteacher from Missouri told me of a remark made by a small-town schoolteacher in Michigan: "A juvenile delinquent is merely a boy or girl who has fallen out of attention." Sixty-some years is a long time to be a juvenile delinquent.

I was born at 5 A.M. on August 7th in Galesville, Wisconsin. The astrologers will tell you that my sun was rising, which probably accounts for my being bent towards incest with other people's children and wives, ex-wives, and daughters and such.

My mother was of Norwegian descent, but she was born in a log cabin in central western Wisconsin, where the Menominee Indians still raided now and then. My father was born on the western side of the state, in Milwaukee. His name was Raymond Nicholas Kienzle.

The first song I learned on the mandolin was the "Ballad of Sam Hall":

> Oh my name it is Sam Hall, it is Sam Hall,
> Well my name it is Sam Hall, it is Sam Hall,
> Well my name it is Sam Hall,
> And I hate you one and all,
> Yes I hate you one and all,
> Goddamn your eyes!

At age three I changed my name to Sam Hall. At the outbreak of World War I, German names became unpopular in the United States, so I changed my name to Raymond Nicholas Kienzle, Jr., and my father approved, since that was what was written on my birth certificate.

Ever since I was four and she was nine I've wanted to make it with my sister Helen, because she was my sister. I'm still planning it. She was a bitch at nine and she never changed.

We played a game at school to "Farmer in the Dell." You know the tune? They changed the lyrics to:

> The hun is in the dell
> The hun is in the dell
> Hi ho the merry-oh!
> The hun is in the dell.

I was always the hun. After birth and the mumps the only time I can remember crying until I got to Hollywood was then. I cried with such rage that I broke through that circle, ran over to the highest point on the school grounds, got on top of it, and said, "Let's play King of the Mountain! I'm King of the Mountain!" And the sonofabitch that got close to me first got it right square in the eyes from my right foot. Thus my present views on prejudices and bigotry were built on a solid foundation.

The story begins at the in-between time of November 8, 1918, the day of the false armistice. I was seven and had become a Lutheran monk sulking under the butternut trees, lying in a hammock, wearing bell-bottomed sailor trousers, teasing my sister to tickle up or go. That night my oldest sister Alice drove my other sisters, Ruth and Helen, my mother, and myself through the town of Galesville, and we all beat pots and pans and lit red torches, honked the two horns, and yelled out, "PEACE PEACE PEACE!! ARMISTICE ARMISTICE PEACE PEACE!!!"

The next morning Alice came into my room to say with heavy doom that it had been a false armistice. I hadn't yet observed that that was the nature of life, so I got goddamn Norwegian mad and ran slamming doors through the house to the front porch. The walls were covered with antler heads, the floor with the tears of my mother and our neighbors, the Beizers. The Beizers' house had been painted yellow during the night to show that they were still dirty yellow huns.

The best epitaph I can think of is:

Born
Lived
Interrupted.

And it happens every day.

MONOLOGUE; CONCENTRATION; ACTION; EYES; CONTROL OF EMOTIONAL MEMORY

I planned a complex day for today, but I cannot begin it until a few other people arrive. In the meantime I would like to start with monologues.

Nothing is more difficult for an actor, particularly in film, than to talk to himself, to thin air, to a cloud, a dog, or an inanimate object and have the audience believe him. Sometimes we're able to make a monologue acceptable just through the convention of the form, but even in theatre it usually will strain credibility. In film we seldom have the refuge of long monologues; we don't stand still for them, but move in closer with the camera to catch each new revelation in seconds of thought, seconds of emotion, seconds of a decision. Whatever is happening, it is of the now.

I remember seeing Olivier in *Hamlet*, both on stage and on screen. In the film, at the famous "To be or not to be" speech, he became thin and unconvincing: he could not contain the space. Olivier has done great soliloquies on screen—in *Richard III*, for example—but those were accomplished by prerecording the sound and holding the camera on the eyes, because in film the melody is in the eyes.

Let's try an exercise.

Sam, how old are you?

SAM: Me? Twenty-three.

NR: I'd like you to walk around in a circle, counting up to ten. Count out loud on the exhale as you step right, and inhale as you step left.

[SAM starts walking the circle, counting.]

NR: Tell one of your stories.
SAM: Stories?
NR: Keep walking.
SAM: I don't know any stories.
NR: How old are you?
SAM: As I said before, twenty-three.
NR: Keep counting.
SAM: One . . . two . . . three . . . four . . .
NR: Did you notice any difference between Sam's first and second response to my asking him how old he is?
BETTY: I was aware as he was answering he had to think about answering.
NR: The second time.
BETTY: No, the second time he just said it, it came off naturally.
MARA: It was more aggressive.
JAKE: It came off naturally, and aggression was part of it as well.
LEONARD: He left out one number trying to answer your questions.
NR: His tone was different, which is more important, I think. It was controlled, controlled and modified by his action. Also the rhythm of his body changed.

This exercise is the simplest I know to demonstrate the value and means of achieving proper concentration. An actor cannot survive in front of the camera by concentrating on the lines he's supposed to say. His concentration must be on what he wants.

The director must help the actor find what he wants in his own terms, not by dictating it to him, not by saying, "This is who you are and this is what you want," but by helping him keep in mind what has just happened to the character, what he wants now, and what's in the way of his getting it. Then what follows in the scene may turn out a surprise, and that's always good.

Harry, do you have a monologue ready?
HARRY: I rehearsed the Gettysburg Address.
NR: All right. Your action is to recite the Gettysburg Address as you walk around in a circle.

> *[HARRY tries to comply, while NICK interrupts him with a series of irrelevant questions.]*

NR: Erica, I want you to do the same exercise with the monologue you worked on.

> *[She does.]*

NR: Any observations?
LIZ: It seemed to me Harry's voice relaxed, and every movement he

made was clear. There weren't any barriers between the person reciting the Gettysburg Address and Harry answering your questions. It all felt very real.

The same thing happened with Erica. She became very clear and pure, and it seemed just how the character should be.

NR: Erica had a wonderful rhythm going as she walked in a circle. [*to ERICA*] How much of an effort was it to keep the same beat going? Your determination looked pretty strong.

ERICA: It was an effort.

NR: You were talking with us. Did you see how, as she walked, she began talking with us?

Who's next?

[MEG volunteers.]

We'll forget about walking the circle for now; let's see the monologue as you prepared it.

Now I'd like you all to move your chairs to form a semicircle around the playing space.

I'm asking you to close in a little bit because I would like you as the audience to participate in the monologue as you hear it, with whatever comes to your mind by association. And I'd like the person doing the monologue to adjust, accommodate, receive, react to the responses that come from the audience. Is that clear?

LIZ: "Participate in the monologue"—does that mean speak out, or go up there to the playing space?

NR: It does not mean go up there.

Meg, are you ready?

> *[MEG pulls a chair to the back wall of the playing space, seats herself at a table across from an empty chair with her back to the audience, and presents her monologue.]*

NR: You brought an association to me, a line from a poem by Browning called "Prospice:" "Fear death?—to feel the fog in my throat, . . ."[17] I felt like saying it. That's what I meant by the audience participating in the monologue.

Meg, why did you move the chair? Why didn't any of you ask why she moved the chair away from us? I want you all to participate with your feelings, your immediate responses. This is more than an

---

17. Robert Browning *The Poems and Plays of Robert Browning* (New York: The Modern Library, 1934), p. 318.

exercise in recitation. There's a great reluctance in all of you here to open your mouths. You can't get anywhere in the theatre if you are afraid. Meg, why did you move your chair away? Why couldn't you have been facing us since he wasn't here anyway?

MEG: I didn't want to use the audience as him. I wanted distance from the audience.

NR: How will you achieve that distance when the camera is in close-up, five feet, a few inches away? This is not a facetious question. As an exercise, yes, learn to embrace the audience.

MEG: Sometimes I don't trust that the audience is interested in what I'm doing, so I rush through just to get offstage.

NR: What breaks your concentration? How does the feeling of distrust get to you? Do you try to analyze it in terms of your action? Do you know what I mean by *action*?

I believe the use of the word *action* and your understanding of that word, is the single most important aspect of your technique. An actor has to act. To act means to do. Action is doing. It is not business, it is not embroidery. What do I want? How do I overcome my problem? Why am I here? What do I want to do? Action implies desire and will.

Your action is what you want to do, what you must do to get what you want. I suggest you phrase your action in the infinitive form of the verb: to do, to get. Your action is your only protection against overpreparation and loss of concentration, against failing to meet your obligation to your audience. Forget the state-of-being school of acting. It leads no place. A state of being is not something you can utilize as an actor, it is not an active force on film. In my experience your action is the only tool that's reliable.

There was a time in New York theatre when everybody talked in terms of intention. To another worker in the theatre *intention* may have full meaning; to me it is what the road to hell is paved with. It's what leads the actor into the almost-emotion, the almost-action, the almost-black, or the almost-white. It is as full as almost-pregnant. Action, to do, is full.

LEONARD: It seems to me your concept of action combines Stanislavsky's concepts of *objective* and *action*.

NR: Your action is your reason for being there, what impels you. Your action has to have an objective. If you want something, your action is what you are going to do about it.

SAM: I find myself substituting the word *motivation* for *action*. I have trouble disconnecting my motive from my action.

NR: Fine. Let's not get snowed under by words. I don't want to be frozen in a concept. You must use words that have meaning to you.

Action is tied up in our idiom with the concepts of *movement* and *activity*, and with "where the action is." In churches it's at the center, you know? I want your action to be specific and meaningful to you, and I want it to be meaningful to other people.

I will keep suggesting this tool to you because it works, but maybe you'll find a different way of approaching it or putting it together. What word can I substitute for *action* so that it becomes more understandable to you? Can I use *reason*? Can I use *job*? I want you to search and find your own way.

Did you catch how Charlotte just entered? There was a quality, a rhythm to her entrance that should interest you as directors.

■　■　■

NR: Jet, you're up.

> *[JET had prepared a scene with BEV, which JOSEF directed and videotaped. The tape is screened for discussion.]*

NR: What was your action, Jet?
JET: I wanted to find out if she was like me, if she couldn't have a kid either, so I wouldn't be alone, so I wouldn't be a freak.
NR: Do you feel Jet achieved her action? Anybody?
PETE: I felt there was very little contact between Jet and the other person. Jet was looking down a lot, so I wasn't sure what she wanted from Bev.
NR: The Indians have a saying: "Eyes find eyes." If an Indian were in hiding or waiting in ambush, he'd look away if he saw a white-faced scout, because eyes find eyes. Here it's important for eyes to find eyes.

I was at a cocktail party at my agent's some years ago to which I'd brought a young actor from New York. He and I made ourselves comfortable on the floor and got to discussing the differences between film and stage acting. Presently I noticed a huge bulk of clothed flesh at my side which then got itself into sitting position on the floor beside us. It was Charles Laughton. He leaned over, tapped the young actor on the knee, and said, "What Nick is trying to tell you, young man, is that the melody is in the eyes, the words are only the left hand."

Film has the magic quality of being able to photograph thought. You must act so your eyes will be visible to us.

The first time a cast assembles to read through a script, I don't concern myself with whether they get the words right or not. I want them to make contact with their eyes. I want to know they're talking with each other. I'll stop the reading ten times on a page if the actors aren't looking at each other. This is particularly important in film, because in film the eyes are such very real and visible facets of the human being, while from the stage they're just blurs to anyone beyond the eighth row.

But the camera work here was also inadequate. It did not capture on film the turbulence in Jet's eyes, her emotion and the way it was being expressed. The camera was not close enough. It should move from a tight two-shot to a close-up. That may mean resetting for the close-up. If the director has an aversion to the zoom lens, he can cut in with a three- or four-inch lens to a big choker.

MOLLY: I felt Jet was basically acting alone, and the other person was just there.

NR: Jet had all the words, but remember, the words are only the left hand. This was not a monologue. The moment Jet chose someone else to work with, it became a scene.

An actor must be sensitive to other actors. Along with awareness of the camera, awareness of yourself and others in space develops gradually and is terribly important, because a scene will not be effective visually if the other person in it is not as strong in her action as you are in yours.

Remember, there is no hero or heroine in literature or in reality who hasn't had to overcome obstacles. I was once offered a film with Bette Davis. It was her heyday and I wanted very much to work with her, it would have been great for me at that point in my career. But I read the script and the hero, her opposition, was cast as a very virile-looking milquetoast whose actions presented no problem for her to overcome. But how can you be a heroine if you have no problems to overcome? How can you be a hero if you have no problems to overcome? In your relationship to another on the screen, it is to your advantage for her action, her point of view, her presentation of conflict to be strong. Then what you do becomes important. Don't ever object to the strength in another person's part.

The actor off-camera has to be just as full as the actor on-camera. Both actors must be alive and working all the time. If there's a reverse on me, for example, you'd have to be just as full as when the camera had been on you to help me come alive so the takes will match in intensity. In the theatre, the ability to upstage is a technique studied and envied by many; in film, it is bullshit. You have to give to the other person because if you don't, he ain't going to give to you. You just can't do anything in film alone.

BEV: I didn't feel comfortable on this stage.

NR: Nothing says that an actor has to be comfortable. You have to be comfortable with your choice of action, but you do not have to be physically comfortable. Sometimes it will work much better for you to find ways to become extremely *un*comfortable.

BEV: I should have used the discomfort.

NR: Right. And that would have fed Jet's emotion as well.

Who else wants to work? Charlotte, are you ready?

> *[CHARLOTTE begins a monologue, and finishes her perfor-mance in tears. NICK asks her to describe her feelings as she began the scene. She says she was upset with herself for hav-ing been late to class.]*

NR: How much did fright have to do with your breaking down and your tears?

CHARLOTTE: I think there was some fear, but more shame, really, and anger at myself.

NR: Why didn't you go with the feelings you had? You must be gentle with yourself, trust yourself, go with where you find yourself. You had done the preparation—not the preparation you had planned to do, but something else. In this case you had to cope with an event of reality, your coming in late to class. What happens in real life if, say, you feel logy, very sluggish, and you have to meet with a group of very bright people? Are you going to fight the way you feel or are you going to go with it? You have to go with it. If you don't, you're going to make a horse's ass out of yourself trying to force it.

Say ten minutes before the curtain goes up, or before you walk on a sound stage, you learn you've lost your life savings on the stock market. That had not been a part of your preparation. It's such a shocker, it blows your concentration. What are you going to do? You're going to have to let it in. And ask yourself: "Why am I here? What do I want to do?" Remember your action. That's your insurance. Your performance doesn't have to sound the way you rehearsed it. If it sounds different to your mind's ear, let it sound different.

I felt you were fighting what was normal and natural to you at the same time that you were doing something very well. You were embarrassed that you were crying. The emotion was full within you, but you were really trying to control it, not expose it. That could have been very good if you had been a little more honest, and not forced. An actor must always have control; otherwise the prop daggers will become bloody. But having control is different from forcing.

The control of emotional memory is an aspect of acting of tremen-

dous interest to me. Charlotte found herself sitting on a keg of dynamite, an emotional charge that she wasn't prepared for. Something
happened to her and she did not know what to do with it. What do
you do when the emotional memory becomes so full that you can't
turn it off? What do you do when a strong emotion, a strong impulse,
a strong need to do something, takes you over in the middle of a
scene? How do you control that great virtuous flow?

Number one, do not disallow it. Recognize it, let it grow, and then
use it. How can you use it without going out of control? How do you
achieve and maintain control?

You may be tempted to take the impulse or emotion as divine inspiration and go completely haywire with it, regardless of why you are
on stage or in front of camera. But you must refer to your action—why
you are there, what you want to do—and subject the impulse to that.
What is your action? That question must become second nature to
you. Your action is your pilot. If your action is strong enough within
you, the scene will happen on all levels—kinetic, intellectual, emotional. Playing the action and subjecting the impulse, the emotional
charge to the action achieves control.

Had I been Charlotte's director and able to get to her in time, I'd
have distracted her from her tense state of being and told her to think
of her action. If an emotional state of being is allowed to take over
completely, so you dissolve in emotion—whether in laughter or in
tears—that is improper preparation, overpreparation: you have such
an inside joke going on that when you do the scene no one else laughs,
or you have so much emotion going on that you're wasted by the
second take. When you feel a state of being taking over, you must
catch yourself.

What is your action? Knowing that will be enough to keep you
alive through a day that may demand fourteen repetitions of the same
scene. A bulb goes out, a cable gets crossed, an airplane flies overhead,
someone slams a door, someone trips— It's not your fault, but you
have to do it again. Your only insurance of staying alive is in complete
preparation and knowing your action, which is part of your preparation. Find the action. Play the action. If one doesn't work, switch to
another.

Now if you can't keep control, that's fine too. You're among friends.
If you feel that tremendous impulse surging in you and it seems it's
going to burst the bounds, let it, have the guts to go all the way.
Follow your impulse, because it may be the event of reality, that
mystical thing, the flight that takes you to the heavens. You must
recognize it when it happens. If flight is about to take place and you

know what your action is, you know what you want to do, then you are not going to go haywire.

Then you can go as loud as you want, but it has to be so true, there can't be one molecule of falsity in it. When you're full of truth at the moment of explosion there will be no mistaking it, and the camera and the celluoid strip will be able to handle it all. Those are very rare moments, and most film performances are modified by the conditions surrounding them. It's very seldom that an actor can give his very best performance. Even the great performances are, in my opinion, less than what they ought to be.

These same problems are likely to come up over and over again in different contexts. It can't happen too often. We're going into everything prematurely, but I don't know any other way to do it but to let it happen, and when it happens, grab it. I don't want anything to go by.

I hate to bore people . . .

[1977]

I hate to bore people, and I think most film biographies are bores. And I resent their being bores because the filmmakers about whom they're written have spent their lives trying to unbore people. Our function is to communicate, tell something, show something. Create a whole. Share a despair. A book, even under the driest auspices, ought to do that; I think that's its purpose. But most film biographies, including those of me, belong in a certain class of entertainment and instruction known in the black-and-white art film days as arty to the mass public that never went to see them. For me the trick always has been to try to get the film into those theatres that would help attract and could accommodate the major number of people possible.

But what shall I do about all of the transitional phrases or pages necessary to make what follows comprehensible to you? The horrible experiences of showing rough cuts of films to film "producers" should have made me trauma-proof by now, but I'm not.

■ ■ ■

I have been under the lash of alcoholism since birth.

I was born in Wisconsin. My grandfather died on Main Street, in front of the office of a doctor called White Beaver by the Indians, while carrying the first buck deer of the season over his shoulders.

My father built levees, docking areas for steamboats, and dykes against floods. He built colleges, creameries, whorehouses, cathedrals, and breweries. Before he was 21, he was the contractor for the construction of one of the first churches on the northern Mississippi. He married his first wife in the Church. He divorced her, and was ex-communicated. He joined the Masons and married my mother, a Norwegian Lutheran. I was born when he was 50, my mother, 39. In my most vivid memories of their relationship, they slept in separate bedrooms. My mother was fond of saying, "Lips that touch liquor shall never touch mine." Who cared when there were so many younger lips?

All during my childhood and Prohibition there was booze in the house, and on the street. At home it was for stealing; I stole my first pint at ten. On the street it was for buying—grain alcohol mixed with sugar and hot water—with money stolen from home. One day a schoolmate downed a bottle of wood alcohol and died horribly. We held a drunken ritual in his honor. Years later in Hollywood the head grip on my crew reached behind the darkened set for his stash of gin and drank from a bottle of carbon tet. He was carried offstage dead.

During Prohibition where I grew up there were twenty-one saloons and speakeasies on one street. I learned to drive when I was 13 so I could get my father home safe from his nightly rounds of speakeasies and bootleggers. Sometimes I'd wait for him in the car and masturbate. At the age of 14 I learned of his mistress. At 15 I made an unsuccessful pass at her. One night at age 16 my father could not be found. I went hunting for his mistress, and found her in a speakeasy across from a brewery my father had built. She led me to a hotel room. He was lying in sweat and puke, with puke pans on the floor at the side of the bed. I took him home and nursed him through the night.

In the morning Doc Rhodes came. He was a dope addict. Before I left for school I watched him heat a substance in a spoon and draw it into a hypodermic. In Latin class I alternated between dozing off and hypertension. I asked to be excused. I went to the S&H Pool Hall and practiced three-cushion billiards. There was a phone call. My mother had tracked me down. My father was dying.

He was dead when I got home. I had never been in a Catholic church, but I genuflected at his side, kissed him, and spent the night in a Turkish bath.

Six months later my mother and I got the doctor into court, but I was so pissed on home brew I couldn't testify, so we lost. The next day I saw the doctor walking on Main Street. I was driving a new Oakland Cabriolet. I was drunk. I ran the car at him across from the cathedral my father had built. A fire hydrant got in the way. Doc Rhodes left town. I got my first ticket for reckless driving.

I learned about Aqua Velva long before I started shaving. No, I didn't drink it. I poured it over the sheets or into the bathtub to clear the smell of my puke.

The pool hall was important, especially on Sundays at noon, after church. I got kicked out of high school seventeen times.

A boy needs a father at certain times in his life so he can kick him in the shins, so he can fight for the love of his mother. The boy misbehaves at one point, runs away at another, while his father remains constant, a gauge against which the boy can measure himself. Take that away and the spine is lost.

■ ■ ■

My sister Ruth, who guided me to my first movie house, was stage-struck. She wanted desperately to be an actress, but no way, not in our family. She released some of her frustrations by continuing to guide me to concerts, theatres, and nightclubs in Chicago during the Capone years. She was working for Edith Rockefeller McCormick.[18] Whenever I got kicked out of school in LaCrosse I'd go to Chicago to live with Ruth and finish the school term. During one of those years she married a scientist-inventor named Shmidling. He was an associate of Lee de Forest in the development of the cathode ray tube for television. Techniques and schemes for heating houses with the sun's rays were a major preoccupation of that ex-brother-in-law. My sister divorced him, so we lost touch. I suppose he remained as poor as Dr. de Forest. Show business, you know? My sister remarried another man on the fringe of show business, and lived out her life as a miserably unhappy millionaire.

I have another older sister[19] who wanted to be an architect. A lady architect? In Wisconsin? In the '20s? No way. At the age of 75 she joined AA, a beautiful, courageous woman for herself, but I suspect she wanted me to become a bank teller. Maybe I should have.

I like women, perhaps not wisely and perhaps too much. I feel rather poetic about women, whether it's savagely poetic or lyrically poetic—but not poetic in the Victorian sense, the pedestal sense. I feel poetic about getting them off the pedestal. Women are stronger than men. They can endure more pain. They're more daring, more imaginative, more adventurous than men.

---

18. A leading Chicago philanthropist of the time.
19. Alice.

■ ■ ■

I won a scholarship to any university in the world, largely due to my work with a radio station. I chose the University of Chicago. I was going to learn something. How to ensure that inspired thought. I took along two gallon tins of undiluted grain alcohol. Two weeks after I arrived on campus I was pledged to a frat and playing football; but I didn't make it through the first year.

While attending the U of C, I was continually standing on the tip of my stiff prick and therefore wanted, as in the old Jewish curse, to go from bed to bed to room to room in every girls' dormitory.

Ask me about *Of Human Bondage*. I was Leslie Howard. A scroungy waitress was Bette Davis. The character of Maugham fascinated me. The scuttlebutt was that the clubfoot was a literary substitution for his homosexuality. I didn't know whether I wanted to be a homosexual or not; homosexual was not in my vocabulary. Did I love and revere men more than women? I think I did.

The head of the University of Chicago drama department hosted a dinner for Miss Ethel Barrymore, then appearing in *School for Scandal*. At dinner Miss B. held forth in a most outrageous way against Miss Edna Ferber's book, *The Royal Family*, which described the handsome queen of actors at a given moment exclaiming, "My God! I'll be late!"

"Everyone knows," said Miss B., "that I've never been late to a performance—or rehearsal, for that matter—in my life, and for her to insinuate as much is nauseating." Miss B.'s voice was chilling and threatening and broke like a rumbling surf across the table into my ears.

"Shocking," a guest pronounced.

"Shocking," added a second.

"Some people simply, uh—" said a third.

"We all know that, Miss Barrymore," rattled another.

She laughed. Another wave hit my shore.

She placed her hand on our host's wrist. "Tell me, darling. What time is it?"

"Seven forty-five. You'll—"

"My God! I'll be late!!" she rumbled, and roared away to meet her curtain at 8:40.

How privileged, how truly *in* I had been, to actually smirk at Edna Ferber in company with the truly adult. A night on the heights . . .

In a Peapod

In the free association, self ridicule, and ego trip of my first attempt at an autobiography I didn't mention filmmaking at all, although it has been and is, with perhaps one or two rare exceptions, the whole mainstream of my life, that for which I have over and over again sacrificed and tried to regiment personal life. Perhaps filmmaking for me is more personal than any of the personal things.

I do not believe in the "auteur theory" as it has been adapted by critics and turned into a gimmick for them to write upon. And I do feel the need to question whether we filmmakers are auteurs in the artsy sense of the word, making the embroidery more important than the theme. Still there is no doubt in my mind—as much as I believe in a fundamental humility toward a script or idea that someone else has proposed—that even the best-written script is a blueprint for the director, and that the director of a film is the true author of the film, who surveys all the contradictions.

And so I think I'm a creator as opposed to an interpreter. As to my style or signature, I don't know my own style, and I'd rather talk about the signature of a Minelli or of a Zinneman, a Ford, a Buñuel, a Kazan, a Rosellini, a Luc [sic] Godard. A signature is as important on a film, I guess, as it is on a painting or a short story, a poem, a novel, or any other work of art. I think that whether it's a good film or a bad film, every film is in some way a key to the director, if he has any signature at all. Otherwise he's a craftsman, and no more. If a director has a signature, it must be because the combination of his personality, neuroses, insight, crudeness or sophistication, and whatever else he knows of himself is very meaningful to him, but not self-consciously. We survive by what we expose of ourselves.

I think I have a signature, but I can think that only because I know how much of me is in my films, how autobiographical are moments I've never experienced in reality, but which have the authority of conviction because they are autobiographical. Perhaps it is sometimes only my own neuroses and my own dislocation that attract attention, and which are misinterpreted as interesting. But if that is so, it is only because I feel free enough to expose them. Whether they are the truth for other people I will find out only when the film is accepted or not by those who see it.

I've heard espousers of auteur theory refer to me as the "poet of aloneness." I can't discuss the need for people to connect without connecting the void, space, and time with the need for people to connect. The need for people to connect comes out of aloneness, the aloneness that different spatial alignments or counter-themes create, or set the stage for, or help to dramatize. But it's the way we see them: a different person will see those spatial alignments in an entirely different way, from a different perspective, and they still will be the same. And natural energy-provided or man-made shiftings of matter in a shifting space, keeping their same relative positions of one mass to another, seem permanent to the temporary viewer, but are always changing.

So how to be an actor in the drama of the world Nicholas Ray supposedly created, but about which he knows not the boundaries, customs, manners, nor morals, nor even the color of the skies and oceans that go to make up a world? I'm not just being cute and reflective when I quote my mother and say, that's not for me to talk about, nor is it for me to conceive. I have no vision of the perfectly ordered world. I don't have the presumption of a social builder or a social critic. I can sometimes say that I have reflected to the best of my ability a part of the life and times in which I've lived from my own prejudiced and/or at times distorted, and kept-in-distortion, point of view; but as an actor, and not always the principal actor, in this little world, I cannot very well be the interpreter of my own interpretation.

And yet intellectually I do respect and I do have feeling for my intentions, and more particularly, for either my success or failure at communication. I respect the failure equally with the success, because success always surprises me, and failure I take for granted. Sometimes it surprises me when things fail, though I'm always fairly attuned to the Sphinx who said, "Don't expect too much." Generally I learn more from my failures than from my successes.

Words are terribly deceptive. It's a pity we have to use them as a main vehicle of communication. We let words go by, believing their meaning is inferred, while it's always open to our interpretation, misinterpretation, or abuse, sometimes unintended, sometimes not. It's always when I realize that I'm dangerously close to something meaningful to me that I resort to the attack or flip phrase or an attempt at humor, sarcasm, satire. I do this in order to protect the privy world I'm trying to approach and expose, hoping to reach a deeper layer of interest in the so-called personal aesthetic. The personal aesthetic must include the artist's economic and sexual involvements and how those relate to what he does every day—and I suppose that's why it's so touchy.

So what am I trying to say? The artist/manager/dictator/planner/logistician/strategist/politician/con artist/director under economic pressure, as he always is when making a film, has to have one little peapod filled with molecules of association to all the senses. That peapod is the repository of all his prejudices, character defects, angers, promises, hopes, conceits, vanities, loves, regrets, sentiments, as well as an automatic censor. Everything resides in the same little peapod which wanders around from bloodstream to air pocket to joints of bones.

Since all those elements must be employed in his work, why does the artist feel he must protect them? And how can he know how to use them without tapping into what is, for him, perhaps the most precious element of all, the imagination? I'm not ashamed of my imagination, and I regularly expose it, but how the imagination works in connecting all the other factors required for creative work is for me a very sensitive area.

I'd like to explore this theme a bit, as it may reveal something of the creative process and how it works in the daily economic and social life of the artist.

I recall a scene in a car at the shore of a lake at the time I was going to school at the University of Chicago. The head of the drama department had invited me to a dinner party for a prominent actress. This bewildered me: certainly I was not so brilliant as a young actor in college as to warrant that kind of attention. After dinner the white-haired professor and I got into his automobile and drove back towards the campus. Lake Michigan was savage black water. For some reason unknown to me, he drove us to its edge and parked. I would have done that too, with Ruth or Henny or Hollie or Francis, but not with my professor.

Instinctually I knew I had to say something. And what I said came out of what was supplied me from the environment, the air and stuff around me. The water helped me stretch my imagination. I began describing the scene that I saw: a horde of Indians in canoes coming out of the black of the night and riding the waves of the lake—by God, a little bit the way Joe Losey brought the Arabs into *Modesty Blaise*. I was fabricating this because I knew the approach of a man who liked other men was about to happen. To impress him was my action. But I couldn't catch him up to change his action. He caressed me. I wanted to please him. God knows I wanted to say thank you, somehow I wanted to say thank you. I said thank you. He unbuttoned my trousers. I wanted to come if he wanted me to come. I stroked his grey-white hair. I couldn't come. We drove back to campus.

That filling of the void by the imagination coming to the rescue is an experience that perhaps very many of us have shared. The imagination is a pretty precious source of protection.

That specific situation also brought to light an attitude in myself not consistent with the social denigration of homosexuals in those days. Later that attitude became very helpful to me in understanding and directing some of the actors with whom I've worked. I believe that I have been or would be successful in exposing the feminine in the roughest male symbol the public could accept. I always suspect the warmth or tenderness or color range of a person who publicly disports himself in either too strict a feminine or too strict a masculine role. For example, I must suspect the sentiment in the suicidal life Hemingway lived, and the ambivalence that could create the number of young writers who called him Papa.

Another situation: somebody who never got to know his father very well finds himself in need of stronger, older male direction. He begins to equate that male direction with male companionship because he knows the need must be satisfied in some way; but he finds that male companionship, unless on a Ward Bond/John Wayne level, is suspect. So what does he do? He builds another reserve of emotion, another source of energy, if he is sensitive at all, which he adds to the peapod.

Why does the artist protect the peapod of molecules? He protects it to avoid the judgments of the world around him, obviously. But the peapod is also instinctually protected by an inner knowledge that the emotions and associations contained within it are the source of the artist's energy and creative spark, his ability to observe and interpret, and possibly also his most beautiful and grossest mistakes. I submit that this is a major chord in whatever statements I make of aloneness.

It is the business of a director to expose himself in whatever ways are necessary in order to communicate, either directly or through the performances of other artists. But it is difficult for somebody as old as I am who has been conditioned not to reveal himself. What happens to the peapod as it relates to the director and his films?

The way the imagination works for me, and I can't assume I'm unique, is that it gives me the ability to lie about myself. I've always found this very important, for example, in my relationship with actors who unfortunately are busy creating their images and who are timid, afraid. I will tell an actor about a situation in which I was involved, in which I was never really involved, but at that moment my imagination is providing me with the situation as if I had been there. That allows the actor to become comfortable enough to think and to permit associations, memories, and daydreams to flow into him so he can have his own moments of decision. As director I somehow want to be of enough help to each actor individually that he will come to believe each idea, action, piece of business, use of a prop, is his own, and only his. I cannot recommend this method of work for others because I know the attrition, I know the connotations and involvement, the wearing and tearing involvement, that it demands. I do it this way, I have to do it this way because I'm not very glib, and I'm always a bit suspect of the rules of the game.

I don't believe in the rules of the game. I just don't believe there isn't an exception every time, somewheres. If the rules were right, I think people would generally embrace them, and expand, and add brightness and color and desirability to the rules. Instead rules are suffered, rules are obeyed instead of enjoyed, and they represent fences and barriers. I don't think they can be very good. I don't think they can generate progress in a man. I've never said that before. And I've never tried to define this molecule of the peapod, but it's a part of what I'm about as a director.

I've always run at the fire bell. Here we have another wellspring of creative energy. It is a very private area, one's will to find out about forms of destruction: self-destruction, genocide, the drama of the disaster, the projection of oneself into either the casket or flaming martyrdom. All contain the origin of symbols with which we've become very familiar.

My friend Les Farber, who wrote *The Ways of the Will*[20], said that the moment the poet, philosopher, psychologist, psychiatrist, writer, or movie director admits that man can destroy himself, then, whether he likes it or not, he is involved with the metaphysical. Adventures into the metaphysical and mysticism are components of another molecule in the peapod. Perhaps my own connections with the metaphysical are too precious or too unformed to permit their being approached by anybody asking a question that could touch and tingle or sever the nerve of communication; but the director must expose, and unashamedly, whatever he truthfully feels about those things, even if what he feels is abhorrence.

The other night, watching the last two reels of *On the Waterfront* on TV, I was again struck by Kazan's translation of "To be or not to be." That's what the film is about. It's not about the waterfront; it's about "To be or not to be." And that lies in the hand of man himself.

There was a period when I examined why I liked certain color combinations, why, for example, I believed that blue and green should never be together. I felt they clashed, even though nature filled everything around me with blue and green. And it took me years before I would buy any painting that had brown and red on the same canvas. Finally—it was a remarkable day to me—I bought two paintings by a French artist just because they had brown and red together. I don't know why, and I don't think it's worth exploring, because there's really no answer, except we are all products of our neuroses. Our personalities, our characters, and our varying degrees of education and its opposite—its damn near opposite, knowledge—are all products of our neuroses.

Some things I just can't explain, some things on color, composition, and either my bad taste or my good taste. Hearing enough influential people repeat that I had a signature of my own, I became unhealthily self-conscious for a while, and not really investigative. But it never occurred to me that because my mother did not drop me on the head while listening to her first jukebox I developed a healthy respect for all expressions in music.

Then there are the very matter-of-fact answers: I did it because I knew it was the only thing I could do. Or I did it because I had to save money someplace so I could add it to the most important scene. Or I was lucky in a decision forced on me by the weather to take an

20. Leslie H. Farber, M.D., *The Ways of the Will: Essays Toward a Psychology and Psychopathology of Will* (New York: Basic Books, 1966).

exterior inside, and the interior turned out to be much better than what I could have expected from the exterior. Or a producer said, "We have to save money, we have to cut out some sets"; so I shot an exterior, and the exterior turned out fine.

There's no self-aggrandizement to be had by making a big song-and-dance about how brilliant I've been. It's so much more often just a matter of a given situation, and a director's days are filled with those situations. To face them I've needed everything within me to be working so they do turn out well, but at the time I don't know that they will. At the time I'm not investigating myself; I'm either responding or I'm not responding, I'm in tune or I'm not in tune, my instrument is working or it's clogged.

Sometimes there are accidents that are discoveries of myself or illuminations of an intention of the subconscious that get on film without my realizing it. If, after wrestling with all the details and influences and pressures and logistics and everything else at work upon and within me as a director every hour of the day, I discover that little surprise and know either instinctually or professionally that I've found the truth of the scene— That's the kind of accident I mean. It's a revelation. It's kind of a wonderful, magic moment when I see it's there. Film is so much of an experience.

BACKSTORY;
PREPARATION;
FALSE START;
DIRECTOR'S RELAXATION

NR: Charlotte, can you re-create how you came in late the other day?
CHARLOTTE: Yeah. There's a certain touch about coming in late. I came in alone. I felt very isolated and unsure.
NR: Can you do it again?

[She tries.]

NR: Just now Charlotte could not get back the quality of her entrance, so she tried to show it.
CHARLOTTE: The first time people had their backs to me, while just now they were looking at me all at once. That made me very self-conscious. What stands out in my mind about coming into a place late is that I'm always so conscious of what other people might be thinking about me.
NR: Yes. Yet if in your entrance you had not taken for granted that this was the only aisle, that this was the only chair, had you circulated among these people to find your way, you would have had the chance to experience true and spontaneous feeling. But what is the self-consciousness, what is it in us? Is it that we want to be liked and accepted? Do we want people to come up and tell us we gave a good show?

Here is the problem: with repetition after repetition, even a simple entrance will go dry on you. Obviously trying to re-create or relive that moment of reality is not enough, neither particularly interesting nor convincing. You may get by with it, but it won't be art. When you are trying to create a living experience for the camera it becomes your responsibility to recognize that intent in yourself and to be honest to the point that you know beyond a doubt you are not faking it. Does anyone have an idea of what Charlotte could do to keep her entrance fresh?

JOSEF: She could put an action to it.

NR: Action, yes, eventually, but it might be more helpful to start with a *backstory*. Creating a backstory is an important first step in the actor's preparation, his process of relating himself to the part he is playing. Even an entrance has a backstory, in theatre as well as in film.

Creating a backstory requires your using the magic IF and asking yourself: "If such a thing happens, what would have happened before that?" In answering the question you must draw on the totality of your imagination, associations, what you have read, past experiences. Start gathering your references—lines of poetry, a laugh, what happened when you smoked your first joint, what happened on your first plane ride, what happened when your purse was stolen. Cary Grant had literally two trunks full of notations on everything from sunsets to burlesque gags that he could use.

The whole quality of a performance is rooted in the IF capacities of the actor. Endowed with physical, mental, and spiritual existence, and sometimes with a talent or a genius on loan, he trains his total personality toward that moment of transition when he is no longer acting as if he were the character, and he becomes the character. It is his backstory that helps him draw on the intimate stuff of feelings, thoughts, and events in order to make the transition from "*If* I were he" to "I *am* he; therefore I want to do this." At that moment of transition, understanding and action combine, the actor prepares, the character develops, and realization begins.

In his preparation the actor is both the violin and the violinist simultaneously. He must make contact with the self, the real thing. When he's in touch with that, then he can change it into something else. In finding out who he really is, he can create an entirely fictional character with whom he's had no bowing acquaintance before, even in fantasy.

There's no escape from doing your homework. An author will give you a situation, but most authors won't be like George Bernard Shaw who wrote *Androcles and the Lion* in seven days and then spent three months writing a preface about the play's background.

Charlotte, I would like to give you the problem now, once more, of trying to re-create your entrance. And I want the rest of you to be thinking about what you would do as actors faced with the same problem.

[CHARLOTTE tries the entrance again.]

Who else would like to try this? Arthur? Do you recall how you came in late that day?
ARTHUR: I took the seat all the way in the back.
NR: Do you remember how you were feeling?
ARTHUR: I felt bad about being late.
NR: Were you breathless?
ARTHUR: Yes, I had been running from the train.
NR: Why didn't you use that just now?
ARTHUR: I was trying to re-create what I did this morning instead of what I did the other day.
NR: Well, it didn't work. You were showing. As actors in theatre you can get by with indication, you can get by with showing, although neither is good for your performance or career. In film you can't get by. A lot of people do, just from the force of their personalities, or because of the time pressures the director is under that force him always to face the possibility of settling for something less than good. But that is not your responsibility. Your responsibility is to do it as best you can, using every resource you've got.

As actors you work with a series of moments that exist for you and eventually must exist on film for the audience. You are like the circus performer who rehearses hours and hours, weeks and months and years, in order to give the audience a few split seconds of excitement and thrill. Burt Lancaster is a great actor who learned about moments of perfection as an acrobat in the circus and who worked just as hard once he learned about the actor's preparation. Who am I? What am I? Why am I here? What do I want to do? *What do I want to do?*

Charlotte, let me give you an example of what I'm talking about, and see if it works for you. Let's take a circumstance and a place: It is the chapel of a funeral parlor. Everybody is quiet; the service has begun. People are at their most attentive. The organ is playing. The body lying in the casket is that of a very dear friend for whom you would have given a great deal. Fill in the rest of the story. Take a few minutes before your entrance.

When Charlotte tried to reproduce from memory her entrance as a latecomer, she couldn't. In this exercise we'll draw on past experience, but a different set of circumstances, to see if that might not be the way to re-create the entrance. There are a thousand variations on these circumstances. This is only an example of the kind of mental construction you may have to depend on in the thirty seconds, minute-and-a-half, two minutes, five minutes before the next take, when you're dry in the part, you know your rhythm is off, and you're not making the right kind of an entrance.

Charlotte, whenever you're ready—

[CHARLOTTE tries the entrance again.]

NR: Now look, you're still not playing the game. What is the backstory? Someone repeat the backstory. Did anybody hear the organ music? What are the sounds? This is a chapel. Had you placed the body in the grave already?

CHARLOTTE: No, it was in a casket.

NR: Where, down here?

CHARLOTTE: No, up about here.

NR: In film especially, please remember, the melody is in the eyes. That is where everything is going to happen. If you do not have eye contact—whether with one other person, a group, or an imaginary object—you're no place.

Let's continue. Someone else?

[Others try the entrance.]

NR: Bev was the only one I felt heard the organ. Was there a specific hymn that you were hearing?

BEV: I was listening to "Abide with Me."

NR: Betty, what happened to you?

BETTY: As I began my entrance I knew I was off, but I felt I could get back on track as the scene went on.

NR: That was a false start. After a false start it's too late. Cut right away. You know if you're not making the right kind of entrance. If your entrance is off, the likelihood is that it will take you quite a while into the scene before you set yourself right, and then it's too late.

ARTHUR: What do you mean by *false start*?

NR: It can be a false start for the actor, a false start for camera, or a false start for sound. It can be that your sound and camera are not in synch. Or it can be when an actor does any single thing, however slight—a hand through the hair, a stick of gum in the mouth—that makes you respond, "Ah, it's off," and tells you his preparation has not been complete. That's a false start for the actor, and it's a false start for the camera too, because the camera's been rolling.

At any such moment, directors, cut right away. Otherwise, you're going to have to go back to it later, after you've completed three or four other setups and changed stuff all around, and that's economically unfeasible. So cut right away, no shame, no blame.

Actors, you then have the problem of repreparing. As you do so, you must ask yourself: Who am I? Begin with yourself. Create a backstory. Create circumstances. What is your reason for being here? Do you feel guilt? Do you feel overwhelming love? Are you making this appearance for opportunistic reasons, to be seen? I saw so very little individuality in your entrances. I saw only minimal recognition of other people. What sounds are you hearing? What are your sensations? What has been your training in sense memory, if any?

By the way, girls, if you are bothered by your hair, it's a good indication that you're about to lose concentration. If your hair becomes more important than what you are saying, then go with that. If the mosquito is there, really dust it away, or kill it. Make a virtue out of it, or it will become self-conscious.

One of the most important skills you can achieve for yourself is the ability, the moment before your entrance, to answer the questions: "Why am I here? What has just happened?" In doing this you will trigger your preparation, everything you've done in rehearsal, all that flood of association, sensation, and emotional memory, so that everything congeals right at that moment. You must be imaginative enough to pull from the moment a poem or story, a set of circumstances, a feeling with an environment that, together with your action, will once again bring you alive.

■ ■ ■

[DAKOTA has prepared a scene, with MARA as director, in which she recites a poem to NICK, who plays her father. The class views two takes on videotape.]

DAKOTA: First it was just a reading of a poem, and then it became a scene in which I read the poem to my father. It was a poem I'd written to him.

NR: I found the second take was better, much more personal, and your action much clearer.

BETTY: The second take was better focused.

NR: That's very interesting. Had we been using both cameras, one on Dakota and one on me, in the editing we could have cut to me when the camera on Dakota went out of focus in the first take, and used the fog to convey confusion from my point of view. That way the technical fault could become an asset.

Dakota, did you feel better in the second?

DAKOTA: Enormously.

NR: Mara?

MARA: I felt very divided between the crew and the actors. When I was with the actors, I felt I was neglecting technical details; when I was taking care of camera and lights I felt I was abandoning the actors.

NR: So many things happen in the making of a film every day, it's quite possible to lose a whole concept amid the multiplicity of demands on your attention. Just as the actor prepares, so must the director. So after all the details of lights, props, color, set-dressing, crew temperament, focus, rehearsal, and the terribly intimate exchanges with actors have been attended to, you must be able to go back to the camera, and you must develop and exercise for yourself a relaxation, a willingness to accept, and a willingness not to take anything for granted. Before you permit the camera to be turned, you must be ready to receive, respond to, and evaluate the scene about to play. And if in the course of the scene you find a lack in your response, you have to find out why, and either redirect the actors, or supply them with something else to work from, until the scene is fulfilled. You have to know when you can say "Print!" And again, this all goes back to knowing what you want, knowing your action.

PETE: I got a good sense of place from the second take, as opposed to the first, which gave me no idea where we were.

BETTY: Both actors' backstories were full enough so their relationship was clear.

NR: My preparation was entirely different for the second take. I found I had to wipe out what happened in the first so I would not be anticipating. It had to be earlier in the morning, and I was watching the weather report on TV.

BETTY: What was your preparation for the first take?

NR: I used the poem of Edna Millay's:

> I looked in my heart while the wild swans went over,
> And what did I see I had not seen before?
> Only a question less or a question more[21]

I wondered what had happened to my daughter. I wanted to tell her of my past glories and tribulations, but we were having difficulty

---

21. Edna St. Vincent Millay, "Wild Swans" in *Collected Poems* (New York: Harper & Brothers Publishers, 1956), p. 124.

Nothing to match the flight of wild birds flying.
Tiresome heart, forever living and dying,
House without air, I leave you and lock your door.

communicating. The verse expressed to me the confusion between us. That was the key to my first preparation, and I carried some of it over into the second. I used the confusion: "a question less, a question more."

I had to make certain I would not fall into self-pity with her last few lines. My action in the first take was to get through the morning, just that half hour, without remembering anything. I wanted to get myself numb and stay numb. If I'd had a bottle of whiskey, I'd have finished it off. Again, it was better in the second take, when my action was to make her feel good. I wanted to protect her from any shame or guilt. It was as strong as that. The emotion came out of the action.

BETTY: I could feel how much stronger it was the second time.

NR: That's what is known as sitting on it.

MARA: What Nick did was very helpful to me as a director. I thought he would be somebody to respond to her, but in a very passive way. But then he asked me, "What is my action?" I told him: "To listen." I really hadn't thought that he'd have an action, but I think it made a difference that he did.

HARRY: Is listening an action?

NR: To listen can be an action.

LEONARD: You mentioned something about lighting to Mara. You whispered something in her ear.

NR: Ah. "The eyes are the melody." You must try to get that kick in the eyes—with the lights, not with a hoof.

LEONARD: I thought it was up to the actors to get that kick.

NR: Dakota had it, but Mara could have helped her, especially working in black-and-white video.

CHARLOTTE: In the first take I noticed that certain lines and images stood out. I came away with only certain words, and I understood only a few lines. In the second, all of that was subordinate to the whole.

NR: I had the same experience.

That's it, you see. This is not some abstraction, the Stanislavsky "Method," in quotes. We are talking about experience. Stanislavsky did not invent acting, nor did Delsarte, Olivier, Dean, Brando, the Barrymores, or Sarah Bernhardt. But people like Stanislavsky and Grotowski, whom I recommend you read very thoroughly,[22] did ana-

22. Nick recommended these texts specifically: Jerzy Grotowski, *Towards a Poor Theatre* (New York: Simon & Shuster Trade, Touchstone Books, 1970); and Konstantin Stanislavksy, *An Actor Prepares* (New York: Routledge, Chapman & Hall, Incorporated, 1948), and *My Life in Art* (New York: Routledge, Chapman & Hall, Incorporated, 1952).

lyze those performances that were great and why they were great, and they sifted and synthesized, and tried to pass information on to other people. You have to become aware of what you are doing and what makes it work, so that it becomes a part of your equipment.

The experience I'm having here is very interesting to me. It reminds me of a discovery I made in the final preparation of the script for *Rebel Without a Cause*. The writer, Stewart Stern, had already gone east, and we were about to start shooting. I had an idea at three or four one morning about the scene in which Jim comes out of the juvenile officer's office to meet up with his family, his grandmother, mother, and father. The father says something, then the mother says something, and then the grandmother says: "Oh, he was never any trouble. He was always such a nice boy, Officer." To this Jimmie would not speak, but my inspiration was that we would hear his thoughts: "Tell another lie, Grandmother, and you'll turn to stone." I was so wowed by my new idea, I was going to go through the whole script and rewrite it so all Jimmy's unvoiced critical thoughts could be heard. Then it dawned on me, Eugene O'Neill had done the same thing thirty years before in *Strange Interlude*, and before that there'd been a Chicago playwright who'd written a one-act play called *Overtones*[23] from whom O'Neill had stolen what I was stealing from him.

It's the same experience I'm having with Stanislavsky. A lot of the stuff I've been talking about I thought I had come up with all by myself. But who am I kidding? It's all been thought of before, and Stanislavsky was writing it down over five decades ago.

So, you know, I don't have an awful lot to say. The important thing for me is to do.

I need two books. One is a play called *The Catalyst*,[24] I don't remember the author's name. The other is by a psychiatrist, I think his name is Wertheimer. The title is *The Criminal Mind*.[25] Who will be responsible for hunting them down?

---

23. No further reference to this play could be found.
24. Ronald Duncan, *The Catalyst: A Comedy in Two Acts* (Bideford, Great Britain: Rebel Press, 1979).
25. Philip Roche, *The Criminal Mind: A Study of Communication Between the Criminal Law & Psychiatry* (Westport, Connecticut: Greenwood Publishing Group, Incorporated, 1976).

Cutting

When I first went to Hollywood there were two or three different schools of film editing besides the idiot school, and I think those were pretty much exemplified by the cutting of Billie Wilder as opposed to the cutting of Darryl Zanuck.[26] Darryl Zanuck would slide into a scene, while Billie Wilder would say, "If you're going to cut, you have to feel it, you have to have a reason." So in a film of Zanuck's, from the straight-on shot you move in a little closer, a little bit over to the right, a little bit over to the left—and it's tepid. With Billie, you're there, and it's WOW! over to the right, WOW! over to the left, BANG! to the center—Billie was a great director of comedy, and also a great director of tension and suspense, as in *Double Indemnity*.

When I first went to Hollywood my experience had not been in film, but in theatre and other media, so I educated myself by talking to film technicians. I met with four editors and one projectionist every Thursday night at the Luau in Beverly Hills. I'd bring along the *Steve Canyon* and *Terry and the Pirates* comic strips as references and discuss the ideas and problems I'd accumulated during the week and not had a chance to resolve over the moviola. I brought the *Dick Tracy* strip too, once in a while. It was mostly too loose and uninterestingly stylized for me, but the compositions were tight, the two-shots were al-

---

26. Wilder was a director, Zanuck a producer and head of a studio.

ways great, the three-shots were always great, and the individuals were always in an interesting perspective to the background.

It's a strange and sad thing to me that the comic strip artist has not been used more in the film industry. I don't consider that the factory of Disney utilizes the talents of great comic strip artists. They hire facile commercial artists who just as easily could be drawing designs for wallpaper, guys who have a certain talent, and the patience and endurance to sit at a desk and draw the same thing 500 times. Though Disney was a great comic strip artist himself, and a minor artist by any museum standards, he represents just a tiny bit of the talent in that whole field. Comic strips are very important in our culture. Some man from Harvard wrote a book called *From Cave Painting to Comic Strip*.[27] Comic strips have been very important for a long time.

So I would point to one of the strips and ask the fellows: "Is this what you mean when you say to get away from the style of the old-fashioned boys—Henry King, Henry Hathaway: long shot, medium shot, close shot? Why can't we do this the way they do in the comic strips?" For example, some of the strips take you from close-up to extreme long shot, but there will always be some key object in the center that leads you out. It's not the kind of long shot that King Vidor used in *Fountainhead*, from the bottom of a gravel pit to the top of a gravel pit—so illogical, and with no emotional foundation.

The editor on *They Live By Night* helped me a great deal by suggesting the cut into the trees swaying with the wind that takes Kathy into the cabin. It's important to remember that your images should either violently oppose or marry with each other.

More generally, those discussions helped me formulate my preoccupation with time and space in relation to film.

A Russian director, Kozintsev, wrote the foreword to Sergei Eisenstein's *Film Essays*.[28] He says that wherever Eisenstein lived you could walk in the door and know right away who lived there. You'd know it by the books and the variety of subjects they covered, by the heaps of paper, the choice of objects. Mostly you'd know it by the contrasts and oppositions, and finally by Eisenstein's refusal, despite his preoccupation with calligraphy and a scientific approach to montage, to bow to any theory or aesthetic at all.

I'd really like to hear somebody talk to me about Eisenstein's calli-

27. Lancelot Thomas Hogben, *From Cave Painting to Comic Strip* (New York: Chanticleer Press, 1949).
28. Sergei Eisenstein, *Film Essays* (London: Dobson Books, Ltd., 1968), pp. 7–13.

graphy studies and make sense of them in terms of his films. Eisenstein never could himself, really. For him, the calligraphy studies were an exercise in intellect and the use of spare time while he was scared out of his ass that he was going to be killed, which he was. I hear a great deal of talk about collisionary editing, analytic editing, logical editing, invisible editing, and I don't understand it at all, I've never heard another filmmaker talk that way. I hear too much concern for result, and not enough for inner logic. There must be some allowance for life and breath and change, for accident, inspiration, the sudden impulse that is a mistake of beauty.

I've told young inexperienced editors to try always to cut on movement, from movement to movement, in order to avoid treating film as something static. Beyond that, however, they must hunt for the truth, and remember a film is not made on the moviola or in the editing room. The art of film has little to do with the art of editing. No editor can breathe into a film what isn't already there, any more than a director can breathe talent into an actor. Whatever quality a film conveys comes from its situation and characters, and never from anything mechanical.

The second concern tonight . . .

11/24/74

The second concern tonight, involving me far beyond my original intent to use twelve or fifteen feet of film,[29] was the voice of an Oriental woman speaking to me—and not about the content, but after the content had been assembled into one piece, one minor block, involving six cuts and trims and as many splices on the splicer. I had spliced a raging green blob, abstract, looking something like a head surrounded by blackness, onto a hemorrhaging red of the same shape, and that onto a Vermeer blue of the same shape again. Together they expressed all I had or had not said to a president of a university.

I was rolling the film back to start position when I felt the rough edges of the splicing tape: I had made a bad splice. I reached for the scissors to trim the ugly edges off the sides of the film. "That's a fine boy. You're doing just fine, and it is so considerate." A dove had cooed at something done, something self-protective. (Do people usually like seeing people protect themselves? From most visual media I would have thought otherwise.)

And now I recall the voice of the old man—not a father. A godfather or a grandfather perhaps, but one who knew of my clumsiness with my hands. His voice was mellow, saying, "You are touching things

---

29. NR was cutting *We Can't Go Home Again*.

with love and precision," meaning the machine would not be hurt and need fixing, and time would be saved for eating or dreaming. Each would be welcome to me.

But now I find I am joyfully working, and pleasures of another kind are being given to myself. Nevertheless I shall go to the store and get some orange juice and fig newtons to sustain the night.

Today was the birthday of my first born.

[1974]

The toilet gushing water-thinned blood over its brim and onto the floor in light and shadow caused a measure of association to *Party Girl*, and Ray wished the blood was his own, that he was quits with humiliation, friend to humility, and experienced in the final experience. His arrogance offended him to the point of vomit, but he would not permit the guts or mind that freedom. Ray knew that the invasion of the professor of literature's gracious poverty was as unwelcome as his own thoughts were to his own—was it still his own?—mind. He ate a quarter more of the tomato, put on his shoes to warm them from the chill of the hardwood floor, and looked for the huge mastiff-husky-Japanese breed dog that had been lying at the foot of the front door. He heard the barking of a dog in the unknown neighborhood and wondered if his host were walking him at this late hour, and if so, why he had not heard them go out. The huge animal could not have squeezed through the window. Ray swept the beige-white shedded hair from the floor of one room, and cautiously opened the door to his host's bedroom. The dog was lying on the floor on the far side of the empty bed. Ray took another swig of wine from the Almaden Mountain Rhine half-gallon jug, stretched his cramping feet and legs out on the sheet that covered the lumpy couch, and went to sleep.

Within moments he awakened to the sound of the film director's voice buzzing through his third ear saying: "I look at this film and wonder what kind of guy is this that made such a film." This remark, followed by a casual "Ciao!" had churned in his seconds of sleep in a reevaluation of a film he'd just seen,[30] and its masterful use of the greatest and most subservient of all media. It was not as a contemporary morality film, with its implications about the Watergate debacle, that the film had interested him. Nor was it as a film of social protest

30. NR had just seen *The Conversation*, which was being cut in a room down the hall from the one Nick was using at F.F. Coppola's San Francisco production facilities, Zoetrope.

that would make people aware that 1984 had already passed them by, and that their national character, once strong, was being destroyed as their government raised fees paid to informers and sneak thieves to steal the thoughts of the young, maturing, and professional men of good will or no will. It was not that simplistic a film, such as Ray would have made twenty years ago, when Claire Booth Luce turned to him in the certainty of Ike's nomination, and said in the presence of the Jesuit father who shared the Beverly Hills house Howard Hughes had rented for her: "I hope to God he doesn't choose Richard Nixon as a running mate."

Ray had asked: "Who the hell is Richard Nixon?"

She had answered: "He is the shrewdest, dirtiest, backroom politician in the Republican party, and we can't afford another Joe McCarthy at this time."

That is the direction Ray would have taken, had he had the idea for such a film as F.F. Coppola has made of a seven-year-old script called *The Conversation*. But Coppola is smarter, possibly because he is ignorant of past events, or because he has already graduated, as Ray and his generation had to graduate, from agitprop into the more humanly connective tissues that some arts can provide. He has made of *The Conversation* a most devastating, suspenseful, magically revealing film about a human being, a master of communication, who cannot communicate.

In Ray's considered opinion F.F. Coppola is the only potential maitre working in the medium of film today—except Ray, of course.

IN CLASS IV

Sense Memory; Showing and Forcing; What Time Is It?

O gentlemen, the time of life is short.
to spend that shortness basely were too long,
If life did ride upon a dial's point—

—Shakespeare, *Henry IV, Part I*

You all have lied who told me time would ease me of my pain.

—Millay

My God! I'll be late!

—Miss Ethel Barrymore

NR: What do I want to do today? Let that become the first question you ask yourselves each morning. The answer may change from hour to hour, but you'll find that asking the question will have a great deal to do with the quality of your alertness throughout the day.

Who has something ready?

[Liz volunteers the tape of her scene.]

LIZ: In the last take I just tried to work on sense memory.
NR: It's a little bit late in the game for it, darling. Your exercises should be done ahead of time, and already working for you. If you're going to do an exercise on stage I'm going to walk out of the theatre.
ARTHUR: I personally find it very hard to do sense memory or emotional memory while asking myself questions like, What would I do if I were a bank robber, or if I were a cowboy?

46

NR: How else can you become the cowboy? Eventually it all has to be integrated. But when you are doing a sense memory exercise, leave the cowboy aside and just do the exercise. But it is only an exercise, just as emotional memory is only an exercise.

ARTHUR: So how are the sense and emotional memories going to carry over into performance?

NR: That will be accomplished through your action. In carrying out your action you must be very specific. For instance, if your action is to succeed in order to avenge yourself, that's pretty general, you know? Sense memory will help you sharpen your action to a point. Ask yourself, for example, What does success mean to me? Search out the answer in detail and try to arrive at something within the realm of your sensory experience. If success means to you the feel of gold dust sifting through your fingers and into the palm of your hand, your action, to succeed, will have a sensory base to it.

Sometimes selection of an action in terms of a poetic image can add color to a performance. Your action is to fly. Do you fly like a robin or fly like a hawk? Which you choose can make all the difference in the world in your character, your concept, your wardrobe.

The final note on your action should be very personal and very specific, and in terms of a sensory experience. The sensory experience is the spine of your action. Physicalize. Particularize. That should help you a great deal.

If any of you have not seen Lily Tomlin,[31] beg, borrow, or steal to get to see her. Her sense memory is astoundingly good. Her concentration is immense. You will realize how the whole foundation of mime is in sense memory. Later on, we will be talking about presentation of character. Watch Lily Tomlin. She becomes a character in five seconds. There's no change of wardrobe, no change of makeup, no reliance on gimmicks.

You know how we make fun of the tourist who says, "Well, we did Genoa in the morning, and got to Milano that night, and then did Milano the next day—" If you tell me you did sense memory last month, or yesterday, you're a tourist, and you can't be a tourist in the acting profession.

Do you relate the technique of sense memory to your daily lives? Give me some very specific examples. What do you do, for example, when you can't remember whether you took your vitamins?

SAM: You re-create what happened before.

31. Then appearing in a one-woman show on Broadway.

NR: How do you remember that? Do you remember if you felt the bottle? Is that a familiar experience to you?

LEONARD: It's very familiar to me, I go through it every night.

NR: That's sense memory. Where did I put that book? Where did I leave my money? What happens when you try to remember? What are some other examples?

BETTY: Cooking. Did I put all the flour in? Is that the right consistency? I use it all the time.

NR: What else?

MOLLY: A smell, a texture—

NR: The general won't help you.

MARA: I can tell if I've put my deodorant on or not by the wetness under my arms. I can smell a person who's just been in the room. I can recognize my mother's scent, or a friend's scent.

NR: Or somebody who's just had sex.

BEN: Whenever I hear a buzz saw and I smell leaves burning, that combination always brings me back to my hometown in New Jersey.

NR: That's very specific. Flying a plane I used to be able to tell by the air currents when I'd reached a certain part of Wisconsin. There'd be a familiar rhythm to the bumps.

CHARLOTTE: If I smell hot chocolate it takes me back to a very specific place and time, and brings up a strong sense and emotional memory.

MARIELLA: I find that foods bring out a lot of emotional memories—Italian sauces, or homemade chicken soup, or hot tea. They make me think of my mother.

NR: Certainly, because sense memory is very closely tied in with emotional memory. Each object you touch can spark an emotional memory.

Training in emotional memory is usually thought to be a fairly lengthy business, while I'm assuming you will come by it naturally, without any training at all. Instead I want you to concentrate on your action, because through your action you will find clues and keys into emotional memory.

I was reading last night a statement of Vakhtangov's that Stanislavsky believed you must play the action first and the emotion will follow. The only thing I presume to add to that is *because*: "I want to do *because*."

Please note that the people Vakhtangov addressed in his book were a group of film directors who felt they were not getting at the truth of the Stanislavsky method in their classes with Stanislavsky Moscow Art Theatre actors, so they went to Vakhtangov who, Stanislavsky had told them, taught the method better than he did. It's interesting. I never knew that.

Really, there are very few guidelines we have to go by, and those have all been gleaned from practical, kinesthetic experiments and observations. I think sense memory and the keys into emotional memory have been among the great contributions of Stanislavsky. He analyzed them so they became a technique, a method.

■ ■ ■

Nat, let's see what you've got.

[NAT begins his performance; NICK cuts it off.]

NR: Do you understand why I stopped him? As a teacher I cannot let you indulge yourselves in bad habits. Whether you are working on a student film or a Hollywood extravaganza, the director has a right to expect you to be prepared.

What we were seeing here was a clear example of forcing, and forcing falls in the same category as indicating, showing, telegraphing, anticipating. Nat did not make proper use of the nervousness, the edginess with which he came on stage. Instead he gave way to a kind of panic or despair.

I recently acted in a film called *The American Friend.*[32] That job was the best preparation I could have had for these classes. It was an opportunity to check myself, to see if what I tell other people to do still works. I got up there the first day of shooting, and I did everything wrong, I did all the things I scream at other people for doing. I was showing, I was acting; I wasn't doing. It took me a full day to get in touch with what was off, and I was able to do that only by playing the action.

How many of you cook for yourselves? How do you boil eggs? Do you time them with a watch or a clock? Or do you just put them in cold water, let them come to a boil, and take them out when it feels right? That's the best way to do it. The first time you put the eggs in cold water, bring them to a boil, take them out, and they're too soft. So the next time you use the clock and time them. Three minutes, they're done. Then sometime when the clock isn't working you say, "I'll try it again, just boiling them." You put them in cold water and let them come to a boil. This time you let them stay in there a little bit longer, and then by a kind of instinct you decide when to take

---

32. *Der Amerikanische Freund*, Wim Wenders, 1977.

them out. You run some cold water on them, crack them open. The yokes are runny, the whites aren't; they're just right.

So the next time you want boiled eggs you try to remember the beats it took you to get them like that. First they came to a boil, and let's see, you walked over to the icebox, then you made some toast, then came back to the stove, took them out, and they were perfect. You do it just that way the second time. The third time all you have to do is just stand there and watch the eggs boil, and feel in your body, in your muscles, when they're ready.

Then you don't boil eggs for a few days, and a funny thing happens. You find you've lost that inner sense, and you're anxious. Have the eggs been boiling long enough? Maybe they better stay in there a little longer. You have no clear feeling about it at all, so you fake it. When you take the eggs out the yokes are completely hard.

In his edginess Nat was forcing, and as a result we did not know why the character was there, what he was really saying, or who he really was. But the energy of anxiety can be of help. Inner turbulence that has not previously been part of the actor's preparation can be used, if the actor knows what he's doing, if he has control. He assures himself of control by knowing his inner action, which has evolved through his preparation.

You must do your homework. Those of you who have been used to going off in a corner for twenty minutes, a half-hour of extensive sense memory and emotional memory just before doing a scene, you won't have that opportunity working in film. Immediately upon hearing "Action!" you must be able to push those stops, call on those references that have helped you develop your character and clarify your action, why you are there, what you want to do.

Before rolling camera I'm going to ask you if you are ready, and each director here is going to ask his cast, "Are you ready?" You must answer honestly. If you go in half-assed, saying, "Well, I don't want to hold things up, I'll be a good guy, sure I'm ready," you're not doing anybody a service. Very often you will not be asked if you are ready, but in my opinion directors who operate that way are cripples.

Nat, you weren't ready, you had not prepared, you did not have control.

NAT: I wrote this last week, and I've been studying it ever since. I guess I've been belting it to death. It's supposed to be about big-time mass salesmanship. First I'm trying to draw the audience in, and then give them the big spiel.

NR: So your first action is to suck 'em in.

NAT: Yeah. I imagined myself doing it in a TV studio, like a commercial.

NR: You say you've been belting this all week. Belting it in what way?

NAT: Going back over it, rereading the lines, trying it in front of a mirror.

NR: That has created more mediocre actors than I can count. You haven't even begun to prepare. What's your backstory?

NAT: I'm embarrassed to tell you this, but I wanted people to be moved when they saw this, I wanted them to cry, I wanted a million different things.

NR: You were playing the result, and the result of that was that there was no actualization.

NAT: But all my life, whether it was in school, playing ball, or in business, I was always told to go for results.

NR: I'm sorry, Nat, but you have switched a word or two in there that change the meaning entirely. Playing the result and going for results are not the same: one is showing, forcing; the other, an objective. Showing is not your purpose at all. Showing diffuses your character. It is fatal for an actor to show. Your purpose is to find out how to do.

It is your action that determines how you say a line. What are you saying? What are you *really* saying?

You might practice this: Say it's a rainy night. You're waiting on the street corner, for a guy or a gal. And the first thing you say when that person comes up is, "What time is it?" Do you realize how many ways you can say "What time is it?" Ask yourself: Am I reprimanding her? Am I blaming her? Am I putting her down? Am I telling her I love her? Am I telling her I'm going to strangle her? Am I telling her she's done it again? That I'm fed up? That she's right on time, and we're going to have a ball? What am I saying? What am I really saying?

It really does no good for me or anyone else to say to you, "You weren't concentrating there, so go ahead, concentrate." On what? On what you are really saying.

Arthur, what time is it?

ARTHUR: I have no idea.

NR: But what am I really saying? An actor knows that words are not his only tool.

If you employ this method, then you will show, by doing. If you play in your action, then your concentration will be on that, and maybe the people will cry, maybe the people will laugh; you're enough of a showman to hope they'll do one or the other.

But perhaps the response to your performance is only lukewarm.

At a certain point you must have lost credibility. Chances are at that moment you dropped concentration on your action, or chose the wrong action. In either case there'd be no chance at all of bringing the audience with you.

Nat, you need to work to get just as far away from the kind of vanity of self-image we saw in this scene as possible. You must learn to know exactly when you are being honest and truthful, and when you are not, when what you are doing is organic to your character, your action, the scene, and when it's mechanical.

Now if you want to take some time to prepare yourself in terms of your action, then you can do the scene again.

Be patient with yourselves, up to a point. Finally you can't do anything wrong, you know. The only wrong thing is not doing anything because you want to be perfect. "Man's greatest misfortune is when theory outstrips performance." Da Vinci said that, and da Vinci was a pretty bright man. These are exercises. Be bold. Take chances. Get off your heads. The difficult we'll do now, the impossible will take a little while.

I was thinking about a man . . .

[1974]

I was thinking about a man who owned and operated a shoe repair (While-U-Wait in neon) on First Avenue and 12th Street. The man was helping a woman with a hole in her stocking into a pair of newly elevated shoes. She tried to pay him, and he said, "Next time. You'll need the money for Christmas. Go ahead now," he answered to her gaping mouth, and went to work on my boots.

My socks had two holes. If there had been only one there would have been no reason for embarrassment. "It gives me great pleasure," said the boot repairman, "to treat my customers individually and help them put their feet solidly on the pavement. It is worth a smile, isn't it?"

His height and mastery reminded me of my father.

22 November 1974

His thoughts of suicide had grown in frequency and determination. His trips to doctors and adherence to their advice became fanatic efforts to prolong his life.

It was difficult for him to make decisions. What a problem! And he wanted to be loved. All his life he wanted to love, retaining the privilege to hate for himself. All his life.

Those who knew of his hatred were equally aware that it could be erased by a favor, a phone call, a promise, a warm greeting, a rumor. Those who knew of his need to be loved knew of his weaknesses in hatred, so they distrusted his efforts to love. It had not been a satisfying life.

14 May 1975

The lines in my face, the wrinkles in my neck that show when the head is relaxed or drowsing towards derangement, the changing color of my hair from the silver after a shampoo to a darker hue depending on how many unwashed pillows it has rested upon, these little bits of the facade, like gargoyles, permit me to say I am old, an old man with one eye (of all things) and a stiff to sagging cock beneath the belly and above the burning feet. Old? I have not told the story of my heart. And I do dare to walk along the beach and choose a pear or peach without my trousers rolled.

Prufrock is not for me. He was, when I was 16 and waiting to become one-and-twenty and hear a wise man say something, anything. But the wise man must have been long departed to another land or sea. No matter. I heard the mermaids! And they say and sing to me. The heart itself will be explored by experts, and I doubt if you or I do qualify, for we are strangers to the vagaries of science and history, but not to the contact of the eyes, the touch of pulse, the sounds of footsteps on the stairs, or the fragrances of love.

[23 September 1976?]

It occurred to me at about 4:00 P.M. Wednesday the 22nd that I have been in a continuous blackout from some time between 1957 or earlier until now. I misplaced my "soul" and have no idea where I left it. Blackouts of not remembering where I left my wallet, or a bottle of booze, or the point of a story must number in the hundreds.

29 June 1977

What is an alcoholic? An alcoholic is a guy who sleeps in a doorway on the Bowery, who wipes the windshield of your car. You know how many women are alcoholics in the U.S.? Of an estimated ten million known alcoholics, about one-third are women.

What is an alcoholic? The head of [X] Rehabilitation Center was a wing commander in the South Pacific who flew over fifty missions, and remembers about five of them.

I was crossing Houston Street on the way to work the other morning. I was in the middle of the street, and a tan sedan going very slowly made its way across the intersection right into the pedestrian crosswalk, boom-bump, into the post. Then he woke up. Hey you! He drove on. He'll get home, but he won't know how he got there.

What is an alcoholic? Who is a criminal?

Dry does not mean sober. To get sober, change is necessary. Alcoholism is a disease of the attitudes. We isolate ourselves and alienate others. And we keep on doing it over and over. Our bodies disintegrate with the continued use of alcohol—and don't tell me again that my body is in chemical need of alcohol when time after time after countless times it has puked and bled under the attack. Our cocks have become limp and our cunts limpid. Our breaths shorter, our cramps stronger, our hearts faster, our blood pressures higher, our livers fatter, our faces yellower, our sight dimmer, our hearing strained, our nerve ends stinging, our steps halting, our skeletons swaying and weaving, our brains rotted. Cuts, bruises, fractures and burns are commonplace.

(Remember, Father's capacity to come back up cannot be counted on to be hereditary.)

The fragmentation of my life (work, methods, emotions, lack of centrality).

Lack of attention to details masked by drinking.

The refusal to think, reliance on spontaneity.

Acceptance of living and begging as a pretentious hobo.

San Sebastian, the two flights.

Eye—frustration of not reading.

Projection of blame.

Not opening or writing mail. Fear of any news, good or bad.

Trauma of L.A.

Arrogance and fear of people.

Suicide, suicide, suicide.

Sex.

Lack of energy.

Despair.

Cirrhosis, two valve transplants, diabetes, circulation, left eye.

ANGER. Where is it centered? Fear? Of what? Guilt? Shame? If so, what can replace it? Why is it frightening? Because it is elusive? What is the most effective antidote to fear? Accomplishment that satisfies self-interest? What is the self-interest? Approval of others? Maybe. But why should it be foremost? Is it foremost?

2 March 1977

Once it was my misfortune not to restrain myself from asking, in front of her friend, a very accomplished journalist, if I could take a young lady from the near North Side to the far South Side of Chicago. I may even have offered a couch or mattress on the floor to her or to both. A white giggle and a black red smile and a stumble over the girl added humiliation to their rejection, and clumsy embarrassment encircled the parade to the door.

The girl was real. I would pass by her, if possible squeeze between her and her companion to feel an involuntary but too welcome sense of her presence, her shoulder against my thigh, the need to touch her hair, protect her head and eyes from my clumsy bulk. The girl was young. A student. The man was also young. I was not. The girl was Semite. The man was Central American black. The totem pole became my cock and the frustration my frieze of life.

One day the girl brought a washcloth to my bath. I never saw her again.

[1977]

Susan has begun the Alernon[33] [*sic*] program. I am a very selfish person, but I nevertheless have a great love for her, if need be would sacrifice my life so she might live, and with no sense of martyrdom. I want to give her *so much*, but yet I am a selfish person and I fear for me that if she engages in the Alernon [*sic*] program I would take advantage of her calm understanding of my anguish and very shortly would be in the bottle again, and then? Death will us part.

[1977]

Well, I guess I'll have to learn someday how to let the others know how much I love them. Someday I'll have to learn I cannot live without her and she can't live with me. Who's freaking her out, relentlessly? Which one? Or is it the mother source, self-hatred, etc., etc.

[1977]

It is distressing to realize at 66 that I have never heard anything positive or wholesome about the nature of money as an acquisition or product, or in any other way.

Exercise: Describe a sunrise to a blind person; woman; man; deaf woman; man.

---

33. Alanon, a support group for family and friends of alcoholics based on the 12 Steps and 12 Traditions of Alcoholics Anonymous.

Color

Just as the close-up, which was not invented by D. W. Griffith, should be used in the aesthetic sense D. W. had of it—sparingly, and at moments of revelation, change of attitude, inner thought, etc.—, so should color be used in film. The use of primary color in film is as significant as the use of a close-up. Color is only revealed by light, which is what made the impressionists the impressionists, and so you have a revelation on your side to begin with. T. Bankhead going upstairs in red at the end of the second act of *The Little Foxes* remains fixed in my memory as deeply moving, whether with disgust or amazement, while in the black-and-white film version the scene was commonplace. But let's get rid of the idea that black and white are not colors.

A few of us have done a lot of experimenting in the use of color and its emotional connection with the audience. These experiments of mine and other directors are within most commercial films.

I'd already shot five days of *Rebel Without a Cause* in black-and-white when Warners realized their contract with the man who invented scope required that everything be shot in color. So I switched over to color and called in John Hamilton, who had worked as a set designer with the Group Theatre, and was a great drunk and a great eye. I made him my special color consultant. We selected our colors from LIFE and other picture magazines. The red-on-red for Jimmy evolved as a result of an improvisation in my living room. I had a red couch. From that we plotted all the other reds-on-reds: the red jacket for Jim; the neutral brown for the kid, into the red; the emergence of Natalie from the gauche red of the lipstick and coat she wore as a 15-year-old tramp on the streets into the soft fluffy pink—sentimental, but a graduation, and important in the development of the personality of the girl. Then the yellow-orange of Corey Allen. All were significant.

Later I used red-on-red for Cyd Charisse in *Party Girl*. Jimmy had been red-on-red on the couch, and it was smoldering danger. Cyd Charisse with a red gown on a red couch was an entirely different value.

In *Party Girl* green was sinister and jealous, while in *Bigger Than Life* it was life, grass, and hospital walls.

I completely reevaluated the use of orange for that film. Barbara Rush had some of the qualities of Rosalind Russell, but not the electricity, the vibrancy. She wasn't a star. I had to give it to her, if I could. I had to find one or two significant ways in which attention would be paid to her. I found an orange dress for her at a fashion show in Paris. I don't think you can avoid orange, and my observation was confirmed when highway departments began using orange instead of red for important danger signs and the protection of its workers. Strange it took us so long to wake up to that color.

Johnny Guitar won awards for its use of color, and I'd insisted on keeping the posse in black-and-white all the way through.

While for *On Dangerous Ground*, shot in black-and-white, I wanted the warmth that color could have provided so much I let both Ward Bond and Ryan and Lupino overplay at times: the emotion was not properly controlled by the aesthetic. Had the film been in color I think I would not have stretched so much in creating the contrast of the violence and the wet, dirt, sleet, slush, and mess of Boston, with the sheen of the snow, the starkness, the pastoral quality. The significance of objects is always lost without color. Not always, but now that we are used to color.

It might be interesting to ask different people, or the same people on entirely different kinds of days, when they're in different moods, what different colors mean to them, and to ask in such a way that they're taken off guard and respond truthfully, and not with an intellectual idea of green as envy, or green as health, or green as jealousy, or green as sanitation, or green as love.

The Black Method

The current style, not method, of acting is a phony naturalism born out of Strasberg and the limited imaginations and supplies of *audace* in the journeymen actors and actresses comprising the great majority of the profession. This has been evident from the time Newman imitated Brando in a Stewart Stern screenplay[34] written for the purpose of cashing in. And Beatty's imitations of Dean (Kazan picture with Natalie)[35] were as studied as Newman's were of Brando. With the accelerated closing of the gap that money brings about, both Brando and Newman began wearing homburg hats, and a death blow was dealt to natural, spontaneous, intellectual- or egghead-ism. Newman's forced intellectualism has been a consistent embarrassment, as opposed to Brando's rare appearances, which to my memory have been simple, unpretentious, and direct. The Black Method has harbored both Brando and Newman. One is a major talent, the other finally has become a fair journeyman actor with enough talent or imagination to believe his own image. Dean, also a major talent, never got the sheets warm at the Actor's Studio—Strasberg kicked him out after three sessions.

But the male actor is not the only blight. The women, especially those on the P.M. TV soaps, manage to make nearly every line they

34. *The Rack*, 1956.
35. *Splendor in the Grass*, 1961.

say sound chewed and beaten, and even jerkier and more false than the hesitant male.

1971

Meeting with Strasberg. Satisfactorily explored our differences in the concept of *action* and its importance. The meeting seemed necessary as a result of Shelley Winters' statement Sunday night that the use of the word *action* was anathema to the actor, as it cut off his creative juices. Lee: "Beware of Shelley's generalities!" He agreed that the concept is correct if the actor interprets *action* as the carrying out of an explicit phrase, such as "I have a bone to pick with you," for example, in which the action is to argue. We also discussed inner actions and action as a monitor against excess, especially when the technique of emotional memory has not been mastered. (He had not thought of that.) He now accepts my acceptance of Grotowski and application of the plastiques as taught by Gerry Bamman,[36] but he will not pay for Gerry, not yet. Important: delineate the difference between *action* and *activity*.

After hearing my program for the term (including the approach to character development) he is in awe, for chrissake, and remarked he knows of no such training being offered any place in the U.S., maybe the world. Bullshit. Has the work and precedent of Vakhtangov been obliterated?

Get Stanislavsky's project book for *Othello*[37] at Drama Book Shop.

3 October 1977

---

36. Gerry Bamman, an actor and close friend of Nick's, assisted Nick in his classes teaching the Grotowski plastiques, a series of physical exercises devised to evoke emotion from the body.
37. Konstantin Stanislavsky, *Stanislavsky Produces Othello*, trans. Helen Nowak (New York: Theatre Arts Books, 1963).

IN CLASS V

TIME WAITS;
ACTION;
ANTICIPATING;
"SIT ON IT"

[NAT and JET perform a scene live.]

NR: I want to convey to you an awareness of the environment in front of cameras on a sound stage. Had we filmed this scene, presumably the camera would have been on a crane, and so could have accommodated all the different moves and angles. But we don't have a crane here, so with each change of angle the camera has to move, which means another interruption, another setup. We would shoot a master shot, then set up to cut in for close shots, set up to cut in for over-the-shoulder shots, set up to cut in for the connection between Nat and Jet—and there'd be a twenty-minute to half-hour wait between each setup. Then we would shoot reverses on Nat and Jet, one two-shot from Nat's point of view for his reactions, one from Jet's for hers, and maybe a couple more if we want an exchange of looks between the two of them. That could mean a minimum of six, eight, nine, eleven times that Nat would have to repeat the scene and not be wasted. Then once this scene was shot he'd have to pick up on the next scene. Since in film the cutting is usually most effective when it's done on movement, from movement to movement, for each pickup he would have to go back and overlap maybe fifteen to thirty seconds of the previous take in order to make the cut less noticeable. And maybe this scene comes at the end of a day after he's already shot one or two others.

How can the actor sustain himself through such a day? Everything that happens on the set will conspire to break your concentration and relaxation, and you're the only one who can do anything about it. I suggest you increase your interest in life, because 60 percent of your time on a set is going to be spent waiting. You'll need every single thing that's happening around you to keep you alive, to keep you alert, to keep you concentrating.

The director of a film would do very well as part of his preparation to outline some activities he can introduce during the shooting of the film that will interest the actors during time waits, those periods when the crew is setting up or rechecking equipment between one take and the next. On *Rebel Without a Cause* I convinced the studio schoolteacher assigned to the set to teach social problems that related to young people. Whether through the manner of the teacher or the subject material, the kids were being fed experiences that contributed to the film. What the director brings to the set, whether baseballs, chess sets, books or magazines, will depend on the personalities and interests of the actors; but whatever his choices, they should help the actors absorb the time waits creatively. In this way he helps them achieve relaxation and focus their energies toward interests that will feed into the film.

My first reaction to Nat's scene was, Thank God, somebody's done something about a drug habit. It's the first smell of reality I've had in this class.

We have been talking about self-image, and we have been working on stripping ourselves down to the essential through simplicity, by just talking with each other from the stance of our individual actions. Nat showed in this scene a tremendous advance towards simplicity and credibility. I stopped him because he was acting—if we had been in close-up on him you'd have seen it. But even though he was acting, he was acting better, acting from a base.

This morning Nat made a statement to me, that until today he thought my emphasis on action as *to do* was a lot of bullshit. It made me wonder if I have been explicit enough, and realize that I cannot take it for granted that the use of the word *action* as a tool of the actor is understood. So in various ways, from time to time and with your help, I will try to clarify and become more articulate about it. The definition we're using here is seemingly complicated, not the usual interpretation of any particular method, but I think it's a little more complete than most.

CHARLOTTE: Sometimes I ask for an action from a director and I get something that isn't an action.

NR: Action is often misunderstood as business or activity.

CHARLOTTE: It seems to me if I'm given an action I should be able to physicalize it.

NR: Not necessarily. You must know what you want, and then what you have to do to get it may result in physical activity; but knowing what you inwardly want is the important thing.

CHARLOTTE: So an action is internal.

NR: An action is internal.

PETE: Should the way in which I carry out my action go along with what that action is?

NR: It certainly should, because your action is an expression of the nature of your character. At the same time it helps clarify your character, his rhythm, how he does what he wants to do. Your action helps you make the transition from *"If* I were," to "I *am.*" Consider this dialectic: content determines form and form conditions content. Now apply it to your choice of action.

What was your action here, Nat?

NAT: Well, first I wanted to go to the couch.

NR: Why?

NAT: So I could say hello.

NR: Wouldn't you say hello at the door?

NAT: I wanted to kiss her.

NR: Why? Are you deeply in love? Is it the first chance you've had to kiss her? Is it the first time you've seen her? Is it love at first sight? Why?

NAT: None of those.

NR: Was it something you planned before entering?

NAT: Sort of.

NR: Did you know that she would be on the couch?

NAT: No. Sometimes she has been.

NR: So on your way to the apartment today you were thinking, "If she is on the couch today I will close the door, go to the couch, set down my briefcase, say hello, and kiss her." Is that what your thoughts were immediately before entering the apartment?

NAT: Not really, no.

NR: Because what if she'd been in the kitchen, or the john? So what were you really thinking?

NAT: I was wondering if I should be sweating.

NR: That's interesting.

NAT: But how could I be sweating when you just had me put cold water on my face?

NR: Not interesting. But why were you wondering if you should be sweating?

NAT: Because of the circumstances.

NR: Which were?

NAT: We were in Saigon. Summer. An average day. Humid. She had sent word to me I was to be at her place between six-thirty and seven.
NR: Did she have that authority over you?
NAT: Yes.
NR: Why?
NAT: The relationship.
NR: Are you lovers?
NAT: We had been.
NR: What cooled it?
NAT: We got too busy and I had to be away a lot.
NR: Jet said it a different way. She said you were lovers, but the dope had taken over.
NAT: I guess you could say that. Sure, the dope became more important.
NR: Then why did she send for you today?
NAT: Because of dope.
NR: Were you waiting or expecting to be sent for?
NAT: Yes.
NR: Of course, or you wouldn't have had your briefcase with you. You might have had flowers or perfume six months ago, no?
NAT: Possibly.
NR: Was there anything special about coming here today?
NAT: Yes.
NR: Is that why you wanted to kiss her?
NAT: No. Well, in a way, yes.
NR: Yes or no?
NAT: Yes. You see a lot has happened in six months. We began snorting and shooting some "H" together, and then I began making some deliveries for her.
NR: She's a dealer?
NAT: Yeah, a pretty big one.
NR: How many deliveries have you made?
NAT: Eight or nine, all local. This one is going to San Francisco.
NR: And you're going with it?
NAT: Yeah, I'm going with it.
NR: So this is a special day?
NAT: Yeah.
NR: Are you afraid?
NAT: Not really.
NR: Sure of that?
NAT: Not really.
NR: Will you get a stake for yourself?

NAT: If she lets me take it.

NR: Why shouldn't she?

NAT: I haven't been too enthusiastic the last couple of times.

NR: Does she know that?

NAT: I'm not sure.

NR: Is that why you should be sweating?

NAT: That and the weather.

NR: Do you want to make this trip?

NAT: Yes I do.

NR: Why?

NAT: To get a stake and pull out.

NR: And quit the habit?

NAT: Maybe.

NR: Do you want to kiss her?

NAT: No. But—

NR: But what?

NAT: But I have to make her know that I can, that she can trust me.

NR: So what's your action?

NAT: You mean, why am I here?

NR: What's the answer?

In *Savage Innocents*, his first film, Peter O'Toole played the part of a trooper whose job was to impose the laws of civilization on the Eskimos. When he was saved for the second time by an Eskimo, played by Tony Quinn, O'Toole crumpled from a standing position to his knees, down the frame of Quinn's body. It was a very honest moment in film. In *Beckett*, in a scene with the same feeling of you-don't-love-me-anymore, I believe Peter did exactly the same thing again. He was not afraid to expose himself in that way, to interpretations of bisexuality or whatever.

If you have an action, to win somebody over, and you choose to do it by self-humiliation, play that action to the hilt. If you choose to expose your emotions, to demean yourself in front of someone, then do it. You are actors. Each one of you presumably has the infinite in your soul. You must not be afraid of it. Therein lies the variety and the greatness of your performance.

NAT: Even before we started you just sat there as if you were expecting me to screw it up.

NICK: Nat, how can you know what I was thinking at that moment? One of the most eminent philosophers of this century said that personal experience does not constitute a fact. I was wondering where people were. Then you started your scene, and your start was very good, and all of a sudden you lost your concentration—

NAT: I screwed it up trying to please. I would like to do it again.

NR: No. For godssake don't try to please. There is no rule for success in the world, but there is a rule for failure, and that's trying to please everybody. I'm sure you're frustrated right now, but what we're discussing is more important.

When I see something in your work and bring it to your attention, the criticism may or may not be legitimate, but if it serves to make you aware, to get you to take inventory of yourself and ask yourself, "Why am I doing this?" then it's served well.

[NAT's frustration mounts and he explodes at NICK.]

NR: Okay, Nat, let the fester break open. Let the pus run down your skin, and then we'll wipe it up. There's been a lot of growing up going on in this class, and I want it to continue . . .

■ ■ ■

NR: Has anybody else in the class had a problem with anger?

[Several raise their hands.]

All right, let's have a momentary discussion on the nature of anger. Of course anger can manifest very spontaneously. It can also manifest after you've harbored a resentment. The anger grows and grows and grows, so by the time you see the gal or guy who provoked you, without even saying hello you want to go up and tear 'em apart. But what produces the anger? What emotions? What experiences?

CHARLOTTE: Rejection. Frustration.

NR: Go deeper than that.

MARA: Fear.

NR: Fear. Fear is perhaps as gut-level a response to a situation as you can fasten on. I believe fear is an emotion you've all thoroughly experienced in one way or another. You are afraid somebody is going to take something away from you. You are afraid you will not be accepted. When you approach the problem of anger in a character, look first for what he is afraid of. Is he afraid of rejection? Why is he afraid of rejection? What happened to him that he is afraid of rejection? What are you as the character afraid of?

Now let's move on.

■ ■ ■

[Two takes of LEONARD's scene are run.]

NR: Which take did you like best?

LEONARD: I liked the first one.

NR: I found the first very good, and by comparison the second made me impatient. Do you know why?

LEONARD: In the first I had my action.

NR: What was your action?

LEONARD: Just myself, what I did with my hands, with my body.

NR: You don't dig what I'm saying, do you. That's activity.

LEONARD: I don't know what action is.

NR: I know you don't. But there was one very simple action you used in the first take and not in the second that made all the difference. In the first you were talking to somebody, whether you deliberately chose that as your action or not. It happens very often that people play actions without knowing it. I believe the reason you didn't like the second take—I hope the reason you didn't like it—is that you lacked any action at all, and so degenerated into self-pity. Self-pity is a most unattractive state of being. If you want a character to lose sympathy with the audience just have him engage in self-pity.

An ability to cry is no indication of talent or technique. Having to play your action over and over again is like the curtain going up not just once or twice, but twenty times a day. Your preparation and your will become very important. When you have to repeat a scene over and over, and then pick up on the next one, and it's the end of a day's work, and you have to be as fresh as you were twelve hours before, your preparation, your ability to use the unexpected event of reality, and your action, always your action, are what will keep you alive. Please try to think things out. Let no line go by without finding where you are in it. Do you agree with me on that?

Usually when we start working in theatre we are hopeful of a great inspiration happening, and then when it doesn't come we get preoccupied with it. We use all kinds of words, invent all kinds of explanations, excuses, procrastinations, we go to all kinds of classes, and still nothing happens. Then we begin to work very specifically, and forget all about the mystical event. By forgetting about it and just doing the work, it happens. Inspiration is not something you can turn off and on like a faucet. You'd do better to employ your own mental capacities and imagination to ensure proper preparation.

So Leonard, how are you going to do it, how are you going to play love on the stage? I lo-o-o-ve you. I lo-o-o-o-o-o-ve you! You chose actions and emotions that were too general and still dependent on that vague world of inspiration and the concept of theatre without work. Your action need not be terribly elaborate to work for you. It need not be something way up in the clouds, so save yourselves the effort and time of searching so far away.

What are the events of a relationship that would make one believe these two people are in love? What are the conflicts? In this case, Leonard, I would suggest to you that the tears are very unattractive. Your emotion is good, and you need to evoke it in your preparation, but wouldn't it be more interesting if it were contained, thus creating a pressure, a tension, so that when you do say "I love you" for the first time, it's a great release? Because you've controlled your emotion, the flood of tears would come from the joy of at last having said the words, and the release. That would give you a scene. But it's monotonous if the character is continually feeling sorry for himself, and then says "I love you" out of that.

I was very pleased to hear Garson Kanin, who's directed some quite notable films and plays and written a few pretty good ones, say on the tube the other day, "Working in films is a ball-breaker, far more demanding than working in theatre."

The greatest difference between acting for theatre and acting for film is that in film, after you've gotten your preparation, your emotion, your reason for being there as strong and full as you can, you have to be able to sit on it, because the camera is a microscope, and because within that limitation there is also a great expanse, so that when you do explode, it's going to be that much bigger, more electric, and you'll affect 50 million people instead of 600 or 650. You have to have just as strong an emotion on film as you do on stage, but you have to learn how to contain it. In that way you create an interest, an energy, a tension, an awareness in the audience that something is about to happen. You always have to have that charge working for you so you can endure a day as an actor and not be wasted at the end of it. That is what film acting is all about.

And Leonard, you must be aware of yourself in space. You must be able to see the shadow you're casting on her face, and so move forward. Can't you feel the heat from the lights? Can't you feel the difference in the temperature of your skin? Nobody should have to say anything to you about it.

MOLLIE: When you say, "Sit on it," I think of holding an emotion and then it evaporating—

NR: I mean contain it. For instance, in a stage situation if you're angry with somebody, normally you'd have to physically extend that anger for it to be seen by the audience, because they won't see your eyes beyond the tenth row. But in film, if you want to tear 'em apart, you feel it just as if you were going on stage with it, but then you must try to cover it up. I hope I don't offend anyone when I say that only actors like to show their emotions. Generally human beings don't like to expose themselves at the real gut level, but use every device they can to hide how they feel or divert it into little rivulets, little trickles coming out here and there—not very healthy. As you contain the anger it will build up, until you are sitting on a keg of dynamite. Then at the point that you do explode, which I call the set point, it will count for something, it will be like Joe Lewis's right cross, and knock the audience into the aisles. Hold it in as long as you can, until it's time for you to act. Don't telegraph your punch.

JAKE: This point about not telegraphing—in boxing there are specific things you can do to get yourself out of the habit of telegraphing, but when you're expressing yourself, when you're speaking, there are certain facial expressions that are habit. Is there a specific technique to control—

NR: By your action. Find your action. Play your action. One action could be to listen to what the other person is saying. What is he *really* saying? If your action is to find that out, you won't be anticipating or letting emotion leak out. You won't be telegraphing, because you'll be listening.

BEV: I'm very cautious of directors and teachers who try to play psychiatrist, who push you to an emotional extreme because they want certain results. Those that can do it without causing harm are extremely gifted people, and very rare. I have seen kids badly hurt by teachers and directors.

NR: I've seen professional actors destroyed. There was a time when everyone in the theatre—and in every drawing room, for that matter—was an analyst. Two actresses of that period ended up in institutions. One was Frances Farmer of the Group Theatre.

Most people have had enough experience with extreme emotion in their own lives that they don't need to be browbeaten into it. I don't think there's anyone who can't find at least one moment in his or her life of panic, hysteria, rage, grief, or despair. A director who knows his job will help an actor use affective memory to contact the emotion, without the actor necessarily having to reveal the particular experience he is drawing upon.

Write this down: A director must never frighten an actor.

On the other hand, an actor has an obligation to his audience to learn how to use everything organic to him in his emotions, the sights he sees, the sounds he hears, what he touches, tastes, smells. And as he expands his access to sense and emotional memory, he must deepen his awareness of the need for control, which is functional in terms of his action.

JET: What happens if an actor loses control while you're shooting?
NR: I don't disallow it. It may be the moment of magic that separates that take from all the others. It may be his flight into glory.

In our daily lives we're inevitably going to encounter experiences that seem to interfere with the practice of our craft, and with what we are trying to become. There are always distractions, sometimes downright interruptions and contradictions. But, you know, great poets have had to work in machine shops. So have composers. But they've known what they've wanted to do.

The likelihood is you won't get a handle on how an action can work for you until you experience it directly. I'll try to convince you, but I'm not going to be able to convince you, you know? You're going to have to have the muscular and emotional experience yourselves, and from that will come confidence. Then it will cease to be an abstract concept, and will become a very comfortable and useful tool. In the meantime, don't take anything I say for granted. Test everything out with each other.

I'm passing out copies of a section from the play *Cowboy Mouth* by Sam Shepard. I would like you to break it down. Go through the script line by line for each character. Ask yourself what he is doing, what is he really doing? I want you to get used to putting in words what your actions are. That means you will have to make the transition: If I were Cavale, this is what I would do; if I were Slim, if I were the Lobster Man, this is what I would do. What is Slim's action towards the Lobster Man? At what point does he want to destroy the Lobster Man? At what point does Cavale have to protect the Lobster Man? Why? Is it part of the game? Is the game directed toward Cavale, or toward Slim's own need just to keep playing the game? Why does he want to keep the game going?
BETTY: Do you want each of us to do all three characters?
NR: Yes, from the point of view of both actor and director, because directors also have to have actions.

I'm curious about your reactions so far to seeing yourselves on the screen. Ask yourselves, "What was I doing?" Try to evaluate yourselves in terms of why you were there. You may see things you hadn't realized you were doing. So? Maybe you'll have a chance to retake those if they're bad. Maybe some things slip your eye. Maybe some things slip the director's eye. Maybe you think some things are bad, but they're very good for the balance of the scene or the whole show. Maybe you see something you'll want to use in the future. Maybe you see an exposure of character you don't like and you wonder, Where did that come from in me? Directors, watch for those moments of exposure. They may lead you down an avenue, into a little pool of oil that you can explore further and help the actor explore. Whatever you see is healthy. It's good. It's there. You're alive and breathing on LaGuardia Place.

"Don't Fuck With a Natural"

Most directors do not know how to communicate with actors. Instead they rely on the externals of composition, camera angles, lighting, lens. It's much easier for a director to relate to the mechanics of the camera—just as it's much easier for an actor to relate to an image of his part and himself in that part—than to relate in terms of action. In both cases a full-blown image is superimposed on the content, and the groundwork is neglected.

To ad-lib a discussion on acting and directing actors is perhaps a lot less complicated than the people who write about acting and don't do it, or who write about directing and don't do it, make it out to be. It's not that writers aren't perfectly capable of discussing and clarifying the crafts of acting and directing, perhaps much better than those who do them, but it isn't their way of making a living, and books require so many words.

I used to try to read books on acting. Even as a student, I found it terribly difficult to read books. I still find it difficult to read books and learn anything. A book may make an impression, and the impression may evolve into an action, but I've never been able to follow a formula.

On the other hand, although I may say everything I have to say about some subjects in just a few lines, when I begin to probe and do a little surgery to find out how actors arrive at that state beyond their own personalities, that state of being able to convince people

72

they are who they are and yet not who they are within a situation, a more thorough discussion is required of many techniques and theories that derive from probably as many schools of stage- and filmcraft as there are schools of psychoanalysis or finance.

So today, for the first time in 25 years, I read the final chapters of *An Actor Prepares*. I was going to say 40 years, and then I looked at the publication date of the book: 1949. This is 1977. Certainly, then, it can only be 28 years. Yet I have been working according to the principles in this book for 40 years. How has that happened? Well, not by accident.

It was severe economic depression time. The cover of an issue of a prominent arts magazine was white bordered in black, and read, "The Theatre is Dead. Let's Give It a Decent Burial." And I, green from the mid-West, untrained and inexperienced (one could be untrained and experienced), was offered a job in a Broadway production called *Her Man of Wax*. There was a hook in it, a sexual one. I rejected it and walked to a theatre housed in a loft at 42 East 12th Street that I had heard called "real," "sincere." I wanted to be real. I wanted to be sincere.

My audition for The Theatre was successful. I moved from a room in a building called Desire Under the L into a five-room apartment on East 13th Street that twelve other members of The Theatre shared with me. My eating habits changed from boiled, fried, or baked cornmeal three times a day to tea and dark bread for breakfast, a cream-cheese sandwich for lunch, and whatever remained of what a seventeen-cent-a-week food budget could provide for dinner. And I began to enjoy a full life.

Contributing to that fullness were my roommates and fellow actors, volunteers from Martha Graham's company (Doris Dudley and Anna Sokolov were my favorites) to teach body movement, voice and diction teachers, Elsa Findlay for eurhythmics, and Billy Lewis, Lewis Leverett, Morris Carnovsky, and of particular significance to me, Elia Kazan from the Group Theatre.

Let me start with Kazan. I consider Gadge Kazan the best actor's director the theatre training available in the United States has ever produced. His achievements as a director are immense. It's puzzling to me that his intelligence and instinct should be so erratically represented by his works.

I met Gadge in work at the loft, and I met him socially through his wife Molly, who was teaching playwriting. I acted in the first play Kazan directed. Earning a living as an actor embarrassed me terribly.

I did it for two-and-a-half years, and only because I wanted to become a director. Kazan had already established a very solid reputation in the theatre as an actor with one or two performances considered among the ten best of the year, but he did not want to be an actor either. Kazan and I became friends because we both wanted to be directors, and knew in order to do so we had to learn the problems of the actor. In mid-adolescence I had my sights set on becoming a director of symphony orchestras. It was painful to admit that I had neither facility nor talent with piano, reeds, strings, or brass. How are you going to learn the problems of the actor unless you act? You can theorize a great deal, and it will keep you comfortable, and prevent you from doing anything. It isn't necessary to be comfortable, but overtalking is a danger. A director who hasn't had experience as an actor is a cripple.

Kazan went out to Hollywood for *A Tree Grows in Brooklyn*, his first directorial job in film, and took me with him as his assistant. During the casting some incredible tests were shot. We decided on Peggy Ann Garner as the girl. She was twelve, had no stage experience, and could not be terribly loaded down with any theories on acting; but she did have a mother who was a lush and a bad check passer. Dorothy McGuire played her mother. Dorothy was well educated, from an elegant background, and had married into a family of northeastern blue bloods. Until then she had been a stage actress. And James Dunn, who played the father, was a drunk who had drunk himself out of the business and had all of the realistic qualities of the character of Johnnie in the story. He could have been a burlesque comic, associated mostly with gamblers, musicians, and burlesque people, and was a constant risk in everybody's mind, as well as a pretty beautiful human being who gave us an Academy Award-winning performance. Kazan's extraordinary technique brought those three very different people with different backgrounds and experiences all together in a unit. He got them all into the same key, and there was not one note jarring.

What I had to learn then Kazan taught me; what he didn't teach me he guided and encouraged me to learn for myself. But he was The Source, the well from which I drank most deeply. He brought the essence of the last few chapters of *An Actor Prepares* to me long before they were in print. That we may each have interpreted them differently in later years is of no matter.

So now at 65 I am once again making the transition from corn meal mush three times a day to a more varied diet. I am twice blessed. And so is the actor who wants to work in front of a camera and reads

Stanislavsky's book. An individual, whether actor, director, producer, or critic, who says acting in front of the camera is easier than acting on stage may not be an idiot. He just runs from the truth, and that's pretty idiotic.

I assume we want in this discussion to distinguish between film acting and stage acting and psychiatric acting out, as well as voluntary and involuntary acting. For the sake of unity, I will speak from the director's point of view.

I made a note during that time working with Kazan: "Don't fuck with a natural." If you're lucky enough to find a natural, let him run, because in him you have a free gift. I wouldn't tell a cowboy who rides fence in the southwest how to walk, but I am going to get a dancer to teach John Derek or Natalie Wood how to walk. Don't direct a natural. But of course it isn't that simple. Most are not naturals and need direction, whether old or young, amateur or professional. I direct every actor, but I try to do it in a way that keeps him hungry for more. I try to make every actor with enough talent and imagination believe that every idea that happens on the set is his own idea.

A lot of people who seek careers as actors never bother to have a method of work. Others who have a method of work do not realize they have a method of work. And still others have to have their bad habits broken without completely deflating their confidence. It's often more fun to work with an absolute amateur.

The approach to getting a performance from an actor and a non-actor, or from a film actor and a stage actor, is sometimes identical, and sometimes absolutely opposite, and conceived on the spot, without any regard for following a plan. I've cast non-actors, people who had never before been on stage or screen, in every film I've made. My personal preference in casting a part is to walk around the block with an actor, find out who he is, where he's from, what he really wants as a person, what his interests are, rather than have him do an improvisation to a scene or read from a script. An actor may make a very good impression, but unless he can project an understanding with some emotional basis to it, both the director and the actor are going to be in trouble.

Whether or not an actor is a natural for the part I've asked him or her to play seems immaterial except for one thing: you can overdirect a very good actor without serious consequence, but if you overdirect a natural, he won't come back the next day; he'll be confused. So the language has to be different, your language and behavior with the non-actor must be disarming.

If you are fortunate, you will have a week or so to get acquainted with him. You must in that week—but if it's only a matter of three hours, you must in those three hours—find a connection so you can help him respond unselfconsciously in front of the camera. The only ways to achieve that, in my opinion, are through concentration and surprise.

In order to achieve concentration with a non-actor you must find within him his greatest want or need at that moment, and transfer it to the situation of the film. It's really no different with the actor, but with a non-actor you have to be able to get him to concentrate without ever using the word *concentrate*, you have to get him to relax without ever using the word *relax*. If you hear a director use those words to his cast with any consistency at all, then suspect the director, because to tell an actor to relax or concentrate on the lines is not going to be of very much help.

On the other hand, if the director can set up a condition that demands concentration, then the actor will concentrate on his action as the character. A character cannot come alive until the actor makes the transition from, "If I were he, what would I want? What would I do?" to "I want this." You may have to help him with some description to give him the right gait, the right look, the right aspect.

Then there's the technique of surprise. In rehearsal you may sense that the scene is close to ready, and that the amateur, this unsophisticated piece of raw material you like, is enjoying himself, but will freeze the moment the assistant director calls "Quiet!" or the cameraman goes up to kick a lamp into place. So you turn on the camera without letting anybody know, and shoot the rehearsal, and then shoot the formality as well, but print only the take that nobody knows about. At those times you have to keep the assistant, cameraman, and technicians quiet, because they have no sense of actors at all, and are likely to bust out with "Print that!" after the rehearsal. Your crew has to be very tight around you; you have to tell them exactly what you're doing.

Other techniques of surprise are use of the hidden camera, or introducing a foreign element into the scene at the very last moment to turn it into an improvisation.

A fundamental for the director, which has only very rare exceptions, is that every sentence, thought, or phrase that is spoken on screen must sound as though it is being spoken for the very first or very last time. The only in-between times are those in quotes to make a particular dramatic point, as when one person satirizes himself or another.

How do you achieve that first- or last-time quality? You've persuaded a non-actor to play in the film with you. You believe the way he's going to speak the lines will be exactly what you want, because in conversation with him that was true and one of the things that attracted you to him. But a lot of things have happened since you first asked him to work with you: during the first blocking with camera he got his first face-to-face look at the camera and walked off the set worried. Then some well-meaning grip or makeup man or script clerk or another actor went up to him and told him he musn't be nervous. By the time you're ready for the first take with him you have a mess on your hands. You then can call casting and tell them you've made a terrible mistake and need a different actor in a hurry, would they get someone out of the company or central casting, you don't care, you just want anybody who can walk, who has been in front of the camera before. But that's a thing that any director with a healthy ego will refuse to do. So you've got some work ahead of you.

Now you have to direct like hell. The non-actor will have accumulated in a period of five minutes to a half-hour as many blocks as has the professional actor in long years of developing external techniques and mannerisms—which also need breaking down. The process with the non-actor and the actor is the same, but again, with a different language, because you can't talk to the non-professional in professional terms. This is why you have to spend some time with him beforehand—whether you go out whoring or drinking, or play cards or baseball—to find out what his life has been, which areas you connect with. If you give importance to the casting at all you must do those things that will facilitate his concentration on what he personally wants, and so enable him to be true to himself, the character that you want. More than confidence he must find his pride, authority, and a freedom from shame of any kind. The non-actor must have the excuse, if he makes a mistake, that he really wasn't himself. He's already embarrassed enough at being in front of the camera.

When you're working with a cast of people, you have to find a vocabulary common to each person in it. Occasionally with actors like Arthur Kennedy or James Dean you will share a language so closely you can speak in shorthand. But that kind of communication is rare, so you must become expert at handling about eight or ten different vocabularies per film, and each must be filtered through your own and then translated.

Let's say after three or four takes your man goes dry. You have to be able to find some way to refresh him. At this point I might give him an action contradictory to everything he has developed so far.

This confuses him. He will think I'm an awful bastard and go back into the scene muttering to himself about the kind of director who would contradict himself in the space of forty minutes. But he's already had enough kinetic experience, he's made enough personal associations to the character to keep the fundamental action alive. And the melody, which shows in the eyes, becomes more interesting, because he's trying to think something out. I'd given him a false concentration, which then becomes a true one, and he's fresh again.

You must do the same with a very long-experienced actor, and you must do it, I'm afraid, in almost exactly the same way. And if that doesn't work, then you have to try something else. You have to be very patient. Bogart, for example, would go dry after six takes. The first time I went over six takes with him, I had to stop on the seventh and close up for the day; there was no point in trying for more. The next morning I began with an insert as a warm-up, and to get away from anything he might have had a block about from the night before.

By the way, I know of no good—I mean really good—male actor who is not embarrassed at being an actor. So within the two extremes of experience you have the same characteristic to deal with: the very new and the very good are both embarrassed.

I seem to be saying that you have the same problems with the over-experienced, aged-in-wood actor, who is wooden as a result, as you have with the inexperienced non-actor, that precious jewel, the natural. The great majority of actors are those in between. They range from the egotistic exhibitionist to the competent craftsman/journeyman. The latter may have technique, theory, knowledge, a real hip familiarity with everything that's happening on the set and in the part, and a mixed bag of tricks he can use discreetly. He may think he's always good because he has craft, he has facility, he knows how to use his equipment. He usually also has a bank account, a first mortgage on his home, a membership in the Rotarians; but he's never had an inspiration in his life. He's had a lot of things he thought were inspiration, he wants to think of himself as an inspired fellow, but he's not, and so all you can do is employ him as being the best utility available, and, if you're any good as a director, make him seem better than he is.

In nearly every film I've worked on, tried to develop into a whole piece of entertainment, I've had actors from every single background, every kind of school that there is. There is no generality that works for all of them. A director must prepare himself to deal with all kinds of training by learning the terms with which his actors are used to working. In *Rebel Without a Cause* Dean's parents were actors who would have been horrified to know they were improvising. Instead we kept it on the simple level of ad lib, so it met their own enjoyment requirements. That way there was spontaneity, there was improvisation; we just didn't use the words.

In the Group Theatre actors were advised just before entrance to "take a minute." The old vaudeville actors took the same minute before going on, but they called it "freezing." And if anybody came up to them during that moment and asked, "How'd the Yanks do today?" they'd grab the nearest stage brace and crack the guy over the head for disturbing their concentration.

You may have to work with people who are very professional, but their profession is dancing or singing. Singers are difficult to work with, because they won't connect with the eyes of the other actors, they look at foreheads. They're trained to do that. They're usually stiff messes, ossified gelatin. Contemporary singers of either acid rock or beat or pop may be exceptions to that, but they'll bring with them another complication, one of false modesty, or false disdain, or of absolutely insufferable ego covered over by a shell of its opposite. There the task of the director is to work to reduce the shame of being anxious. It's difficult, because you're no better than an analyst, and you're not going to change anybody's character. The character is there, but the affectation can be changed, controls can be instituted.

There are those actors who will ask the director to demonstrate what he wants, and then they'll take over immediately, and then maybe you'll be able to breathe a little more into it. You may do this only once or twice during a film or in rehearsals, but just enough to give the actor confidence, to get him started. It's like getting the writer to put the first letters down on a piece of paper.

But you don't have time to give acting lessons to everybody. There are certain self-indulgent actors who feel they are doing a favor to the audience by appearing, and then proceed to exercise their own usually psychotic needs. These fellows mistake creative activity for confusion, or confusion for creative activity, in my opinion. And they have every question to ask, just like a child who doesn't want to drink his milk, because who knows which cow the milk came from.

From the moment you see an actor come onto the set, you must sense enough of what has happened to him just before to know if there's something there to be used for the scene. You must know the material better than the actors. You must know what you believe the actions of each actor to be, and also have options in mind, so if an actor has chosen a wrong action, there is another choice ready for him and he won't be left floundering. Actors by themselves can take a scene and rehearse it only so far.

This method, which is perhaps the most difficult and time-consuming and demanding method I know of anybody using, requires a relationship between actor and director such that everything said between you, either in the preliminary contact or between takes, is of a terribly intimate nature in its content and associations. It is my recommendation that the director of a film always keep the exchange between himself and an actor away from the ears of other actors. You must not violate an actor's confidential, personal information, because if you do he's going to shut off the flow between himself and you and the other actors as well.

At the same time, a director must expose himself, if only by lying. I'll tell the most atrocious stories imaginable about myself to get an actor to release himself without feeling ashamed, so he can say, "But he did five, ten times as bad as I did, and he's the director. If he's that bad, I can be that bad too." But this assumes you have been able to convince the actor with whom you are working that his basic equipment, in addition to the script, sets, props, and director, is himself, his memories, associations, and imagination. Of all those things the most important is imagination.

No director I've ever known has been able to breathe talent into an actor. Don't try it. You can't breathe in talent, but you can breathe in imagination. And that you have to have in abundance, because no director is talented enough, in my opinion, except a Welles or a Chaplin, to play all the parts. You need your cast, but you have to know how to make them a little bit better than they are.

And then the film director has to know everything there is to know about stage equipment, plus everything there is to know about stage communication, plus as much about theatre, acting, musical composition, vocal training, current events, politics, involvement, and anything and everything else as he can absorb. There must be nothing a film director can't or shouldn't do. Abbie Hoffman put it well when he lectured at the Art Institute of Chicago one night during the Chicago Conspiracy Trial. He said, "What is art? Fuck art! Art is what you're doing! What is politics? Fuck politics! Politics is living!"

I understand there are young people making three-minute, five-minute films to fulfill course requirements in school. In this way the young filmmaker becomes a person withdrawn from his society. He does everything alone. Finally, I don't think you can make a film alone. You need the lab, you need the guy who sells the film, you need the guy who makes the camera. You need your wife and your friends to provide transportation, to do things for you. You just can't make a film alone. To me the raison d'être, the obligation, of the director is to provide the audience with a heightened experience, a heightened sense of being. If a director can't say hello to other people, how is he going to say hello to an audience?

If I were asked, "So what's the magic formula for becoming a director?" I'd say, "Don't be afraid to be a sonofabitch." If you want to be a director with the thought that therefore you will be loved, forget it, you're in the wrong business.

A director must be unselfish. It's a complicated, wonderful profession, but thankless. Drop it before it's too late, and you'll find life easier, quieter, and more respectable. Otherwise love the stage. Love it more than you love your home. A director feels the joy of creating only when this joy is shared by all those who surround him.

THE CAMERA;
INVOLUNTARY
PERFORMANCE

NR: I want to clarify how I feel about the camera. I don't have a reverence for the camera. I have a reverence for the celluloid strip, but not for the camera. The celluloid strip is perhaps the most servile medium we've ever had. It recognizes neither time nor space, only the limits or extensions of our imaginations.

The camera photographs thought. It's one of the magical properties of the lens. The camera photographs thought, and extends time with thought. That's why as a worker in film your intellectual level is very important. As you follow with camera an actor moving in space, and the reactions of other people to the actor's movement in space, time is extended. Time presents you with space in which a director may reveal his intended conviction, his unintended fallacy, or a genius of which he is unaware.

The basic pattern in shooting film is pretty much long shot, medium shot, close shot. In close-up the microscopic value of the lens can extend what would take a split second into twenty seconds, thirty seconds, a minute, as the actor moves from confusion to clarity to decision, or gets a new idea, or reveals something, or has something revealed to him. Just count up the number of feet of film you have used. That's about as simple an expression of the relationship and extension of time and space in film as I can give you.

The camera is for use. It's a tool, an instrument. It has to be in awfully good condition, but that's because it has to progress the story, it has to reveal things for us as we wish them to be revealed. We can always rent another camera.

Did any of you see André Previn and Isaac Stern on television last night? At the end of the program Isaac Stern spoke about how we glamorize and glorify the instrument. He said that in the mystical idealization of the instrument there is always a danger of the instrument becoming more important than the music. We use the instrument in order to make music; we do not use the music to show off the instrument. Is that clear? If it is not, please let it become clear. That is what Stanislavsky meant by his life in art.

When my son Tim called the other night to talk about his latest adventure as cameraman I asked him to try to recall for himself, now that he's first cameraman, the way the first cameraman on his last film handled his crew. Was he serving them or were they serving him? Was he successful at his job—not so much in terms of what got onto the screen, but as a leader of a small group of people upon whom the film was depending for its success or failure? Why was he successful?

Ask yourselves the question: Is it the art in your life, or your life in art? Think in concrete terms. Here are a piece of wood and some strings. You as the instrument have to be as well-tuned as a Stradivarius. Why? In order to make music.

Directors, before you set the camera down, you must rehearse with the actors without the camera. Without that rehearsal you won't know where the camera belongs. The actor must have the freedom to move wherever he wants at whatever time he wants. If he goes out of camera, out of light, you always can reset the camera and reset the lights. Rehearsal is the time to decide which camera to use and what that camera is going to do. During rehearsal, imagine the camera on your shoulder, walk through the scene. Watch the actors' movements and look for your angles, hunt for the significant moments, for the truth of the scene. You must be very attentive in order to catch the rhythm.

My personal approach is first to hunt for the truth of the scene, and then to try to make the camera act for me, to put the camera in the position of an actor as soon as I can. This is not something everybody should do, not at all. If it has meaning to you, spell it out for yourselves, how it has meaning for you, when it has meaning for you. You may encounter a director who claims to work from a theory, who says he shoots everything from the eighth row of the theatre, and therefore the camera is objective, impersonal, and so on and so on. But he hasn't developed a technique at all, he's just developed an attitude. An extraordinarily good director like Preston Sturges might make such a claim, but he'd just be demeaning himself, trying to be modest. He could not work that way because his imagination wouldn't let him. A good director will violate his own theory constantly. I'd be a horse's ass if I said I had to do things a certain way every time, because then I'd be sacrificing content to style, maybe even impeding the progress of the scene. I cannot superimpose my style on you, nor on the content of the film.

SAM: You usually use only one camera.

NR: Yes, unless it's a huge mass scene. I've used two cameras, and even three, four, and five cameras at times. With one there's always the risk I might not get that moment again, but then I might get it better. It becomes both the director's and actor's problem, to get back that moment.

Let's see some work.

[The class views the tape of BEN's scene, as directed by HARRY.]

NR: Ben, I liked what you did here, it seemed that you were very full, but you should have worked right into the camera.

HARRY: I asked Ben if we could do it that way, but he wanted to work off an actress.

NR: Then you have to show the actress, or else— It was a thought piece, you know, and you were not giving the camera a chance to get into the eyes. Any particular problems you faced as an actor, Ben?

BEN: I had problems going in and out of my character.

NR: It would have been much better had you made a very pure connection directly to the camera, talking into your own reflection. You can use the camera lens that way, you can find your reflection and talk to your own eyes. It's different talking to the lens than to a mirror.

Had we gone for another take I would have tried to get you to turn around—not by telling you to turn around, but by creating a circumstance so that you'd feel the impulse or need to turn around.

LEONARD: Ben kept his emotions on simmer so he could turn them up to a boil when he wanted to. Is that a technique you think we should be aiming for?

NR: You know I admire that very much. You don't come across it often. But aim for it only if it's comfortable for you.

Time is very expensive on a film shoot. A day can cost tens of thousands of dollars. You will not necessarily be given the two to four hours of preparation time you might normally take before going on-stage. I cannot limit the free use of your instinct, imagination, and intuition in finding what works best for you. I can only offer you a method within which to find your own method to rely on with confidence as your muscles get stronger. You have to find the method within the method that is comfortable for you.

Never let the mechanical, the technical, take precedence over the quality and substance of your emotional preparation, your emotional memory, sense memory, and imagination. In film you always have another chance, another take. Joan Fontaine, who starred in my second film,[38] who won the Oscar twice, prided herself in knowing exactly where her key light was and being able to make a wardrobe change in thirty seconds without causing a moment's delay for the crew. And all her talent dried up in that overawareness. Robert Wagner was the same way. I'm sure he knew every possible mechanical gimmick; he just didn't know how to act.

It may seem you're being given a book full of dos and don'ts, but I hope you don't make dos and don'ts out of anything I say. Good rules are made especially to be broken.

Who else has something on tape? Jake?

[JAKE's scene is screened.]

NR: Jake, that's very extraordinary. Was this from written material?
JAKE: No, from a situation. A guy comes home, and his old lady just stares at him. She follows him around the house and just keeps staring at him. Whatever room he goes in, she just keeps staring at him. It makes him feel guilty. He doesn't know what he's done. And he wants her to talk to him, anything, just so she doesn't keep staring at him.
NR: What were you working for?
JAKE: My action was to make her respond.
NR: Was that your only action?
JAKE: Well, my overall action was to make her respond, and how I went about it changed each time I tried something that didn't work.
NR: In viewing the scene on tape did you catch any time when you went out of character, lost concentration?
JAKE: A lot of times.
NR: Not a lot of times.
JAKE: Well, there were times when I really saw a face. I was looking into the camera and I really saw a face. I saw the face, I saw the

---

38. *Born to Be Bad.*

perspiration on the face, the eye blinking. Sometimes I was intimidated by that stare, both as the actor and as the character. And to get the sense of his own power, the character would turn his head and close his eyes to get away from the stare and collect his thoughts—

NR: Now, let me interrupt for just a moment. What were you working for? Were you working for that to happen?

JAKE: Yes, yes. Personally, me, yes.

NR: Right.

JAKE: But sometimes when I turned away, and the character was thinking of what his next move would be and how he'd deal with the stare—

NR: That is where you went out, just as you're going out now. As you speak, you're alternating between "I" and "the character," just as at one point in the close-up you went into third person.

JAKE: I didn't realize that. That's interesting. But that's what I was trying to say. There were times when the character and I got confused. That's when I felt I went out of it.

NR: How would you protect yourself against that happening in a performance?

JAKE: I really don't know, but I think if I had a clear, defined action I would be able to separate me from the character.

NR: I think in the course of rehearsal you might put down all your external actions, so you have those in mind very clearly. Then also put down the internal ones, break them down a little bit more so you're not playing just the one overall action.

For instance, in the first take, the action behind your first line, "I blew the rent money"—with which I can identify, and perhaps it's because I identify so much with it that I question it—seemed more complicated than just to get a response. It was to challenge, it was to provoke.

JAKE: Yeah, that's exactly what he's trying to do, to provoke her. He tries that, but that doesn't work, so then he says, "I love you." He's trying to make her feel pity, sympathy for him. He's saying, "I love you, and you're not returning this love." And that doesn't work. So then he tries insulting her and says, "I don't want to fuck with you, you've got a fat ass." And that doesn't work. Then finally he decides—it's an unconscious decision—to physically threaten and frighten her. So there is a series of mini-actions and an overall action.

NR: Who directed?

JAKE: Peter.

NR: Was he helpful?

JAKE: Yeah, very helpful. I just wanted to have a clear action and character. He looked at the scene, selected the critical moment, and he amplified that moment. So he focused it.

NR: When you went into the close-up, what direction did he give you?

JAKE: He suggested on the third take that I take everything that I had just done and pick it up right from the strangling episode, and work from there.

NR: The strangling episode evoked something strange in me. I felt the pressure just above and just below my Adam's apple. I felt it in my own body. I also felt my own hands feeling an Adam's apple. There was a dual experience going on in me. I usually don't go backstage and talk to actors, but this kind of experience would prompt me to do that, to ask: "Hey, what were you doing there?"

JAKE: I felt her neck. I saw what she looked like. I saw her eyes darting about the room, flickering. I saw the stare break, and I—

NR: Did you feel the pressure on the Adam's apple?

JAKE: I felt myself I was being choked.

NR: The same thing was happening to me.

JAKE: It was almost as if I was confusing whose neck I was choking. That's when my speech started getting squeezed.

NR: I'm very impressed. You say you had no breath control, but you did. For a lot of people in that situation without good training in breath control the larynx would close off.

There was an interesting self-deflation here too, from the first line, "I blew the rent money," to his whimpering at the end.

MEG: One problem that I have as an actor is that I can't let myself go, and here Jake let go all the way.

NR: Were you conscious, Jake, of using any controls?

JAKE: Control in what sense? You mean the actor's control of his equipment?

NR: Yes.

JAKE: Yeah, definitely. But I didn't have any emotional control, I did not want to block anything out. There was one point where I was really on the verge of being frightened. When I broke down and sat back on the chair after the strangling I was personally frightened.

NR: You were on the edge.

JAKE: Yeah, that's the perfect description.

NR: That's the chance you have to take.

What happened to you was a beautiful example of the involuntary performance, although a performance can never be completely involuntary because there is always at least the willingness to appear. After an involuntary performance the actor is kind of stunned and bewildered, he doesn't know what just happened to him. He is in shock at having caught sight of his own evasions, tricks, and clichés, or at sensing something of his own vast and untapped resources, or at being forced to question why he became an actor at all. At such moments the director knows he has found something, released something which nobody in the world could have told the actor was there.

PAOLO: Can you give some examples from your films?

NR: I would say the entire performance of Sal Mineo in *Rebel*. The love scene between Natalie and Jim. The milk bottle on the forehead. The fight between father and son on the stairway. John Derek in *Knock On Any Door*, when he cried for the first time since he was two-and-a-half. Burton's soliloquy on top of the hood of the jeep in *Bitter Victory*. The scene at Romanoff's bar in *In a Lonely Place*. Gloria and Bogie in the kitchen. The performance of Burt Mustin, the farmer in *Lusty Men*. Some of the farmers of Colorado in *On Dangerous Ground*. Nearly every climax of Mercedes McCambridge in *Johnny Guitar*. Every one was dangerous. I kept asking myself, am I too far over the key? Dare I go that wild?

JAKE: I didn't want to go for the third take, especially with the last sequence, but Peter said, "Let's do that one moment. All the rest has been preparation for that."

NR: How did you feel about it, Peter?

PETER: It scared the shit out of me. I was really unsure after the second take what to do.

NR: You did the right thing. Even if you already had the scene on film exactly as you wanted it, it would be perfectly legitimate to do one more take just for protection, especially if you got it on the first or second takes. Something could be wrong with the film, something could happen at the lab.

In this case it would have been a mistake not to have gone on. When you as director find yourself oversolicitous of the actor at a moment like that, you must check that it's not because you yourself are unable to cope with the emotion. You must go on, even though you don't want anymore. You must go on to help the actor, even if the performance is bad or unsuitable. It's a necessary catharsis. Just going up and hugging the actor isn't enough. It's better to go on with the scene, to stay involved, and not walk away from it. You did the right thing.

JAKE: At that point I trusted Peter, because he came up to me, just looked at me, and asked me if I was all right. He talked to me. He suggested I was feeling fear, but he suggested that I do the scene again anyway. It was my trust in him that made me realize that I was okay.

NR: It's like going up on the trapeze again after you've taken a spill off a giant swing. You just get up and do it again.

In the last couple of scenes the levels of response, of interaction, have been very high. I hope we can keep it up, and keep topping ourselves with this kind of awareness.

Did you get *Cowboy Mouth*? We're going to have a fine time with that.

IN CLASS VII

SCRIPT BREAKDOWN

I want to take this five-page section from *Cowboy Mouth* and break it down. I want to approach it as if it were the whole play, a complete entity.*

I think Sam Shepard is one of the craziest of today's young contemporary writers. He and Patty Smith were engaged in presenting *Cowboy Mouth* for the first time in New York in the spring of 1971, and they were having trouble with it. About three days before the opening they and the director, Bob Glaudini, called me in on it, and by the time the play went on I'm not sure I understood it at all myself. Bob Glaudini played the Lobster Man, and Ralph Lee, a very good puppet and mask designer, designed a wonderful outfit for him. The play opened and closed. When I first heard a scene from it in class I thought, Jesus, that sounds familiar. Is that *The Lobster Man*? I'd even forgotten the title.

I have an affection for this kind of writing. I have an affection for material that's out of the ordinary. This is very contemporary, and it has a good ear to it. The author puts a stethoscope to usually hidden places.

One reason I've chosen *Cowboy Mouth* for your exercise in breaking down a script is to have you explore how you'd relate to the Lobster. It's a very difficult acting problem. Even though the Lobster wore a marvelous lobster costume, it was difficult for Sam Shepard and Patti Smith to relate to him.

The locale is a dusty motel on any southwestern highway you've been on. Set it on the plains of Illinois.

---

* Sam Shepard, *Cowboy Mouth* from *Angel City and Other Plays* (New York: Urizen Books, 1980), pp. 211–216.

You've seen the scene performed by Arthur and Jet several times in class, and I assume by now you have read the script many times. You must determine from your reading exactly what the author is trying to tell you. An author will usually set his central idea in the exposition. Shakespeare seldom goes beyond the first fifteen lines of a prologue before he has told you the entire content of the play. What would you say is the central idea of this script?

ERICA: To find out about the Lobster Man.

NR: To find out about the Lobster Man. Arthur? . . . Arthur, you haven't read the play through, and that was apparent in the way you performed the scene.

What is the central idea? You have to find that out. Let us for the moment assume the central idea of the author is: *The games we play only lead to other games; therefore games are futile.* That may be a wrong choice, but we can't be sure until we break down the script into actions. We may find our actions in constant contradiction to the central idea, in which case either the actor is wrong or the author is wrong. For now let's take the author's word for it.

It is his idea. It is not yours. The director and the actor do well to begin with some humility. As an actor you may experience the trifling and momentary joy of ad-libbing a line, and believe you've had a great creative experience. At that point I suggest you take inventory and ask yourself, "Does this contribute to the central idea?" It may bring a free gift or a nice lift to the scene, or it may very well destroy your character and the impact of the scene altogether, just as though you had taken an incorrect or nonsupportive action.

Directors, how do you feel about the central idea, about people playing games? You must find your own personal point of view, your own philosophy about people playing games, however you want to phrase it.

You've read the script, you know what you are playing, you know whom you are playing. Now start at the first scene. What happened before that scene began? What were the events? You must lay out the backstory. Here you have to know very specifically what happened up to the minute before the first action of the scene.

What do you draw on for your backstory? Draw on research, association, dreams, your family, your experience at the concert, at the gallery, at the cafe having a cup of coffee. Draw on yourself within certain events. Those events should relate to events that could have happened to the people involved in the story in which your character is participating. What are events? Events are not just car crashes,

O.D.s, stumbles over flower pots; they are sunsets, arguments, pleasures, fears, laughter. What was the event that came out of the sunset?
What were the events that caused the fears, the laughter? Be specific.
Be very, very clear about it. What kind of a room were you in? What
kind of subway were you on? What was the stink on 50th and 8th
Avenue? Was it eye level, nose level, hip level? Did it make you want
to get out of the city? Who were the people you were with? Were they
beautiful? Loving? Hateful? What were your feelings?

So many things will come to you as a result of exploring your
backstory that you had better keep a pen and paper beside you. Write
down your associations, whether sunsets or floods—whatever crosses
your mind. At some point as you work on your backstory you must
activate an inner monologue. The scene may take place in a tearoom,
while your association is to a locker room or maybe a beach. That
association implies an historical connection somewhere in your mind,
in your experience; there is something there for you. First impressions
are fertile soil in breaking down a part, in investigating not just your
actions, but colors, moods, and relationships. Sometimes they'll come
from music you hear or what you are reading, sometimes from how
you feel about the day. If you listen to yourself, your equipment will
tell you if you're being phony. Risk the mistakes. Some you can afford,
some you can't.

The director now has an interesting problem. You now must relate
the actors' backstories to your own. You must find points of reference
to your own sum total of personality as you exist right now, because
everything that happens on that soundstage, every moment, must
be personally important to you. You must be involved with every
toothache, every hangover, every case of nerves, whether it's a property man's or your star's. You must attune yourself, make the total
experience of the script your own, so that when the actors come on
stage you can project, not by telling them that they have to feel one
way or another, or that their scene is the most important, or that they
are the most important, because they ain't gonna believe you. It must
be clear in the way you behave, the way you perform your functions,
the way you convey your knowledge and your enthusiasm. Your job
is to help the actor contribute. You cannot play every part in the
script on film, but you must be able to play every part in your mind.

Until now you have been using your minds, but at this next stage of
breaking down a script you must tap your feelings. You all have some
background in emotional memory and sense memory; you have techniques, in various stages of development, for drawing upon your feel-

ings. Through your imagination and through the specifics of your backstory you must arrive at the *what-I-want*. The *what-I-want* is an oversimplified but useful, nonintimidating way of referring to the will. It is interesting that very few qualified doctors of psychiatry and psychoanalysis have written thoroughly and convincingly on the matter of will. Stanislavsky has written better on the subject than most, although another book, *The Ways of the Will*, by Dr. Leslie Farber, comes to mind.

Each character in a play has one overall action, one thing he wants to achieve more than anything else. Directors, you must know what the action of each character is, and still you must be receptive to whatever the actor brings to you, without changing your central idea, your concept. The actor's final choice of an overall action must be in terms of its contribution to the realization of the central idea. The central idea is the spine of the play.

The spine is made up of many vertebrae, many individual actions that help support the spine, or feed or progress the main action. Somebody once said—and this is reaching way back into my youth—that the spine of a play is like a trip on a train, made up of a thousand little stops along the way. Each stop is an action, and within each action are beats—transitions in color, tone, mood—and each beat has its origin in your backstory. You can almost see the beats working.

I would like you to separate the beats indicating changes of attitude, action or activity, entrances or exits, within each action. Write them on the script or on a separate page so you have space enough to amplify and break down in this way each action of each character. Give yourself options. Go all the way with it.

Now what you want, your desire, is very important to you, so make a special column for it in your notes. Go through the script line by line, for each character, and ask yourself, "If I were this character, what would I do?" Find the sub-actions within each beat. Let each sub-action grow in strength and clarity as you make the transition from "*If* I were he . . ." to "I *am* he." Maybe it will be the same action, line after line, that constitutes a progression to the next beat, or maybe something happens so the character has to change his tactic. His overall action, his overall purpose, remains the same, but within that his sub-actions change. You may find that a sub-action doesn't work in relation to your overall action, it doesn't further your progress towards what you want. Or your action is right, but you're approaching it the wrong way. Maybe you have to win him over by flattery rather than demand. Each action you choose should be specific. To be general is no good. That's what is wrong with most performances, they become generalized.

You must get used to breaking down a script on paper. As you do, it will become easier for you to do it in your head, as you're talking with people. Directors, your directions to actors will become much briefer, you won't get bogged down in rationale. In my director's script I put a blank page opposite the script page so I can put down the overall and individual actions of each character. I may write down one, and one more. I want the actor to find his action, but that action may not work; I'll have another one ready for him.

LEONARD: What are some ways to deal with the possibility that the director's idea is different from the actor's idea of his action?

NR: The best way to deal with that, and it's going to happen, is to prepare yourself by finding the spine, the overall action, for each character, as it contributes to the central idea of the script. If you feel that because of an actor's choice of action your central idea has no chance of being realized, you can suggest an alternative action. He may not accept it, but he must have enough faith in you to try it anyway. Even if your idea proves wrong, it can still stimulate him into finding his true action. That's the nature of the creative process between actor and director. Or else you can give the other actor an action, or help the other actor find an action, that will conflict with the first actor's action, making it more difficult for him to play, so he will try harder, and then the other one will try harder, and then you'll have a scene.

NAT: Shouldn't the actor's action have to do with the character he's playing against?

NR: It is your action, not the other person's action. Unless there's a conflict, something in your way, you're not going to be interesting, so don't direct the other guy in the conflict. You each will find your own actions. If you can't, the director will help you. The writer has already implied the nature of those actions; it's only a matter of searching them out in terms of your own personalities, experiences, and imaginations.

NAT: But could I as an actor say to the other guy, "This is my action."

NR: Yes, you may say that, and he'll take account of it. What you may want to retain for yourself, however, are your inner reasons. Those you needn't reveal to the other person. Your inner life is your own. But don't be afraid to expose yourself.

As director, your actions will change every day, because you cannot expect to achieve consummation of the event you are filming always in the same way. You must be at least as various as the actors. Actors and directors must do their homework continuously, throughout the film.

Up till now you have been so involved with theory and technique that you've surrounded everything with words, words, words. It's good for actors to have an easy flow of a lot of words so associations can arise and be investigated, but directors have to be able to put down the theme of a scenario in three or four lines, or a character's action in three or four words. That's what it's about: bam, bam, bam, bam.

BEN: To get the action down to a single sentence seems very limiting. Since an action also encompasses an objective, putting it in only one phrase almost demotes it to an activity.

MARA: But if you can get your action down to one phrase, so that that phrase says very specifically what you're after, then it's cleanest, strongest, and most playable, and all the activities and sub-actions fall into place in relationship to it. I know if I can get my action down to a word or two, that helps everything else.

BETTY: I have so much I can draw on, it's hard to choose just the right action.

NR: But I want you to make the choice anyway and then go with it. Carry conviction to the hilt, it's the only way you'll grow. You can't be all things to all people in all concepts.

NAT: Do you break down the script before you start rehearsing?

NR: Certainly I do. Before I go on the set I have to know exactly what I want because most casts won't know what they want because they don't have a method of work. When this class is over I want you to be able to answer me when I ask, "What's your action?" I want you to tell me loud and clear, very simply, in three words, six words, ten words maximum.

Slim's first words are: "Now what'll we do?" In this case his action may be to start a new game, or continue the old game, or support the new game, or end the game. In terms of the specifics of a backstory Slim's words imply, among other things, that Cavale and he were doing something else just before this. If he has any time, the director will suggest to the actor an improvisation on a different kind of game that Slim could have played before the scene began. But maybe the director won't have the time, or he may not employ a method of work that permits him to set up an accurate improvisation and variation. Within his preparation the actor must find some way to say the lines as if for the very first time. How does he go about it?

Suppose the game he was playing was Scrabble or Detect This

Tune. Or say his game was singing a song about eyes—blue eyes, brown eyes. An argument starts: "Goddam it, you're cheating! That wasn't about eyes at all, that was about brown hair!" –"No, it was about eyes!" –"Stop this shit!" –"Let's get the Lobster Man up here!" Why?

For some reason known to them, Slim and Cavale invite the Lobster Man up. Why do they invite the Lobster Man up? Be very simple about it.

CHARLOTTE: They want to get to know him.

NR: Why do they want to get to know him? He is not a usual person to see around a motel, is he? He is interesting. Is it any wonder they invite the Lobster Man up, the Lobster Man who has claws and is shiny orange-red? What does the script tell you?

What does Slim want? He tells the Lobster Man, "Have a seat"; and from there to where "Lobster Man grunts" Slim has one overall action. The director should work with the actor—but the actor can't rely on that, he must work with himself—to find which action best stimulates his imagination, his responses, his desire. Each of you must find your own individual actions through the scene.

The Lobster Man grunts and Slim asks, "What did he say?" Here some possible actions for Slim could be to size up the Lobster Man, to find out about him, to find an opening for conversation, to make an opening for conversation, to force an opening for conversation—all in order to feed into the investigation of who and what and why the Lobster Man is, in order to feed the new game. The game has changed, and he wants to get the new one going. I'm mentioning specific actions here only to stimulate you into finding your own actions.

The grunt, by the way, ends the first beat. A beat may signify the end of an action, or a change in an action, or the addition of a new color to intensify an action. At that station stop many things can happen, but you have to keep your action in mind or else you'll knock the whole train off its tracks.

Does the Lobster Man have hair under his claws? Does the Lobster have eyelashes? What protects those bug eyes? Slim and Cavale evaluate the Lobster Man differently, but come to the same conclusion. How do you, personally, relate to the Lobster Man? It's important that you read the play all the way through in order to understand the author's conception of the Lobster Man.

LEONARD: About the Lobster Man, is this actually a lobster, or is this a man dressed as a lobster?

NR: This is a lobster, as far as you know. This is a Lobster Man who serves delicatessen objects at the motel. And now something in your imagination must be able to say, "If that's true, if the Lobster Man is a waiter at the delicatessen at the motel in Solinas, Texas, or Amarillo, how did he get there?"

LEONARD: He is a lobster.

NR: He is a lobster. For all intents and purposes he is a lobster.

LEONARD: Now it's really strange—

NR: Oh, it's not strange. You see him every day—

LEONARD: Because if he's a man dressed as a lobster, that's one thing, but being a real live lobster—

NR: As far as you know he is a lobster, and you accept him as a lobster. There he is. He looks like a lobster, he walks like a lobster, and it is perfectly possible to stage the play with a fellow coming up with some crabs and clams. This is a Lobster Man, and the author has written: "The Lobster Man enters."

You have an obligation to your audience to create the Lobster Man. Suppose the Lobster Man were a waiter at the Sheraton Hotel, or the Hilton Hotel, and you, Cavale and Slim, can't stand playing games or talking to each other anymore, so you want to keep the Lobster Man there with you. What kind of room do you see yourself in? First floor? Second floor? When you're talking to the Lobster Man, who are you talking to? You flatter him: "You must be a very interesting fellow." You start conning a little bit.

Is there anyone who has not at some time been at a hotel, sent for room service, and tried to get something extra? The waiter comes up, and maybe you give him a tip before he brings what you order. Or maybe you're without money, so you ingratiate yourself with him so he'll bring you free food. You've all pulled a con, haven't you? Be honest with yourselves. You've been conning since you were six months old. From your mother's breast you switched to your father's pockets. So you con the Lobster Man, make him feel special. What purpose does it serve? It gets your game started.

Arthur, Jet, why did you treat the Lobster the way you did? It was not clear why you brought him up to the room. There's no law against having fun, you know, especially if your action is to boost your spirits or protect yourselves from drowning on the floor; but you have an obligation to yourselves and to the audience to be clear and specific about whatever you're up to. How dare you take it for granted that we're going to be interested in the self-indulgence you presented us with the other day? Would you be? If you would be, then you'd better develop your taste and see a lot more plays and a lot more films.

Now the game begins. How does it begin? Slim makes a long speech. What does Cavale do during Slim's long speech? Mark it down. During

Slim's speech, besides a close-up on Slim, there may be a close-up on a reaction from the Lobster and a close-up on a reaction from Cavale. If you're the Lobster or Cavale you can't be dead in those moments, because the director will point to you and tell the camera-man, "Hey, come in here, I want a four-inch, right here." Find out what your reaction is. You may not have one line to say, but you have to be full, darlings.

Let's move on to Cavale's speech. Put down Cavale's action for the entire beat. Have any of the women come up with an action for Cavale here? Yes, Meg.

MEG: To try to get Slim's attention.

NR: Fine, that's a part of the game. Dakota?

DAKOTA: To get Slim uptight or jealous.

BEV: That could be a reaction to Slim's action. Could Slim's action be to gain control?

NR: Right, and that would feed into a later action. That's a very good question. What kind of person is Slim? We haven't come to that yet. We'll come to that later, through the work with actions. That's why we do this work, to find out who the characters are.

We detect in Slim his old game, the game of trying to get control. Slim is not a very imaginative fellow. By accepting the Lobster Man into his hotel room he is certainly more imaginative than most, but still not very imaginative. He's using old tricks, playing a con game.

As for Cavale, her action during Slim's speech comes into its flowering in her speech, and it's a similar action to Slim's. They both want to play a new game, but if, like Slim, Cavale tries to flatter and con the Lobster Man, she does it by trying to pierce his brain and imagination. She doesn't talk about the shit on the floor and room service; she talks about nightmares, aspirations, and dreams.

This is a new dimension to the game that feeds into the line we're drawing. From those thousand stops of the railroad car we're drawing one continuous line.

I see the end of the second beat as being at the next Lobster grunt. That grunt is a station stop.

BEN: Does a beat apply just to the individual actor?

NR: No, it applies to the whole scene and everyone in it.

Now Cavale, somewhat more sensitive and only getting a grunt in response to her questions, says: "I think we oughta try a different tactic." Well, that's a very obvious clue to the action of the beat: to change tactics, to a different tone, different texture, different color, different maneuver, without changing the action itself. Let's look at how she does this.

Slim says, "Like what?" On that line Slim has a sub-action that is very important to his character. What could that sub-action be? It could be to tell her to go ahead and take the ball. It could be something else.

CHARLOTTE: So in a scene there's usually one large action that comes close to the spine of the character, and then within the beats there are other smaller actions.

NR: Yes, absolutely right.

BEN: I can usually find the sub-action, but I have trouble finding the big thing, the overall action.

NR: So work on it. It's not going to happen for you with just this one session today. On the other hand, as the basis for your selection, ask yourself, "Does this action advance the story? Does it advance the theme?" Be patient with yourselves. But work, sweat it out. You have all the tools I can give you that you can absorb at this point; anything more would be confusing. Take this scene. Take another scene. Go through the scenes you've already worked on.

PETER: You use the word *sub-action*.

NR: Try the word *color* instead.

What could Slim's sub-action be? Arthur?

ARTHUR: I found at this point I was unprepared for what went on.

NR: You were not prepared?

ARTHUR: No.

NR: But that was obvious. You were not playing an action. Or if you were playing an action, it was not the right action. Or if it was the right action, it was not intense enough, it was not important enough to you, Arthur. I like the action of throwing the ball to her, challenging her. There's no such thing as a pure emotion; there's no such thing as one simple action either. What does this action indicate to you of Slim's character? What does he want to do?

ARTHUR: He does not want to stop the game. He does not want to go outside.

NR: That he doesn't want something may be considered an action: to reject. You can work with that. He wants to stand pat, he wants his way. His way is right. That's the foundation of this fellow. Slim is not an adventurous man; he's reactionary. He doesn't want to go outside. He's scared.

So Slim is a very conservative fellow. Now let's make the transition from, "*If* I were Slim, how would I act?" to "I *am* Slim, and I know the need to get out of this room, and I know I'm paralyzed within this room, so I'll have to stay here and bear the conflict within me."

So the need in Slim for the game now becomes that much more intense, even deadly.

Now. Cavale suggests a different tactic with the Lobster Man. She suggests "just ignoring him for a while." Here, Jet and Arthur, we come to the great big rupture in your scene, caused by a lack of humility in your interpretation of "ignoring." Lines went haywire, actions went haywire, Arthur got thrown higher than a kite. The whole play went out the window. During your presentation of the scene, I encouraged you to go with it. I hoped if you wanted to play the action, to use the Lobster to make Slim jealous, you'd play it to the hilt. You'd find room on the chair to sit next to him, put his claw around you. I thought maybe something would come of it that I hadn't foreseen.

MARA: When they were doing the scene I kept asking myself, "Who is being ignored?" I thought Jet and Arthur should be ignoring the Lobster Man, but Jet and the Lobster Man were ignoring Arthur.

NR: Which was completely the wrong action to take. Jet and I talked about this already, so I trust I'm not offending her. And where were you, Arthur? Where was your perception? Why did you sit there during the scene and not participate? It's because you do not have your action established as an element of your equipment and vocabulary. What is your action? What do you want to do? What happened to you just before this? You want to stand pat, you want your own way, but your overall action still is to play a game and use the Lobster Man. And there he is. You want to put a drink in his claw, you want to do anything to keep playing your game. That is your action.

Now let's see how Slim's conservatism, his need to stand pat, is sustained. Two simple lines, "Like what?" and "I never would," reveal the nonadventurous nature of this fellow who wants to play games, and is now playing games with the Lobster Man. He reinforces his action, to play another game, when he says "The whole point in bringing him over was so that we'd have something to do." See how the character's overriding action remains intact?

You've observed how drastically Arthur was thrown in the scene, and you know that happened because Jet chose the wrong action for Cavale. I'd like to concentrate for a moment on Cavale. From my point of view you can take it pretty much as a rule of thumb that women are a lot more adventurous than men. Cavale, more adventurous than Slim, is ready to start on something else. She's very specific about it when she says: "Let's go down to the deli and leave him here alone." By leaving the Lobster they will either heighten the game or else they'll find a new game downstairs.

And there's another element in her action. She knows Slim is afraid to go out. She knows he wants to stand pat. Her knowing that adds a color to her line, doesn't it? There's a taunt to her line that becomes a sub-action, while the main action remains the same. The foundation for the sub-action will have its roots in her backstory, if you have been thorough in developing it.

Now Slim says, "He might rip us off." Here's our nonadventurous fellow again. He's finding another excuse to stand pat, to pursue the game. To pursue the game becomes a means of protecting himself physically from the hazards of the outside—from a sunstroke, or tripping down the stairs, or running into somebody he hates, or buying poisoned food at the deli. The actor must build his backstory fully, because in his backstory will lie the intensity, the degree of conviction with which Slim says, "He might rip us off." You must work for those associations that stimulate and reinforce your action. In front of the camera you cannot afford to let any line, any inner association evaporate or go unheeded, or you risk becoming a mechanical, calculating actor. Nothing is casual. If you find yourself saying, "Well that's just a casual line, that's just a throwaway," find out why you're saying that. Are you trying to cover up something? Are you trying to give a different impression of yourself than who you really are? Are you trying to disarm someone? Take nothing for granted. How many times do you use the term *rip off* in a day?

Cavale says: "So what. We don't need this shit." What's her action behind that line? What does she want to do?

PAUL: She's putting him down.

NR: How is she putting him down? Think of the central idea.

PAUL: She ends the game.

NR: So we have two actions going here now: to threaten him and to end the game. Slim asks, "What about my drums? My guitar?" How do those lines fit in? Arthur?

ARTHUR: Well, the drums and guitar are his functionary pieces.

NR: But what are they really? They're really a further support for standing pat, staying put.

So what does our adventurous woman say now? Read her next lines. What do they mean? Does anyone even remember hearing those lines? Here's one of the most important moments in the whole play, and if there is a spine to her character, this is the spine to her character: "And like the Chinese say, sweetie, fuck the dream, you fuck the drum." If you fuck the dream, you fuck up who you are.

"Fuck the dream, you fuck the drum." When I went home the other night I couldn't think how to give that line some meaning. My immediate associations to it had me putting two different poets together:

Archibald MacLeish wrote a poem in which he said, "Man's fate is a drum"; Duke Ellington wrote a song, "A woman is a drum." What do we have here, man's fate is a woman? There are a lot of ways you can play around with Cavale's line.

But I'm not just playing with words. I'm working with feelings, conviction, thought, want, desires, and the will. There is nothing very tiny, small, or peppy about the profession of being an actor. The demands are tremendous. You have to attack yourselves every day of your lives.

Now let's skip to a later beat, to the moment Slim pulls out a switchblade. Why does Slim want to destroy the Lobster? Is it part of the game? Is the game directed toward Cavale, or toward Slim's own need to keep the game going? Cavale says: "Slim! Cut the shit!" What is her action there?

MARA: She's mocking him.

NR: Can you use the infinitive form?

MARA: She wants to mock him.

NR: The switchblade is out. Slim is insisting on his game. If I were Cavale my action would be to change his game.

MARA: At this point I think the game is over.

NR: Then so is the play and we may as well bring down the curtain. She wants to change his game. She has to change his game. Why? Because otherwise the games will stop. She doesn't want the games to stop. Keeping the games going is what these two characters are all about. It's what the play is about. Are you going to violate the author again? She doesn't want to end the game, she just wants to change the way he plays it. That's conflict, isn't it? And the conflict leads up to the climax. But don't anticipate, don't play what's ahead, be right here now.

Cavale wants to change his game. Now what's Slim's action in the next beat?

ARTHUR: Outright aggression.

NR: Put that in terms of action, to do. What does he want to do?

ARTHUR: Lobster Man is doing something to him, and he wants to know what that is.

NR: He wants to find out what the Lobster Man is doing to him. How would you find that out, Arthur?

ARTHUR: By cutting it out of him?

NR: Cutting it out of him means what?

ARTHUR: Killing him.

NR: And what does that do?

ARTHUR: That ends the game.

NR: That's right. So what does Slim want to do?

TOM: End the game.

NR: You can play that, Arthur. It gives you a purpose. It gives you a reason for the attack. She wants to change your game, the way you play it? You'll end the game! Right?

What is Cavale's reaction to Slim's wanting to end the game? She wants to protect it. Before, she wanted to change his game, and now the change threatens her. Do you see what is happening? You have turbulence. Have you ever thrown a glider? A glider climbs on turbulence.

Why does Cavale want to continue the game? To extend the game to new heights? To get high? She hasn't had her high yet. To save the show? To protect herself from hearing the Lobster's scream? To protect herself from having to put the Lobster in boiling water? Any of those. All of those. State it in whatever terms you want.

I have a note for Cavale that takes us into another dimension, another texture: Cavale now wants to protect the game, she wants things to continue as they are, because she senses in the Lobster Man there is something much greater than what they have so far perceived. She senses, but she does not know. She does not yet know the spiritual life of the Lobster.

Now why are we this meticulous? Because all these aspects we've been exploring up till now contribute to the climax of the scene, the emergence of the Lobster Man as the rock-and-roll savior. Everything you've done up until now by way of preparation must preserve you from anticipating that moment, from telegraphing it or letting its charge leak away. It has to be a great moment, full to the brim.

Keeping in mind your introduction to the problems of working in film as opposed to those of working in theatre—the immediacy, the time factor, the distractions, the demands to repeat over and over and over again the same actions or beats or adjustments, the camera being wrong, the sound being wrong, the lights blowing out, whistles blowing, planes flying overhead—do you wonder at all anymore that this method has made an even greater impact on the screen than in the theatre? Do you wonder that those who have background in method have made more advances on the screen than those who come from—forgive the expression—the London School of Dramatic Art? I saw one of the most disgraceful performances I've ever seen last night, by an American trained in London at the National Academy. It was exactly what we're trying to get away from, the calculated performance, the intellectual performance, the performance of planned business and inorganic invention. You cannot survive in film if you take that approach. You will dry up within the first three hours of shooting.

It is not enough to want to be an actor. It is not enough to want to be a star. It is not enough to want to have attention. It is not enough to want to be free enough to exhibit yourself and demand money for your trouble. It ain't no place near any of those things. That is why we're investigating this method and trying to find how it works for us. This is your life insurance.

Naturals

Of the actors I've worked with Arthur Kennedy, Bob Mitchum, Jimmie Dean, and Bogart were naturals.

The quality of being and of acting at the same time was perhaps as true of Bogart as of anybody I've seen on film. He was always very well prepared—he knew what the scene was to be, he knew his action, and the details came naturally to him—but he wouldn't learn his lines until the last moment. But Bogie, like Bob Mitchum, had a truly photographic memory. When word got out about how he and Mitchum took advantage of this ability to achieve spontaneity, soon every new actor who had touched the fringe of the Actor's Studio was asking for his lines, saying, "I never rehearse lines because it interferes with my spontaneity." Then we'd have to go twelve takes while he'd learn his lines.

Arthur Kennedy was a beautiful actor to work with. Where it might have taken me five minutes with Mitchum and ten minutes with Susan Hayward[39] between takes to get them into the right groove, when something went wrong in one of Kennedy's scenes, by the time I'd cut, walked over, and gotten my arm around him, he'd know everything I was going to say. And the next take would be perfect.

John Wayne was a natural. I thought the Broadway drugstore critics who hadn't yet been asked out to Hollywood were just terribly imperceptive about him. He was a much better actor than most peo-

---

39. In *Lusty Men*.

ple gave him credit for being, almost daily full of nice surprises. But he was not flexible about himself. He couldn't conceive that I would be serious in wanting him to do O'Neill's *A Touch of the Poet*.

With Bob Ryan there was always quick intellectual reception. I cast him opposite Wayne[40] because I knew that Ryan was the only actor in Hollywood who could kick the shit out of Wayne. That conflict was going to be real, so I'd have two naturals. I created the situation and enclosed them in a tent, using the space for tension, so you could expect that the moment Duke dropped his right, Ryan would stiffen, and pretty soon they'd bring the tent down around them. But the tent didn't collapse, and instead became the setting for "No man is an island," another expression of tension and space.

O'Toole had to be directed[41] and I think he still has to be directed. He seems to repeat himself time after time, an aspect of his character that I've never found particularly attractive.

James Mason[42] just needed the key or the freshening up of an idea. He is the most constantly improving actor in the business. A beautiful man, beautiful actor.

Burton is a natural, if he has the right thing to work with[43] otherwise he is awkward. At one time he was an astonishingly good actor, and beautiful to work with. Then he married Elizabeth Taylor, and his values changed.

Quinn needed direction[44], but he is perhaps the best character actor we have in American cinema and one of the best leading men I've ever seen on the stage. In many performances of *A Streetcar Named Desire* Tony was better than Brando. Both had a kind of animal poetry.

When Marlon Brando began, many of us thought he was the first impeccable actor we'd seen. There was just no way he could make a mistake. But then there was one despair-ridden decision followed by another in succession. And then he did very good work in some films that were not terribly popular, and you're only as good as your last film, and goodness is measured by box office returns. He did just fine in *Godfather*. I did not read the book, but I'd wager the ending, the scene with him and the child, was something he added. He was always a contributing actor.

And Dean was a brilliant actor. His imagination was fresh as a new day.

---

40. In *Flying Leathernecks*.
41. In *Savage Innocents*.
42. In *Bigger than Life*.
43. E.g., *Bitter Victory*.
44. In *Savage Innocents*.

James Dean:
The Actor as a Young Man

First there was the revolver.

Jimmy kept a Colt .45 in his dressing room, where he also slept. He had come back to Hollywood at the age of 22 for *East of Eden*, but everything that he did suggested he had no intention of belonging to the place. He had come to work; but he would remain himself. He found in the Warners studio a sanctuary of steel and concrete. At night he could be alone in this closed, empty kingdom. Perhaps the revolver was a symbol, of self-protection, of warning to others.

He rode a motorcycle. He dressed casually, untidily, which invariably was interpreted as a gesture of revolt. Not entirely true. For one thing, it saved time, and Jim detested waste. It also saved money. (This is a simple consideration, often ignored. Most young actors are poor: T-shirt and jeans for work, later to become a mannerism, was originally a quick and comfortable way to cut down the laundry bill.) Some days he would forego shaving if there was something more important to do. And what's wrong with that?

Like the revolver these habits were self-protective. Riding a motorcycle, he traveled by himself. Sleeping in a studio dressing room, he had complete solitude. He could leave, but nobody else could come in. He shied away from manners and social convention because they suggested disguise. He wanted his self to be naked. "Being a nice guy," he once said, "is detrimental to actors. When I first came to

Hollywood, everyone was nice to me, everyone thought I was a nice guy. I went to the commissary to eat, and people were friendly, and I thought it was wonderful. But I decided not to continue to be a nice guy. Then people would have to respect me for my work."

Soon after shooting on *East of Eden* was finished, he went to his dressing room and found the gun had disappeared. He was furious, but this was only the beginning. A few days later the studio authorities told him he could no longer sleep in the dressing room. (It came close to violating safety regulations, and Warners had had a couple of disastrous fires.) He refused to believe them until he was refused admittance at the gate that night.

There were name and number plates on each office door at Warners. Next morning Jimmy took them all down, changed some around, and hung others from ceilings and fountains, causing widespread confusion. Then he rode away on his motorcycle, vowing never to make a film there again.

Cat-like he had prowled around and found his own preferred corner. Then it was forbidden him. A wound to the pride of a cat is serious. Ask any of us cats.

Not long after I had written the first outline of *Rebel*, Kazan invited me to see a rough cut of *East of Eden* in the music room at Warners. The composer, Leonard Rosenman, was there, improvising at the piano. And Jimmy was there, aloof and solitary; we hardly exchanged a word. That he had talent was obvious, but I respected Kazan's skills too much to give full marks to any actor who worked with him.

My office at Warners adjoined Kazan's. One day Jimmy dropped by. He asked me what I was working on. I told him the idea and approach. He seemed warily interested, but didn't say very much. A day or two later he brought in a tough, dark-haired young man named Perry Lopez, whom he had met in New York. He told me that Perry came from the Lexington Avenue district: "You should talk to him," he said.

A few more such encounters and I decided to get Dean to play Jim Stark.

But he had to decide, too. It was not a simple question of whether or not he liked the part. Neither he nor Warners were sure he would ever work there again. And after the smell of success began to surround *East of Eden*, agents and well-wishers were eager to advise him. It would be foolish, they told him, to appear in any film not based on a best-seller, not adapted by a $3,000-a-week writer, and not directed by Elia Kazan, George Stevens, John Huston, or William Wyler. He was not the kind of person to take such advice very seriously, but intensely self-aware as he was, he could not fail to be troubled by "success." If there were aspects of it he enjoyed, it also played on his doubts.

One evening we had a long passionate discussion with Shelley Winters about acting and show business. "I better know how to take care of myself," he said. This attitude lay behind his choice of work. He had quarreled with Kazan during *East of Eden*, but retained a respect for him, and would have been flattered to work for him again.

There were probably few other directors with whom Jimmy could have worked. To work with Jimmy meant exploring his nature; without this his powers of expression were frozen. He wanted to make films in which he could personally believe, but it was never easy for him. Between belief and action lay the obstacle of his own deep, obscure uncertainty. Disappointed, unsatisfied, he was the child who skulks off to his private corner and refuses to speak. Eager and hopeful, he was the child exhilarated with new pleasure, wanting more, wanting everything, and often unconsciously subtle in his pursuit of it.

Late one evening he arrived at my house with Jack Simmons, at that time an unemployed actor, and Vampira, the television personality. (Jack was to become a close friend of Jim's and appear with him in a TV play. Jimmy often extended sudden affection to lonely and struggling people, several of whom he'd adopt. He had few permanent relationships, so his companion of the moment was most likely to be an adoption of the moment, or a new object of curiosity. He told me later he had wanted to meet Vampira because he was studying magic. Was she really possessed by satanic forces, as her TV program suggested? "She didn't know anything!" he exclaimed sadly.) On entering the room he turned a back somersault, then from the floor looked keenly at me.

"Are you middle-aged?"

I admitted it.

"Did you live in a bungalow on Sunset Boulevard, by the old Clover Club?"

"Yes," I said.

"Was there a fire there in the middle of the night?"

"Yes."

"Did you carry a boxer puppy out of the house in your bare feet across the street and cut your feet?"

I had.

He seemed to approve. He had heard the story from Vampira and came to find out if it were true.

On Sunday afternoons I used to invite a few people in to play music, sing, and talk. Jimmy always came to these gatherings and enjoyed them. We were exploring on both sides. Was he going to like my friends? Both of us had to know.

One afternoon he stayed on after the others had gone. Clifford Odets came by, and I introduced them. Jimmy was peculiarly silent and retreated to a corner. I went out to the kitchen to mix some drinks. Clifford later told me what had happened:

There had been a long silence. The distance of the room lay between them. At last, in a grave voice, Jimmy spoke:

"I'm a sonofabitch."

Clifford asked why.

"Well," he explained, "here I am, you know, in this room. With you. It's fantastic. Like meeting Ibsen or Shaw."

Clifford remembered this as one of the most flattering remarks ever so sincerely addressed to him.

Jimmy approached all human beings with the same urgent, probing curiosity: *"Here I am. Here are you."* At encountering a new presence, invisible antennae seemed to reach out, grow tense, transmit a series of impressions.

Sometimes there'd be an extraordinary, unbearable tenderness. Michael and Connie Bessie, a couple I'd known for many years, arrived one day from New York. After I'd introduced them to Jimmy, Connie sat down on the couch. Without thinking she picked up the cushion beside her and cradled it in her lap.

Jimmy watched and, after a moment, very intent and quiet, he asked her, "Can't you have a child of your own?"

Connie was dumbstruck and left the room. I went after her. We had once wanted to marry. She and her husband had just adopted a baby.

Just before Christmas I went to New York to interview actors. Jimmy was already there, and I visited his apartment, for there were things I had to know, too. It was on the fifth floor of an old 68th Street building without an elevator. A fairly large furnished room with two porthole windows, a studio couch, a table, some unmatching chairs and stools. On the walls, a bullfighting poster, capes, and horns. Everywhere piles of books and records, some neatly stacked, some spilling over. A door led to the kitchen and bath, another to a flight of stairs to the roof. It was evening. The only light came from the scrap wood and fruit boxes burning in the fireplace.

He played record after record on the phonograph. Where did he first hear all those sounds? African tribal music, Afro-Cuban songs and dances, classical jazz, Jack Teargarten, Dave Brubeck, Haydn, Berlioz. Many of the books were about bullfighting. I remember *Matador* and *Death in the Afternoon*.

I introduced Jimmy to my son Tony, a Plato of sorts, to see if they'd get along and to see him through the eyes of his own generation. Tony stayed in New York and I went back to Hollywood. Later he told me he saw Jimmy several times, mainly at parties at the 68th Street apartment or in rooms of one of the half-dozen young actors and actresses he made his most frequent companions. It was always the same group, and no one ever wanted to go home. Jimmy played bongo drums, while another guy danced calypso and imitations of Gene Kelly. Conversation ranged from new plays and movies to (as dawn broke) Plato and Aristotle. They read stories and plays, going right through *Twenty-Seven Wagon Loads of Cotton*.

Jimmy also went to more orthodox parties. These were larger, given by people he knew less well. But he didn't like crowds, they made him insecure. Ignoring the talk and games, he would find his own melancholy corner.

He swerved easily from morbidity to elation. The depression could lift as completely and unexpectedly as it had settled in. Once it was cured by going to see Jacques Tati in *The Big Day*. Unshaven, tousled, wrapped in a dyed black trench coat, glasses on the end of his nose, Jim's mood was dark as he entered the theatre. But after ten minutes he was laughing so wildly, the nearby audience complained. He ignored them, there was nothing else he could do, the spell of delight had got him. Before the film was over he had to leave, which he did in a series of leaps and hurdles through the aisle. Back on the street, he stopped at a pastry shop. Then down the sidewalk, eclair in hand, with the Grouchian walk and the inquiring, bulbous-eyed face, he turned into Tati's postman.

Another sad, grey, rainy New York day he decided to buy an umbrella. Umbrellas were everywhere in the store, rack upon rack. But which one? Finally he let Tony choose one for him, an ordinary three-dollar model. Jimmy seized it as if it were the one he had been after his whole life. He played with it as a child with a new toy, exploring all its movements, flipping it open, pulling it shut, twirling it over his head. In the street as the rain poured down, suddenly brilliant and exhilarated, he became Charlie Chaplin.

It seemed that anything interested him. His gift for mime was uncanny. A friend wanted to audition for the Actor's Studio, and Jimmy offered to do the scene with him. They chose a fairy tale, a fight between a fox and the little prince. Immediately and with a ferocious longing Jimmy concentrated on the fox, and his imagination winged. He did not imitate; the stealth, the grace, the menace of the animal seemed to enter his body. He *became* a human fox.

He became other people with obvious passion and relief. "If I were he," he would say—and bless him for that, for it was a great part of his magic as an actor. It was the magic IF Stanislavsky had learned about from all the great actors he'd interviewed. But Jim hadn't learned it, not from Lee Strasberg, for chrissake. Nobody learns it, and nobody can breathe it into another.

Like the fox he was wary and hard to catch. For many, a relationship with Jimmy was complex, even obsessive. For him it was simple and probably much less important. He was intensely determined not to be loved or love. He could be absorbed, fascinated, attracted by things new or beautiful, but he would never surrender himself. There were girls convinced they were the only ones in his life (often at the same time, there were so many people and things in his life at the same time), when they were no more than occasions.

When he was poor and unknown in New York, he had reason to be grateful to several people for food and companionship, yet this was not enough for him to trust them. Returning to New York after *East of Eden*, he sometimes used his success to be cruel.

A young photographer he had known quite well in the struggling days wanted to buy a Rolliflex camera. He asked Jim to go halves with him: the price was $25. Jim was affronted: "Why should I get a second-hand camera with you when I can get all the new stuff I want now."

He complained of his companions: "They bum meals from me." One day in a restaurant he wondered out loud, "Where are my friends?" Four of his closest ones were with him at the table, but before they could answer he abruptly got up and walked out.

"I don't want anything seventy-thirty," he liked to say. "Fifty-fifty's enough for me." He came back to this idea often.

Every day he threw himself upon the world like a starved animal after a scrap of food. The intensity of his fears and desires could make the search arrogant, egocentric, but behind it was such a desperate vulnerability that one could not but be moved by it, even frightened. Probably when he was faithless or cruel, he believed he was paying off an old score. The affection that he rejected was affection that once had been his but had found no answer.

The night before I went back to Hollywood we had dinner together, as we had done every night of my New York stay. We ate at an Italian restaurant, and Jim ordered the food with great ceremony, taking pride in his knowledge of obscure dishes. I felt he had come to trust me. And that he would like to do the film, though if this were so, other difficulties would lie ahead, including the situation with Warners and the objections of his agents and others who were beginning to hitch their wagons to the new star. And though I knew what I wanted in the story, I had only thirty pages of script.

I was mulling this over when he looked up at me. Something in his expression suggested he was about to impart a special confidence. He was restless, more so than usual.

"I got crabs," he said. "What do I do?"

I took him to a drugstore and introduced him to Cuprex. Outside in the street, we parted. He thanked me for the help, smiled, then said:

"I want to do your film, but don't tell those bastards at Warners."

I said I was glad, and that I wouldn't tell Warners anything except that I wanted him. We shook hands on it.

1968

ARTIFICE; USE OF OBJECTS; PLAYING SHAKESPEARE; "HIT-THE-MARK" ACTING

[TANDO directs and acts in a scene he also wrote.]

NR: What was your action here, Tando?

TANDO: To harass the people, to intimidate them, to make them dance to my tune.

NR: To turn over White Charlie.

TANDO: Yeah, that's right.

NR: That's why you went to the park.

TANDO: No, I was in the park already, and this old witch showed me two faces, called me a tramp. I just decided I was going to find me some people and take 'em apart.

NR: That was your backstory. This scene was inspired by a real incident that took place in the park, wasn't it? It was very clear what the scene was: people sitting in the park, doing their own thing. But you thought it would be interesting and help expose the rather fancy theme if there were a couple of masks brought in.

When you introduce masks in a scene, you take on a whole style and culture—whether Far Eastern, Italian, African, Spanish, Icelandic, Eskimo, Mexican—of masks and theatre, and must do so with some responsibility and awareness. Everything else that happened in the scene could have happened, but not the masks. They were a gimmick, a superimposed device, neither essential nor organic to the scene.

SAM: So how do you define what is artifice, what is just a technique?

NR: Lily Tomlin grows masks out of her own face, in one twist of her body. What she does is organic, and extremely difficult, very much to be admired.

If it enhances the scene, progresses the scene, helps reveal what you feel is the truth of the scene, it is not artifice.

In *Rebel Without a Cause* an idea was born in improvisation and rehearsal to shoot the mother's entrance into the living room from Dean's point of view as he is lying on the couch, to turn the camera around 360 degrees to bring her into the room. I had the idea, but I didn't know how to do it, I didn't know there was a wedgehead that could accommodate the angle. The shot came to express my feeling toward the entire scene: here was a house in danger of tipping from side to side. It was organic to the scene.

A couple of films later I caught myself doing the same thing in a scene with Cornell Wilde in *Hot Blood*. I was in the middle of the shot before I realized I was imitating myself. I caught myself in a stunt, and I was embarrassed.

SAM: So it doesn't matter that the scene in *Rebel* calls attention to itself in that way.

NR: Not at all, because it was intended, and legitimate in point of view.

■ ■ ■

[NAT and JOSEF perform a dueling scene from King Lear.*]*

NR: When using an object as significant and prominent as a sword in a Shakespearean piece you must be able to give that sword some reality, or else you have no reality. And so we go back to sense memory, as always, and not very complicated sense memory. In this scene, Josef, you handled your sword like a butterfly net. Do you have any idea of the weight of a sword of that period? Handling a sword as heavy as that in the way you were handling it would have flattened a very healthy person to the ground. This was a perfect case of two actors uncomfortable as hell. I don't think I've ever seen two people so uncomfortable and in need of business. Director, what could you have been thinking? You are taking this course as an actor as well as a director so you can achieve some comprehension of the problems of the actor. You must know how to help the actor. Actors, in developing an activity or business, you must make the objects you choose have some kind of significance, make them work for you.

Objects were always terribly important to me in theatre. Someone who had worked with von Sternberg told me how he raised hell when the significant objects of a scene were not highlighted in some way or another. That stuck with me. If you're going to do it, go all the way with it, not just a little bit of the way. For *King of Kings*, I went to the set late at night to put silver paint on the leaves of the trees of Gethsemene—not to make them appear silver, but to give them life.

A good property man is a remarkable adjunct to a film company. In *Brecht on Theatre*[45] there's a description of the actor coming in and choosing a hat. It's tremendous. It would be a marvelous monologue for someone to do. Osgood Perkins, Tony Perkins's father, would base his whole preparation on his relationship to his props.

On *Rebel* my property man's name was George McGonnigal. I said to him, "George, I don't know how to open the film. It's Easter, and the guy doesn't have any toys, the guy doesn't have a gal, the guy doesn't have parents. All he's got is some booze. I'd like the man carrying the packages to have, besides the Easter lily, a bunch of toys for the kids in the family that he's going to visit." George came back with about twenty mechanical toys, one of which was the monkey that Jimmy cuddled in the opening titles. He needed someone to be close to.

Questions?

NAT: What's the best approach to developing the right accent for Shakespeare?

NR: When Gielgud was presented with the Order of the British Empire and became Sir John, it was in recognition of his contribution to the performance of Shakespeare, of his playing the sense of the lines, not the pentameter. If you are going to try to develop in a few weeks the accent and inflection that it took him years of constant playing in repertory to master, you're going to get pretty bogged down. The importance of this exercise for you is not the stylistic one. What the exercise demands of you is already within your frame of reference. I want you to find your action as the Duke of Burgundy, and to execute it speaking your native language, without putting extra blocks in your way.

LEONARD: Which is more important in playing Shakespeare, text or action?

NR: The first great Shakespearean players that came over here played the mines out West. Among the miners the books that were best known were the Bible, *Pilgrim's Progress*, and the plays of Shakespeare. If an actor went up on his lines, he could be sure that somebody from the miners' audience would feed him his next words. I think text is terribly important, but without the actions behind the

---

45. Bertolt Brecht, *Brecht on Theatre*, trans. John Willett (New York: Hill & Wang, 1964).

lines, the psychoanalysts of this world would be deprived of the foundation for many of their theories and practices.

There was a school, an era more than a decade long, of London acting we called "hit-the-mark" acting. The film actor would ask, "Where do you want me to stand, where's my mark?" and the director would say, "When you come in through that door stand at this X." One of the reasons those directors resorted to hit-the-mark acting was because they didn't know how to talk to actors. They were afraid of actors, because they hadn't had the experience of acting.

Then there was a remarkable confluence of energies and talents. When Richard Burton won an award for his performance of Hamlet in London, it was because he broke all the rules of hit-the-mark acting. I went to Stratford with Peter O'Toole to see *Coriolanus* with Olivier. Olivier was unbelievable, but when he was offstage, in spite of a wonderful supporting company, the play lost color and became uninteresting—except for the leader of the people, who was fascinating. I asked Peter, "Who *is* that?" He said: "Next to me he's the best young actor in England." It was Albert Finney, who had trained at Bristol. At the same time Joan Littlefield and the Unity Theatre, a left-wing theatre, were making an impact on the West End stage, and then Peter Finch and the Workers Theatre of Australia came to London, surrounding Joan Littlefield and introducing the Stanislavsky method. A couple of Australians, Peter Finch in particular, had a very profound influence on British theatre.

But the majority of directors still direct from storyboards and diagrams, or by laying out marks for actors to hit. Since neither the director nor the other members of the company are going to adjust to you, I'm going to remind you from time to time that this is a technicality in acting for film that you will have to accommodate. I hate to see it, because there's already enough for actors to cope with, and the camera can be moved.

You know, whenever I saw Burton and Olivier together, I never heard them talk about the profundities of acting. They talked about each other's legs. Burton would kid Larry about some entrance or other, and Larry would say, "But I have *legs*!"

ACTION INTO THOUGHT; THE HERO

Does thought come before action or action before thought? Until now we have been dealing mostly with thought. We've deduced, we've imagined, we've thought what the character would do, and out of that we've derived an action. Today I'm going to try to present the other side of the coin: action into thought, or action into thought into feeling into thought into action.

I have said that we translate action as meaning *to do*, "I want to do." Action implies desire and will. This morning I wrote a couple of gibberish notes:

> To want to do, and then do it, and it is done, and then I may think about it. I thought about it, and the more I thought in detail, the more aware I was of an emotional response coming into being within me, and that feeling began to affect my thinking.

That's the whole cycle.

Let's take a milkman. An old-fashioned milkman is walking down the sidewalk from his truck to deliver the milk. He's carrying two tin trays, full bottles of milk in each one. He sees a baby tottering on the sill of the attic window of a frame house. He drops the milk bottles, runs over to the house and catches the baby. Two hours later he's a hero with his picture in the paper.

The more I thought in detail of what I had done: I dropped the milk bottles, I rushed to the building, and I stood beneath the window where the child was tottering. The child fell, and I caught her in my arms. Afterwards flashbulbs flashed, and people told me, "Jesus, you were great!" There was one fellow in particular, and a woman who came up and hugged and kissed me, and I was invited to City Hall. I had a wonderful feeling, I loved everybody.

Now: *This feeling began to affect my thinking:* The man shook my hand and patted me on the back, and it made me glow inside, and suddenly I wanted to hug him so I could share my fullness with someone. I feel good about what I did, but I didn't do it because it was going to make me a hero.

See how the detail grows? As the detail emerges from thinking about what I had done, I re-create the whole event for myself, and a feeling comes into being upon which I may act. This is a very important dynamic for you to assimilate to make your concept of action full and complete: in this case the action comes first, then the thought.

As for pure or abstract thought, the theory of relativity, for example, there is a rumor that Einstein dreamt the formula, and wrote it down the next day without reference to anything except that which was within him. I used to read *Evolution of Physics*[46] in the late thirties. It's still one of the greatest mystery stories I've ever come across, abstract thought at its best. But if Einstein dreamt it, it is not abstract thought, because first he dreamt it. He dreamt, and out of that came the theory.

There is an argument for pure thought. I think you might find it among the Tibetans. But don't they meditate first? Find out where the action is. It's not always in Las Vegas.

About the hero: I have found in writing or directing a hero, the hero has to be just as screwed up as you or me so that I can identify with him. Heroism need not be bravery or courage as we know them. Heroism can be resistance. A guy makes a mistake, embarrasses himself, and I know I could make the same mistake or embarrass myself like that too. He goofs off, and I say to myself, "If I were in that situation, I'd goof off too, I'd do just what he did. That cat's been inside my life." Then the same fellow does something wonderful, and I know, "If I were that guy at that moment I would have done just what he did. I would have done something wonderful too, something heroic." But the guy hadn't planned it that way, believe me. Watch for that in your heroes as you write, cast, direct.

Another thing about writing a hero or leading character, or build-

---

46. Albert Einstein and Leopold Infeld, *Evolution of Physics* (New York: Simon & Schuster, Touchstone Books, 1967).

ing a character as an actor: try to find the keg of dynamite he's sitting on. That was Clifford Odets's advice to me while I was working on *Rebel*. Jim Stark was sitting on a keg of dynamite. That one single concept helped me tremendously in building the character. Or it can be a keg of laughter, that's dynamite too.

NAT: If that's how you define a hero, what's an antihero?

NR: An antihero is a hero, but he defies the popular concept of a hero. Richard Burton played an antihero in a film I made called *Bitter Victory*. He defied the popular concept. He could make mistakes. By background he was a scholar, and as a scholar he wasn't considered suitable for military command. He went into a guerilla operation with a superior officer who was jealous of him, of his humanity, and his humanity brought about his death. Humanity isn't supposed to do that.

MARA: Is the word humanity or is it humility?

NR: Humility is an essential ingredient in being able to admit your humanness. Humility does not mean kissing ass. There's a good deal of selectivity in humility. Perfectionism is its opposite, it keeps you from being able to admit your mistakes, take criticism, and to accept the mistakes of others. There are actors who can talk up a storm about the technique and theory of acting, but who never *do* anything. But that's not going to be any of you.

By now you've had a pretty good introduction to some of the major problems you will face as film actors as opposed to stage actors. At this point the work begins. Now we will concentrate on the development of character.

As an assignment over the next few weeks, I want each of you to select a character from existing literature or your imaginations, and I want you to develop that character with all the skills, techniques, and imagination you have. I want to know who he is, why he is there, what he is doing. You may use wardrobe, makeup, props, existing scenes, or scenes from your imagination. You will be given two and one-half minutes, and not one second more, to make your entrance and make your presentation. That's more time than you'd get in a professional setting, by the way, in which you'd be more likely to get thirty seconds. Each character will be presented individually. Other characters may be imagined, but you may not work with anyone else.

Have any of you ever seen a flamenco singer perform? He's playing his guitar, and he steps up before the audience. He's about to sing.

> [NR demonstrates, claps a flamenco beat, bellows the start of a song.]

He has something to say. He makes it clear: he has a thing to tell you.

You ought to be able to reveal your character in three lines. You must be able to name your action in a phrase. This will take mental discipline, work. You have to be motivated. You have to be able to use all parts of you, your quiet parts, your bold parts.

In the course of your preparation, questions will come up. Investigate those, and more questions will come up. You will need to use everything possible to project as fully as possible from the very beginning of your presentation.

Pete, in preparation for this, take from our lab funds enough for three minutes of composite single-system color film per person. Get it as fast as you can.

I'm trying to jam an awful lot into this course, perhaps too much at times, though I don't really think so. I think you are all capable of handling everything that we've dealt with up till now. With this next exercise you will certainly have the opportunity to demonstrate whatever holes there may be in your training, as well as how you've progressed. There has been a remarkable progression in each of you. And then you fall back—but that's to be expected, par for the course.

H. H.

I have come to a block point in my autobiography. The same block has appeared several times before, and I have pushed it aside and found emptiness beyond.

A decade ago in Paris, with constant encouragement from Lazareff and Jones,[47] I put in months of labor writing. I wrote myself into a shroud of despair and ponderosity, and the sound of my voice oinking out dark sounds during casual bistro or marketing conversations became repugnant. So I burned the book and drove to my island home on the North Sea. En route I thought of the night of the false armistice and the death of my father.

The blocking point during my writing in Paris was the same as it is here on Spring Street ten years and a month later: Howard Hughes. Putting together the words that tell my relationship with H. H. and the effect he has had and still does have on my life is the most difficult experience I've had with words. In Paris and now death was/is heavy around me—his, my father's, and mine. I loved them, one by one, self included. Such loving has never been in season. I hated my father for dying too soon, while in earlier years, when it was normal to want him out of the way—because he was a rival for the warmth of my mother, a witness to my fear, scorner of my pimples, withholder of

---

47. Pierre Lazareff, whom NR first met while working at Voice of America, and James Jones, author of *From Here to Eternity* and *The Thin Red Line*.

122

money, knower of my sexual agonies, punisher of all my indiscretions, and an embarrassment in his work clothes and accent—, I hadn't been strong enough to kill him.

But Hughes— Howard Hughes flew around the world in four days and saw five sunsets. He made a real film when he was twenty-one. He invented strategic instruments. He bore a battle scar from Ava Gardner on his upper lip. He wore tennis shoes and drove a dirty Chevrolet.

He was his own test pilot. He once crashed a plane into two houses in Beverly Hills, and, having been pulled from the wreckage by a stranger, he dictated the defects he'd observed in the plane and reviewed his will in the presence of an aide, a girl, and Dr. V. Mason. Then he turned to the doctor and said, "What are my chances, Verne?" –"Fifty-fifty, Howard." –"OK. You can knock me out now." He had bequeathed ninety percent of his fortune—even then it was immense—to medical research.

He wrote me a note on my return to RKO to tell me I was wanted. When I refused to make *I Married a Communist*,[48] he didn't fire me. Mitchum told me that a guy out of the DA's office had told him in a drunken moment that my office, my house, my car, my everything had been bugged to the teeth, and that Howard Hughes had learned about it, and had called his executive producer, Sid Rogell, and said he wanted all the bugs and harassment taken off Nick Ray: "I don't want that boy hurt." And he asked nothing in return.

And that was the end of the story of *I Married a Communist*.

I detested his party politics. There I felt superior to him, and I should have been grateful. He had every reason to believe I was a communist, and he defended me. He offered me wealth and power in a small town, and when I refused it he was not vindictive. He knew I drank. He was a mechanic and a dreamer, and he flew airplanes, and I flew once, with Howard Hughes.

I studied and lived with the most outrageous egocentric of our times, Frank Lloyd Wright. I marched with the frail body and brilliant mind of Lord Bertrand Russell, drank a martini with FDR, and rejoiced at my father's death; but I flew with Howard Hughes.

One day I was having a drink in the Beverly Hills Hotel Polo Lounge with Taffy Simms. Howard came to our table. Smiling and looking a little lost, he asked if he could borrow a nickel for the telephone.

---

48. A film offered to directors as a test of communist sympathies during the McCarthy witch-hunts.

As I pushed over some change, Taffy laughed: "Howard, phone calls are now a dime." A few minutes later I went to the can. Howard was there. He said, "Line's busy," and kidded me about dating Taffy, who also worked for him, then went back to the payphone. I knew that he rented a bungalow and two suites from the hotel, and one of the suites was only a corridor away from the payphone. Do you think it odd that he wanted public privacy? Do you think it odd that Ralph Nader uses only a public payphone? I don't. But Hughes was screwy. Sure he was.

It is a ridiculous sorrow, which I can't let disappear into the bottomless bucket, that Howard Hughes is dead. The absent man. He, Russell, and Wright each had gaping holes into which the critical fist could punch with comfortable security. The flaws in Hughes were more real than Russell's writings or Wright's buildings, more touchable, more in common with most of us, more decipherable. He had enormous wealth—not rich-uncle wealth, acquired wealth. Russell and Wright were paupers, and each took giant strides and risked life and fame. Hughes was his own test pilot and his secrecy was a headline. I argued with Wright, marched with Russell, and flew with Hughes. Four absurdities, and three were giants. Is it wrong to say something loving about a man whom it has always been fashionable to ridicule?

For the *NY Times* Classifieds:

MAY ANY FILM MADE ABOUT HOWARD HUGHES NOT DI-
RECTED BY NICHOLAS RAY BE PUT TO REST IN A VAULT
AND MAY THE VAULT HAVE SEVEN ROOMS AND MAY
EACH ROOM HAVE SEVEN SHELVES AND MAY THE FILM
BE SHIFTED EVERY SEVEN YEARS FROM SHELF TO
SHELF TO ROOM TO ROOM UNSEEN AND UNREMEM-
BERED.

1977

Nicholas Ray in high school yearbook, 1929.

Nicholas Ray appearing for the WPA, late 1930s.

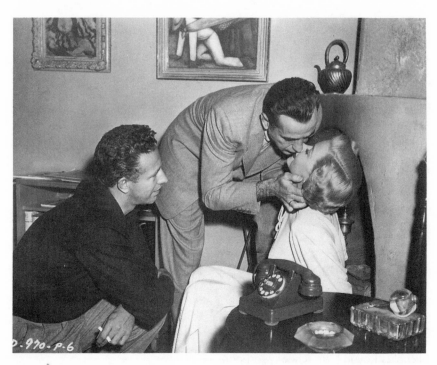

Nicholas Ray, Humphrey Bogart, and Gloria Grahame shooting a scene
from *In a Lonely Place*, 1950.

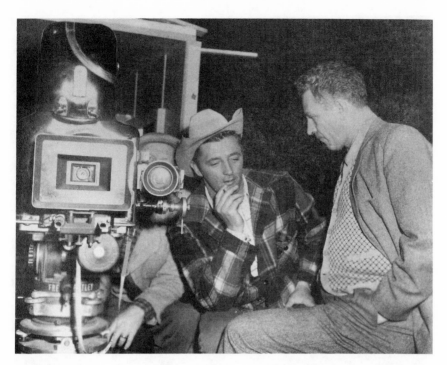

Robert Mitchum and Nicholas Ray while shooting *The Lusty Men*, 1950.

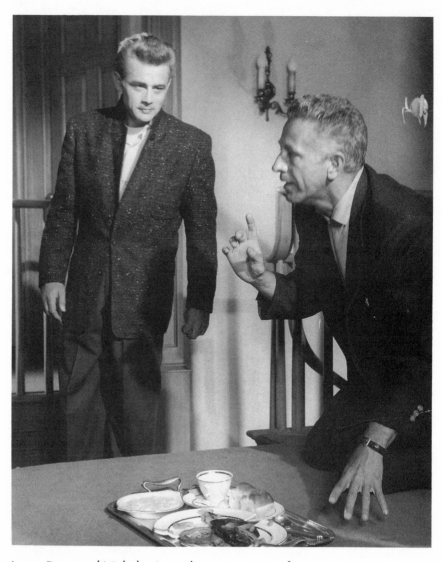

James Dean and Nicholas Ray rehearsing a scene for
Rebel Without a Cause, 1955.

Dennis Hopper and Nicholas Ray in New Mexico, 1971.

Nicholas Ray with crew members, Europe, early 1960s.

Nicholas Ray presiding over the courtroom set for the film about the
Chicago Conspircy Trial, 1969.

Nicholas Ray at Harpur College, 1972.

Nicholas Ray and class at Harpur College, 1972.

(l. to r.) Alan and Mrs. Pakula, Nicholas and Susan Ray at the San Sebastian Film Festival, 1974.

Nicholas and Susan Ray, 1975.

Nicholas and Susan Ray, 1976. (Photo by Michael McKenzie.)

Rip Torn, Nicholas Ray, and Marilyn Chambers discussing *City Blues*, 1976.

Nicholas Ray playing a forger in *The American Friend*, 1977.

Nicholas Ray in *Hair*, 1978.

Wim Wenders and Nicholas Ray at Mets game, 1978. Behind them, Mr. and Mrs. Fred Roos.

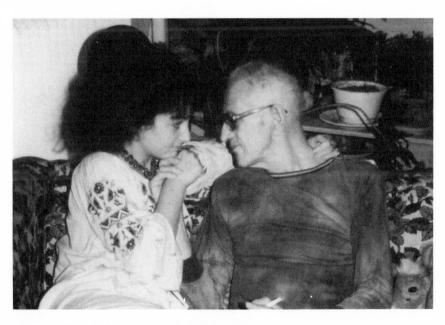

Susan and Nicholas Ray, Christmas 1978.

(l. to r.) Martin Schäfer, Stephan Czapsky, Ed Lachman (behind camera), Nicholas Ray, Susan Ray, and Chris Sievernich during production of *Lightning Over Water*, 1979.

Nicholas Ray, 1979.

CHARACTERIZATIONS

[Class members screen their characterizations for discussion.]

ERICA

NR: The scene Erica performed was somewhat distorted from its original context in the play by an additional set of circumstances, a mental improvisation, in order to fulfill the exercise of presenting a character. For my taste and from the standpoint of the exercise, that set of circumstances showed on film and immediately clued me into the woman's state of being. I didn't know her action, but I knew where this woman was at. Erica has, I think, a remarkable proclivity for fastening onto the essence of a character. This was evident in the first take we shot yesterday.

Did you notice, Erica did not light her cigarette. A lit cigarette in the mouth is commonplace, but with an unlit cigarette in the mouth she reveals something about her state of being, her attitude—or else that she's inviting someone to come light it for her. And if it doesn't get lit, it takes on even more meaning. That's what is meant by the use of an object.

When we shot the two retakes today it was very difficult for Erica to recapture the freshness, the first-timeness, she had in the first take. That's why I'm curious about the intensity of her preparation, and whether she can rest on her natural facility. I'm dubious about the strength of her characterization and how long she would be able to maintain it through the onslaught of take after take, day after day, in the development of her character through the entirety of a film.

Every word must sound as though it is being spoken for the very first or very last time. To achieve that quality your preparation must be meticulous to the detail, so you aren't missing any beats, actions, sub-actions, or adjustments. If you're relying just on the spirit of the moment setting upon you and releasing your genius, forget it. You have more reliable tools to put your faith in.

ERICA: For some reason I find it so difficult, you know. I grope for things that aren't even there. It's so hard in front of the camera to recapture the same momentum, my own natural way in my life, to get it all into the character. It's hard to explain. I'm going to go home and write about it—

NR: No, let's discuss it here, because this is a universal problem. Each one of you will face it, and more than once; not one of you will escape.

Erica, you had three takes, you had one-and-a-half to two hours of preparation here, as well as what you did before you got here. Your rehearsals were intense and full, the first dress rehearsal was full. Then you were interrupted, the mikes had to be set. For you that waiting time became a period of automatic, if unwilled, relaxation. But that was your time to reconcentrate. On what? On your preparation. On refreshing your action. Is that action still working for you? If not, what's your backstory? Is your backstory still working for you? If not, intensify it. If the transition into the attack isn't strong enough, make it strong enough. Be more specific. How did he grab you? Where did he throw you? From what distance? What did you bump up against? Were you exposed, did you have to cover yourself? What part of your human dignity was diminished, destroyed? When has this happened before? What did you have to do then to recover your dignity? What do you have to do to recover your action? What do you have to do in order to get what you want?

PETE: On a movie set are there as many interruptions as we have here, or are you just presenting us with obstacles?

NR: While shooting a film you will encounter a multiplication of the distractions, a multiplication of the changes of angles, a multiplication of the takes and of the times that you have to reproduce, recreate, sustain, and reenergize. You will encounter a multiplication of the interruptions you're up against here.

You will learn to prepare yourself in your relaxation exercises, and by the end of the day you may have to repeat them twenty or thirty times. Old sources won't work on certain days, so you will have to find new ones. But your concentration should be pretty well taken care of by knowing your actions. If you know your backstory and actions, you will be adequately prepared, so when the director tells you, "Concentrate," you can tell him to go climb a tree.

What does it mean, concentrate? What does it mean, relax? What right does the director have to tell you to do those things? He has every right in the world, but he also has a right to be ignorant, which you do not have. A director is going to be too damn busy to pay attention to each actor and create a new scene every take to keep you refreshed and alive, you can count on that. As actors, it is your responsibility to refresh yourselves, so don't expect any kudos or extra change in the pocket for it. You must be prepared. And don't be ashamed or embarrassed at starting from the beginning, over and over again.

BEN as Lenny Bruce: Comedy; Bigger than Life

NR: Did you ever see Lenny Bruce?
BEN: No, this is just from things I've read.
NR: At what point in his career did he do this routine?
BEN: In 1964. By then he'd been busted four times.
NR: I thought he was perhaps the most talented young performer in American theatre at the time. I took my attorney to see him work at a club on La Cienega Boulevard. Lenny gave us forty-five minutes to an hour of solid entertaining. He had a tremendous ability with an audience, working on them the way a poultice sucks poison out of a wound. He ran through his whole history with narcotics and his whole history in the courts, and he also devoted quite a bit of time and effort to the subject of Jerry Lewis, whom my attorney represented as well. At intermission I turned to the lawyer and said, "What are you going to do, Mike, slap an injunction on him?" Mike said, "Hell no, he knows too much." And he did.

I'd like to recount an experience. I had been offered a musical, *High Button Shoes*, to do on Broadway, and I turned it down, like the guy who turned down *Gone With the Wind*. I went back to Hollywood and ran into an old friend, Phil Silvers. I asked him, "What's going?" He said, "Here I am married to Miss America and I can't even get work except a comic role in a goddam musical." Of course the musical was *High Button Shoes*, and it ran for about a year-and-a-half.

Phil got the job in *High Button Shoes* as a result of a performance he gave at the Copacabana. His opening was just days after the death of his comedy partner of twenty years. Every day for two weeks Phil had gone to the hospital to rehearse the act with his partner as if he were going to live.

Opening night, during the first act, the dinner act, which is the toughest in the club business, Phil started to fall apart a little bit, but was able to make it through. When he came on for the second set, every comic in the business was in the audience. Milton Berle was there, Henny Youngman was there, Sinatra was there, Dean Martin was there, Jerry Lewis was there, J. C. Flippin was there, Jimmie Dunn was there. Phil began with a parody on "Old Man River," a strong opening, but then he began to crack a little. Then—I forget who began it, I think it was Berle—the guys in the audience began to heckle him, one after another. This went on for about an hour in one of the greatest jam sessions I've ever seen in my life, a jam session of comics. Each one topped the one before him, they couldn't be stopped. While B. S. Pulley was up on stage singing, "When you're cryin', keep on laughin'," Joe E. Lewis, who'd flown in after his dinner show in Cleveland, came down through the audience with two seltzer bottles under his arm and loosed them on Pulley and Phil. And Phil just sat up there laughing, because the greatest comics in the world were paying tremendous tribute to him.

Bergson writes in his "Essay on Comedy" that comedy very often produces tragedy, and tragedy produces comedy—and to my observation, an unexpected warmth as well. Where does theatricality come in? How comfortable are we with bigger than life? We should be very comfortable with it. It is our obligation.

So if I were directing your scene, Ben, I'd take an entirely different approach from the one you chose. I'd have you fight against self-pity, against anything that felt like self-pity descending upon you, because you're a showman, godammit! Now my direction might be entirely wrong, but this is the way I would feel about it, and so you as an actor would then be obliged to conform to that direction. The function of the artist is to communicate. Certainly the function of the stand-up comic is to communicate. If he doesn't, he won't get the laugh.
BEN: But he's not looking for laughs.
NR: But he is looking for attention. My premise is that you did not satisfy my attention. I saw no reason for looking at you.

I would guess the session you're working with was recorded about the same time as the one on La Cienega Boulevard; but I had no idea to whom you were talking, I could only assume it was to an audience. I have to know when you come onstage why you are there. From your entrance I couldn't tell. I didn't know if you were wanting to get ahead of other comedians or not, if you were in competition or not. The way you did it, your entrance would need more than a spotlight to bring you to our attention. Your entrance was indication. A great deal of what you were doing was indication—showing, rather than actual doing. That left me dissatisfied.

If you're addressing an audience in a nightclub, you're going to have to contend with chairs scraping, people being seated, waiters taking orders, spilling drinks. How are you going to get their attention? A difference between stage direction and film direction that's worth keeping in mind, and that a lot of theatre directors making the transition to film can't handle, is that in theatre the movement is mostly lateral, while in film the movement is through depth. Instead of entering from down right or down left center, try it from upstage right or upstage left.

Harry, don't cover his entrance with the spotlight, keep the light focused center stage. Let Ben walk *into* the light. Make a clean entrance, Ben. A clean entrance means you make your approach out of view of the camera.

While the convention is for comics to come out with a hard sell, here you want to try something new, to center the audience on you, very slyly. In this case, starting from silence might well be a more effective attention-getter, just as it is for the conductor raising his baton. In film the effect is a little easier to achieve than in theatre, because you have the focus of the lens, you have the lights directed toward you, you can be isolated, and you can exclude all the other sounds from the sound track, even though they're there, so long as you're concentrated. But your concentration must be down to a pinpoint as to who you are, what you want, why you are there, either belligerent, hustling, or in good humor. Or else you have to be completely fragmented. But there can be no in-between. Otherwise you're lost. If it's almost the first time, you're lost. If you're almost there, you're lost.

BEN: What I'm interested in are the possibilities of working directly with the camera, as if the camera were another person in the scene.

NR: You see that done occasionally. In the British theatre, for instance, there's the aside. It's common to Venetian, French, Portuguese, and Greek theatre as well. Sometimes it becomes the entire style of the film; the actors direct themselves to the camera and the camera's the audience. I like the way Woody Allen does it in *Annie Hall*. When Jerry Lewis does it it becomes a stunt, but Woody does it with a fluidity that I like very much.

You must find a way to address the fourth wall. Some comics I know will have some specific person in the audience in mind, or else substitute someone—"My mother's here tonight—" and by engaging that person they'll engage everyone. Bob Hope might use Crosby, or his gardener, or maybe he'll use himself in a mirror. I would think at his worst moments he does. Will Rogers used specific people for different bits that he did. He'd tell one thing to a drunken Indian, another to a cowboy, and another to a politician, a particular politician. The film actor has to do the same thing, because all he sees is a lens and some lights hitting down on him. He has to create from his imagination the sensation of an audience.

Another possibility and useful rule of thumb: gauge the mood of your audience and start from there. If you begin in the same place as the audience, you'll have the opportunity to take them into any kind of fantasy in the world; but a fantasy that does not begin with a reality is in danger. You must first establish your credibility. And don't telegraph your climax, don't telegraph your punch line.

PAOLO as Caligula:
The Unexpected Event

NR: Which take did you like better?
PETER: In the second he played his action, while in the first he played the emotion, he played a state of being.
NR: That's it, that's the difference between the two. It's remarkable, it's so clear. Paolo, you did very, very good work with difficult subject matter. You said you worked out the action line by line, but in the first take there was not that beat of sizing yourself up in the mirror. As a result, I felt an absence throughout the opening. As you approached the mirror in the second take, I asked myself, how is he going to let us know it's a mirror? But you did, in the sizing up, the appraisal of yourself. That was a definite action: to size yourself up. It made such a difference.

I was distressed in the first take by the collapse at the end that I saw in the simple gesture of your releasing the paper to the floor. The gesture seemed to me artificial and contrived, and a denial of everything you had just gone through. I said nothing at all to you about it, but in the second take you held the paper. Where did that adjustment come from? I believe it came from the fullness of playing your action.

I asked Paolo if he had heard the voices downstairs, because if he had I was going to raise hell with him for not having used that intrusion of reality in his scene. As Paolo is talking to the mirror, there's an image of the too many dead, and he could have related the voices downstairs to the dead. All the pictures of his past atrocities he saw in the second take which he'd not seen in the first, those echoes of the past, could have come alive with the intrusion of those voices.

One of the reasons I've stressed your reading the last two chapters of Stanislavsky's *An Actor Prepares* is because the point is made very clearly that if some distorted or unexpected event of real life happens during a scene, you must learn how to take advantage of it. For instance, a scene may be playing very well when a lighted candle, which has been stable during rehearsals or in previous takes, suddenly falls to its side on the tablecloth. If the director doesn't cut right away and the actors don't go up on their lines, this unexpected moment of reality can become a great adjunct to the scene. The actors can use it while continuing to play their actions and say their lines. There is no need for anyone to ad-lib, "Oh look, the candle has fallen. My tablecloth!" You're working in a visual medium, this has been seen. If it's allowed to continue, the scene will most likely be heightened by the new energy needed to reset the candle and extinguish the burning napkin. With a turbulence that has not been part of the actors' preparation, the scene will gather a new intensity in its lines and relationships. In that intensity the words can be spoken as if for the very first time.

Shelley Winters was playing in *A Hatful of Rain*, and on the way to the theatre one day she slipped on some ice and sprained her ankle. It was painful, but she played the entire performance, and used her discomfort all the way through. A lot of things had to change—movements, pitch of voice. Her action was intensified because she had an unplanned obstacle to overcome. Her concentration was stronger, and that enhanced the intensity of the relationships. It was a beautiful night in the theatre.

In *Rebel Without a Cause*, in the juvenile officer's office, the character Jim is thrown to the floor, gets up, sits on a chair, and says he wants to hit something. Ray tells him: "Hit the desk." He does. We rehearsed that scene so Jimmy would be able to hit without hurting his knuckles, but when we began to shoot, it was clear that in the intensity of the scene he was hurting himself. I resisted the temptation to cut, and he continued to play the scene. Tears came, and pain, and the scene was very intense and meaningful. We finished the shot and even changed setups before I took him to the hospital and learned he had broken a knuckle.

BETTY: What if something is happening in your personal life at the moment you're working on a part, and it breaks through your concentration—"Oh my God, my son's on the operating table right now!"—can you use that technique in such a situation?

NR: Yes, I think you can. How do you keep fresh during the eighty-ninth performance of a play? You use the realities of the given moment. A nickel falls on the floor and you pick it up, or a lit candle flips over on the table. You use the intrusion of the thoughts of the moment in just the same way. Don't fight them.

Say you have lines that are, for whatever reason, very difficult to handle. Try admitting into your preparation some of the thoughts passing through your mind at that moment, no matter how completely opposite they are to your action. As they come in, don't fight them. Go with them, while remaining determined to carry out your action and using the words as they were written. See what happens. You will have to try harder to talk, which will strengthen your connection to the words and the person to whom you are speaking. It makes no difference what you are saying, whether it's out of an entirely different century or not. By admitting those thoughts of the moment you will achieve an interesting tension.

Can you think of any real-life situation as an illustration? You're at a party. You want to close a deal with a fellow there, and he's throwing a question at you. Then someone calls you: "Hey, phone call!" But you have to convince the guy to sign the paper, right now. If you leave him to go to the phone, he'll go cold. He's got the pen in his hand. You know what you want to do, but the phone call intrudes and causes a tension in you. Allow the tension. That way you will maintain control, and you will never go up on your lines. Your rhythm will change, and what you are saying will take on an additional emotional impetus, and so it will stay fresh.

MARA: If that's how an actor makes it through a long run of a show, how do you know what he'll give you to work with?

NR: You'll still get your cues.

MARA: Sometimes.

NR: You'll get enough to key you in to the sense of the scene. And even if you don't, you can use the same technique: admit the confusion, let it in. You still know where you are, you know who you are, you know what you want to do, no matter what the other guy does. You'll find your way through.

Let's go back for a moment to the situation in which you have to say lines that really don't have much organic place in your structure at the time, lines that feel awkward. Another way to approach the problem while you're rehearsing is to start listening to yourself, to the words you are speaking. As you do, the words will begin to sound different, they'll take on different meanings. What seemed rational now seems irrational. You develop a different kind of concentration, a different slant, and your rhythm changes.

This past weekend I found myself repeatedly using the word *manipulate*. During an interview, I called a film *manipulative*. I began listening to, questioning, what I was saying. Isn't every film manipulative? Isn't every script manipulative?

LEONARD: Some films are, obviously.

NR: It's more than just some, don't you think? But if the overall purpose of a film is to manipulate, it's usually not very memorable. A film whose intent is to manipulate offers a vicarious experience, an experience through nonidentification, through detached, objective titillation and sensory response, but it denies the full cycle of emotional response.

Hitchcock in *Psycho* was extremely manipulative. He studied and made use of psychiatry and the analysis of human behavior in order to achieve a sensationalist scene. A lot of people were frightened by it, and that's what he wanted. I found that very manipulative and repulsive. It left me with no insight into the character, no perception that would help me recognize another psychotic person or detect a tendency in myself. Yet another director might make use of the same techniques with entirely different results I would not find repulsive.

Anyway, as I was criticizing a recent blockbuster film for being manipulative, I asked myself, "What am I really saying? What do I mean by manipulative?" I realized what I was talking about was not so much manipulation as overall purpose, and really what I was talking about was the low quality of films. In listening to myself, I slowed down to think, and a whole new meaning emerged.

So you take the simplest action: to find out what I am really saying, or to find out what he is really saying. If that's what you want to find out during a scene, your attention is going to be different. If your attention is different the top of your head is going to be different. As you adjust rhythm and attention, the lines will come alive.

BETTY: Rhythm

BETTY: Seeing myself on screen, two things struck me: I was aware that my head was up, and it shouldn't have been; it's a mannerism that doesn't belong to the character. The other gesture I kept repeating, without any idea that I was doing it, was to pull my lower lip in. I don't know why I do those things, they must be things I do in real life. Somebody's got to remind me to check myself.

NR: If you feel you need to be checked, most likely you're right. Did it feel as though she, the character, had used those gestures before, had rehearsed them?

BETTY: No, they weren't rehearsed, they're just habits.

NR: Nervous energy.

JAKE: Betty, I couldn't understand a word you said. You should do it without the Southern accent.

NR: I think she hit the right key for handling an accent. It was a regional accent that's very difficult on the ears. The convention in theatre is to hit the accent in the first act, especially if it's a heavy one, and then reduce it as you go along. By the way, the tempo of speech for film should generally be about 20 percent faster than it is for theatre.

I think what you're reacting to, Jake, may be more the rhythm than the accent. To me, the transitions weren't full because they weren't followed by a change in rhythm. Rhythm is very important, so I'd like to pursue the subject for a moment. A change in rhythm can touch off and refresh an emotional memory, take after take.

BETTY: My body wanted to move, and I should have let that come out through my voice.

NR: By all means. The actor has an obligation to find the rhythm of his character and to know that that rhythm will change. What in the character would impel a change in rhythm? How could you choose different rhythms?

BETTY: A transition into a hot room would bring about a different rhythm.

NR: That's interesting. Or what about when the author gives you wonderful descriptions of rivers running and horses flying? What happens to your rhythms then? Do you take a rhythm from those words? Yes, you do, you must.

LEONARD: How do we as directors—

NR: You have to search the character, help the actor search her character. What happened to her just before? What kind of environment is she coming from? What were her activities? How does she move when she has to catch a train or a plane? Is she always on time?

LEONARD: Those things affect rhythm?

NR: Yes. As you clarify all the little things, the grain of the character begins to emerge. Then put the character into a different situation, an unusual one. He'll be fighting his normal rhythm, won't he? How does he feel? Does he suddenly begin to limp? He has never limped before. He's late, running with a portfolio in one hand, a typewriter in another, trying to catch a plane. Why does he suddenly begin to limp? What is it in his action, in his character? Does he really want to catch that plane? Wouldn't he rather procrastinate? If he would, and he's running to catch a plane he doesn't want to catch, isn't it possible that irrationally he would develop a limp? You see how it becomes interesting.

Today was hot as hell, but while I was working I didn't notice it. How can that happen? It happens because of the strength of my action and concentration. If I walk home from the subway up Spring Street and my foot begins to hurt, and I think about the foot hurting, I drag along, and it's as though the loft were two miles away. My God, aren't I there yet? I can make another trip three hours later and, preoccupied with an idea for an exercise, I'm already at my front door, having walked rather rapidly, feeling no irritation at all. I couldn't tell you whom I saw or whether it was raining or not.

What does the character want to do? Where is he from? You have to be sensitive and attuned. Suddenly you get an idea: maybe he needs a cane. Something happens and he begins to use the cane as a toy. His mood changes, his rhythm changes, and he expresses the change through the toy. What else can affect a character's rhythm?

BEV: Another person in the room.

NR: A relationship, certainly.

LEONARD: The way the other person moves.

NR: What do you mean by that, Leonard?

LEONARD: Let's say Betty is doing her scene with Charlotte and Charlotte keeps moving around in her chair, shifting around, and then gets up and walks in front of her.

NR: So irritation happens. Irritation would change the rhythm of the words, the tone and the volume of the voice.

We know that it's not good to take on another character's rhythm or another character's tone, right? If an actor takes on another actor's tone or rhythm and the director doesn't catch it, the scene is in trouble. As actors, how do you avoid that situation? If you find you're trapped by the same tone, the same rhythm as the other person, or when a monologue becomes monotonous, try another activity, something as simple as tying a shoelace. What gives a cotton-picking song a different rhythm than a spear-driving song? It's the activity. The proper selection of an activity is organic to your action, but you must be imaginative. Betty, could you have been knitting?

Or let's say you've got a real rhythm piece going on in your head. You've been hearing it all day long, you can't get rid of it. You walk into a roomful of people, and you're bouncy with that tune in your head. Your voice is distinctive, it stands out from the others in the room. The others begin to pick up on it, on your mood, on your rhythm. That can work well in a scene, if everybody picks up the same rhythm. It becomes a jam session.

Does thought change your rhythm? The way you open a door? The way you sit down? The way you light a cigarette? Ask those questions in terms of your character. What makes that character interesting? It's all in your imaginations and in your varieties of experiences. Invent something. Try it out. If it isn't right, try something else. If it works, stick with it, develop it, search out its colors.

DAKOTA:
The Crew; Personal Objects

NR: This scene got off to a false start. Dakota, when you made that movement of rising from a kneeling position to your feet, the camera couldn't follow you, and that caused a visual gap. It would be impossible for a cameraman, no matter how expert, to pick up that fast a movement. Please try to help the people who are working with you, you are only helping yourself. The members of the crew are going to do whatever they can to help you get your best possible performance on film, but you in turn must honor what they are doing and cooperate, because you are not a single sole agent making the film.

If the cameraman feels he can't follow the actor, he has to cut. He cannot cut without telling the director; he must get a signal to him, because maybe at that moment the director is watching the actor and not paying attention to the monitor.

Dakota, you can smooth the way by telegraphing the move and taking it more slowly. By telegraphing I mean making a small move to clue in the cameraman. In this case you come up on one knee, for example, take a beat, and then rise to your feet—but slowly. That way you give the cameraman a warning, so he's free, he's ready, he knows where he has to go.

What else did you see here? I want to ask the director, what was the reason for the side angles?
BETTY: I wanted to show the distance between her and the box.
NR: What about where she put the box, does that have any importance? What does the space mean when she sets the box down?

Generally, Betty, I was impressed with how you handled the switcher, following the actress, almost as if you were a conductor who did not need a score. You had that degree of familiarity with the scene. But you did not concentrate that familiarity into your crew. You have a responsibility to your cameraman, to your scriptclerk, to your gaffer, to your grip. It's not just that they have a responsibility to you.

Dakota, what was your relationship to the box?

DAKOTA: It was supposed to have been my son's toy box, where his ashes were put.

NR: What does that mean?

DAKOTA: It holds all the memories.

NR: Are they tender memories?

DAKOTA: Yes, tender, and also mystical.

NR: Is it something that you are compelled to get rid of?

DAKOTA: Yes.

NR: Something you want to get rid of?

DAKOTA: No.

NR: So the box holds very tender memories, very personal memories, which date back much earlier than your son's death. You have to get rid of the box but you don't want to—

DAKOTA: You're right, I didn't use it, my hands were tense.

NR: You held it as if a black widow spider were about to crawl out. I felt hostility toward the box. I felt you felt hostility toward it. You had some beautiful moments in this scene, very touching, very moving moments that would then disappear because there was no relationship, no connection between you and the box.

DAKOTA: The box replaced an urn I was working with.

NR: I don't care if you're using an ice-cream cone, that ice-cream cone has to be the urn. Whatever it was, right now the box is the urn. You are playing the scene, for better or worse, and this is all you have, and this has to be complete. You cannot write a footnote at the bottom of your performance: "The box should have been an urn."

The use of personal objects is terribly important. You must develop their significance and connection to you. Among other things, an object can provide you with the activity that will help you rebuild the emotion that may have been lost during a time wait, during rehearsals, during multiple repetitions.

Have you ever handled an urn?

DAKOTA: I didn't work hard enough to make it a part of me, because an urn is cold, and it means death. I think it was a big problem that I didn't go to a morgue—

NR: Oh, but there's so much more. You've tried to tackle something immense. Please, at this stage of your development, work with material to which you have a solid personal relationship, material that is well within the realm of your imagination, so that you can make full use of yourself. There are certainly ways of approaching this scene: revolving it around a death in the family; doing the research with an urn; going to a mortuary. As an actor you must do at least those things to know what you are feeling, to discover your emotional connection to the object and what you are doing. But you must start with yourself.

DAKOTA: I know I don't match the material, but I thought if I started with it now, maybe ten years from now I—

NR: Fine, I am all in favor of choosing material like this, if for no other reason than that it may caution you not to do it again. In the meantime, work with what you know, and avoid the temptation of those fan magazine fantasies that are so soothing to our vanities.

Before we break for the holidays I'd like to make a party to which everybody comes in character. I'd like three or four of you to get together and work out the logistics. I don't know how you feel about opening it up to friends. If you want to do that, then those you invite should be in the profession and also come as characters.

A New Theatre[49]

Thank you, Richie,[50] Wendell Phillips, Stage Group for inviting me
here.

I'd like to address myself to something that always excites me: a
new theatre is starting. So long as a new one is starting there's another
burst of hope on the horizon. There is also the promise of an awful
lot of work, very hard work, a lot of self-torture, a lot of people facing
themselves; for those entering the profession of acting for theatre or
film know they will have to put themselves on the line every day of
their lives, both on and off stage. This is a profession so fundamental,
so much of the essence of life and living that it has been very easy to
put on the pages of slick magazines with glamour ribbons attached
to it, because people do not like to recognize what really goes into
making a performance, what goes into making an actor.

The Stage Group now forming in San Francisco is under the leadership of a man whom I've known for forty years. When I first met him,
Wendell Phillips was a member of one of our very noble institutions
in the theatre, the Group Theatre. At that time I was matriculating
in a somewhat less glamourous group originally called the Workers

---

49. Edited and revised from the text of an address to The Stage Group, San Francisco,
July 15, 1977.
50. Nick had been invited to speak at The Stage Group by Richard Bock, who had
been his student at Harpur College and played a leading role in *We Can't Go Home
Again*.

Laboratory Group, and then called the Theatre of Action. Thirteen of us lived in a five-room apartment on seventeen dollars a week, and we worked at learning our craft twenty hours a day. At 9:00 we'd be up taking classes in body movement from Martha Graham or Anna Sokolov, at 11:00 there'd be instruction in voice and diction, and at noon we'd take a dime for a cream cheese sandwich or subway fare to a museum. Eurhythmics was at 1:30, at 2:30 we began improvisations, and at 4:00 or 4:30 we'd rehearse until it was time to go out and perform.

We performed on picket lines, in union headquarters, in subways, at universities—wherever we could perform, because there is no actor unless there is a spectator. That's why Stanislavsky said the actor begins the study of his profession in the cloakroom. Learn to respect the spectator. You must not be above hanging up his coat, showing him to his seat.

The great thing about the theatre in the thirties was that everybody was involved. We all knew what everybody else was doing, and we all cared. We really cared. Theatre in the United States seems to thrive in periods of depression. It didn't matter that we were poverty-ridden, that we had to burn bedbugs off our beds twice a week, that we didn't get paid for a performance. We survived, and we survived with each other.

We survived. There really is no place in the theatre or film for *I*. I lived for a while with the Eskimos in the Arctic. You know, they have no word for *I* in their language. They say *this unhappy one, this happy one, this joyful wife, this miserable husband.* I tried to trap Eskimo airline stewardesses on Canadian Airways into using the word *I*. No way. I tried for two years to write letters without using the word *I*. I had to stop writing letters.

Nobody ever does it alone. Wendell Phillips can tell you of all the pains, rivalries, and tortures, economic, artistic, personal, mental, physical, and spiritual, that go into forming a collective effort. It's one of the most endearing and wondrous things I can think of that a man so long in the theatre could still want to have that happen. I think it's beautiful.

I can see all of the work ahead of you people as you start this theatre, work not only on yourselves, not only in learning techniques, learning everything you can about music, speech, cultures, myths, colors, spectators, but work in having to keep the theatre clean; because by the time you open for your first performance you will know that it is not important that you are on stage, but that the stage is there for you to be on. It's a joyful life. It's the most wondrous life available to man, but it's a tough one, especially for women. I get kind of tingly inside when I think of it, the beautiful growing pains that those of you who are part of the Stage Group are going to have.

And those of you who are not active members of the group, keep your eye on them. You're very important to them. Watch their every advance. Support them. The spectator must not feel himself above those that have come to the stage to offer a heightened experience and sense of being. Don't ever set down a star. Remember that a star is a star because he generates his own light. Don't ever, as so many people recently have taken delight in doing, set down a man like Frances Ford Coppola for being over-budget when he has put every-thing on the line to protect the integrity of his film[51] so that it gets to the audience the way he knows it should be. Such a man you applaud. You don't wait in ambush for him.

Theatre provides something that film and the tube cannot. It's that personal or physical contact, the direct confrontation. How many times a day are you forced to realize how difficult it is to talk to one another? If you're walking down the street of a strange neighborhood in a strange town, how many times do you call over to a stranger, "Hi there! Good morning!" An actor cannot exist unless he has a warm feeling toward his fellow man.

Q: What about the leftist theatre in this country?
NR: Where is it?
Q: Then.
NR: Then? I was very much a part of it. That's what I meant when I said we played picket lines, unions, union halls, subways, strikes, universities, factories.
Q: Do you think theatre in the sixties evolved from that?
NR: I wasn't in this country very much in the sixties, but in what I saw when I came back here I'd say there was no real awareness of the tradition of the American theatre.
Q: Do you feel that the kind of ensemble theatre you were involved with in the thirties can exist successfully today?
NR: Yes, and I hope it does, and I hope it continues being born and reborn, generation after generation. I was telling Wendell today, one of the things that I missed most in my career following my theatre experience was that wonderful feedback, that wonderful ability for self-criticism that we had amongst each other, and the wonderful sharing of experiences. It was a terrible absence later on.

---

51. *Apocalypse Now.*

On *Richard III*

I thought I was going to see Richard II.

I did see Richard III. He I did see. I saw him better than ever before in a span of years marked by Fritz Lieber through Lord Olivier. This Richard III in the being of Ron Liebman suited me. So did Joan Copeland's Margaret and Mendy Wager's Buckingham (as a kind of forties Hollywood agent, a Bert Allenberg, but I was comfortable with him). And Geoffrey Horne's King Henry was fully realized. It's a pity the director couldn't see some wisdom in committing an act of distortion and manage to subvert the plot and rid the stage of Richmond, Catesby, the woman, and the dream—good God, the dream—long before the evening ended. Perhaps Tyrol, the only other actor to address the audience with talent beside those mentioned, could have been woven into the crown by the magic of a fool. Were it not for Liebman and Copeland, who faltered only once, the presence of a legitimate fool on stage after Act III would have helped.

Perhaps—no certainly—there was other talent on the stage. Elaine Hackert is a gifted actress with a long track record as a contributing performer. And the fellow who played Hastings at times showed fine texture through the void surrounding him, and maybe there were others; but whatever method of direction was employed by the director and his/her staff did not serve to release the other talent to the audience. "It's a one-man show," said Wager. "I played it without makeup," said Hackert.

142

I saw it and my stomach sank, and sleep is distant. And I must teach this morning at the Strasberg Institute. I would rather have had Richard's nightmare and the sleep surrounding it than face the thoughts I'm facing now or dissect the purpose of my present work.

1977

THE PARTY

On Friday night we are having a party, a work party. We will hold it at 528 LaGuardia place. We'll take two cameras with a switcher, sound tapes, and film. Anyone who has tape recorders, please bring them. We will have to buy three guns.

The event is a costume party for the characters you have presented in this class. I have prepared an outline of the scenario. The dialogue is a blueprint. The words you say will come out of your individual actions. I will discuss your actions with each of you, as they must be very specific.

[NICK reads the outline.]

MOLLY will be the scrubwoman assigned to clean up the place and get the floor ready before the party. That's the job she does to earn her tuition for class. Only the work lights are on. All we see is a dimly lighted entranceway as MOLLY enters and says hello. She moves into more light. She is carrying a bucket and some heavy rags. "Hello?" She advances. There's the sound of a toilet flushing. She looks for the sound, sees the light through the crack of the ladies' room door.

TAPE RECORDER (SOUND OVER)
Merv shows the wa-ay!

NAT comes through the door carrying a tape recorder. He is consumed by his preparation. He nods his head.

144

MOLLY
Where are the lights?

NAT nods to the switch. MOLLY hits the lights.

MOLLY
Why are you so early?

NAT
Preparing.

MOLLY
Why didn't you use the men's room?

NAT
No lights.

The toilet flushes again.

MOLLY
Who else is here?

NAT shrugs. MOLLY goes to the ladies' room. She finds
CHARLOTTE at the window in the washroom. Deep study, no
words. There seems to be an overt hostility between them.

MOLLY
I have to clean up this place.

CHARLOTTE
What character are you playing?

MOLLY
Myself. So far. Cleaning up your messes for my
tuition, and then I can act.

CHARLOTTE
Cleaning up our messes so then you can make your
own.

MOLLY
Shut up.

> CHARLOTTE
> You're breaking my concentration.

MOLLY fills the bucket, exits the washroom. We see others coming out of the woodwork, seated in groups, all in various states of preparation. Some have been there for hours, some all night.

We cut to NAT. He's practicing for Merv Griffin's entrance by singing a very saccharine and sentimental song into the tape recorder. As NAT becomes Merv he becomes the welcomer.

DAKOTA enters, commences her action.

We see PAOLO downstairs dressing himself as Caligula, a lone figure on the red floor, in a semicatatonic state of preparation.

> DAKOTA
> Am I late?

MOLLY begins scrubbing. DAKOTA practices, getting ready for the attention of others. She complains she may slip on the wet floor. MOLLY reacts to that.

PETE enters, sees NAT. Immediately he leaves. We hear CHARLOTTE's voice to NAT:

> CHARLOTTE (VOICE OVER)
> Where's he going?

> NAT
> He's jealous. He wants to be the host.

PETE pokes his head back in.

> PETE
> I'll announce myself.

> NAT
> So announce yourself.

> PETE
> When the time comes.

MOLLY
(from the floor scrubbing)
Don't do it yet.

CHARLOTTE
Don't do what?

MOLLY
Announce yourselves.

She splashes the water.

You'll slip. If you slip you'll kick me.

CHARLOTTE
I'd like to kick you, honey.

PETER makes his entrance sliding on a piece of soap. NAT
continues to sing.

LEONARD, JET, and ERICA enter. NAT introduces them.
HARRY and TANDO enter. SAM enters. BEN and BETTY
enter. They all track over MOLLY's cleaning work. In the
meantime MERV is announcing.

CHARLOTTE (to MOLLY)
You're stupid.

MOLLY throws the rag at CHARLOTTE. CHARLOTTE ducks.
ERICA comes to MOLLY's aid.

ERICA
I'll help you.

ERICA gets down on her knees to help.

MOLLY
Give me a cigarette.

ERICA does.

Dancing begins. And now there's dancing all around and
through the two women on the floor scrubbing. They have to

talk between legs. CHARLOTTE returns. She gets on her knees too.

CHARLOTTE
You're supposed to scrub the floor, right?

MOLLY
You got it.

CHARLOTTE
You're an actress, right?

MOLLY
Who knows?

CHARLOTTE
You'll ruin your hands.

ERICA reacts to this.

CHARLOTTE
Get rid of this crap.

She sees NAT from point-of-view of the floor.

CHARLOTTE
Nat!

He crosses and bends down to them.

CHARLOTTE
Get rid of this crap for us.

Whatever NAT says to CHARLOTTE at this point says 'I love you.' CHARLOTTE responds as if she were Juliet. BEN overhears this, and intently watches CHARLOTTE as she returns to the floor.

PAOLO has entered by this time, has been introduced by NAT, and he observes the relationship between CHARLOTTE and NAT. And why is it his reaction is in the character of Caligula?

Now the lesson begins. CHARLOTTE shows what actresses really do in order to clean the floor. They don't use a bucket and water and rags; they use sense memory. So the three start scrubbing the floor with sense memory, and continue to do so throughout the scene. As they get started we cut away for a minute. We come back to them and they're still scrubbing.

ERICA's walkie-talkie beeps over the music tape.

> "CHARLIE" (V.O.)
> Hello Angels. Charlie here. The killer, well hung—
> with a knife, girls—has entered the building.
> He could pass for an Italian. That's all I know
> for now. I'll get back to you.

The three Angels begin to scan from the knees upward looking for the possible killer. ERICA, of course, is the leader of the angels. And the director of them. At this point JET enters with a flourish as only JET can. She is a prostitute whose objective is to score.

At this point MOLLY, by crawling through legs, comes onto the monitor and sees herself as a glamourous, all-giving prostitute on the couch. We have to have that tape ready. We will select different tapes from our classwork to which we will cut from time to time. The video monitor will be going all the time; music will be going all the time; people will be referring to themselves; and we'll also see your characters as you first portrayed them.

PETER and MARA have a relationship that has to be worked up. ERICA continues her action to keep the Angels together, so when MOLLY is distracted by her performance on the monitor, ERICA pulls her back to scrubbing and trying to identify the killer from the knees up.

At this point MOLLY has a brief action with CHARLOTTE that leads CHARLOTTE to discover PAOLO as the chief suspect. He's Caligula, and he must be the killer. She fingers him to the others. He makes a pass at MOLLY. BEN watches. DAKOTA becomes very active and breaks the attention on PAOLO, because attention is what she wants most of all. JET also wants it and a conflict begins between JET and DAKOTA. This is interrupted by whatever is happening at the time, we don't know what yet.

There will be more developments Friday night, until the Angels bring things to a conclusion with their traditional "FREEZE!" as they point their guns in three different directions, each fastening on the person they believe to be the killer.

The whole class freezes, and one of you will be the killer. None of you will know who the killer is. Then we will have the conclusion.

Now that is the structure of the improvisation. Before the end of the day, determine which character you will play. I don't want you all to play junkies. It may take all night or a couple of days before we finish, but we'll begin at seven o'clock Friday night.

Bring your wardrobe, makeup, and props with you and change at the studio, because you do not want to attract attention on the street. It's tourist time in the City, and adventure time for kids just out of school for the holidays, so make your entrances casual.

If there are to be any refreshments at the party, fine, but there is to be no drinking of alcohol until after we finish work, neither before nor during.

As is an all-too-usual practice in making a film, we will be shooting out of continuity. This will be as close as you will come in this class to the working conditions on a set. Try to approximate on at least an elementary level the discipline required by those conditions.

Homage to the Film Buff[52]

I have never been a film buff. I remember the first film I ever saw. It was *Birth of a Nation*. I was nine years old. I remember the name of the theatre, the Casino Theatre, on Main Street in LaCrosse, Wisconsin. My sister Ruth took me there. About thirty years later I frequented a bar on Wilshire Boulevard. There was a nice old gentleman there at the bar. I'd engage in conversations with him. Then I moved to a different bar at the other end of the Boulevard and never saw him again. I learned later he was D. W. Griffith. If I had been a film buff I would have known.

Sometimes you film buffs annoy the hell out of me. But I'd like to pay a tribute to you. An actor doesn't exist unless he has a spectator, and at least you are spectators. But you're a lot more than that. You analyze, you probe, you remember, you collect. And observations, analyses, and the putting of definitions to things can be terribly important and very useful. But, of course, unless it is done within the cradle of love and experience, and with the ability to observe and participate in life at the same time, then it's meaningless, isn't it?

Sometimes there emerges a man like Henri Langlois, perhaps the greatest film buff of our century, who was also an artist. He must have been an artist, he died without a penny to his name. He lived

52. Edited from the texts of talks at Wheeler Hall, San Francisco, 13 July 1977, and at Dartmouth College, 13 July 1978.

in a cold-water flat. One day he felt ill. His phone had been turned off, so he had to run downstairs to call the doctor. But he collapsed on the way from a heart attack. He created the Cinémathèque Française.

The cinémathèques, the archives around the world, are the places where you as film buffs, as serious students, as participants in the art of making films, can go to attach yourselves to films, to reject or revolt against other films, or to contradict that process. Thanks to cinémathèques and archives, works that you feel attached to are preserved, so that you can exploit the opportunities they offer for your own artistic growth.

I think the reason you film buffs annoy me is that you ask so damn many questions, and I'm always afraid I won't have the answers. And I resent it if I don't have the answers. But hell, I don't have any answers.

I once asked a question of a venerable old Eskimo. A long silence fell between us, and then he said, "Excuse me, but it is only the wisdom of the question that makes me ponder so long." Certainly my question was not a wise one, it was just a confusing one. If I pause after the questions you ask me, I assure you that it will be because of their you knowwisdom. Any questions?

Q: Have you a favorite film of your own?
NR: Lots of them at lots of different times. I like the first one, *They Live By Night*. That's just fatherly. I began *They Live By Night* as I was finishing a musical on Broadway. I chose a cameraman, George Diskant, who had never been first cameraman before. I said to him, "Every mistake in this film is going to be mine. Everything that's done here is going to be mine. I want to find out if film is for me, and if it's not, I'll go back to Broadway." George said, "Sure." I said, "I want the head of the camera right at stage floor level." He said, "That will mean cutting through the stage floor. Give me forty minutes." Twenty minutes later he was back and the camera was set. That's how we worked for three pictures.

There are very few films I've made in which there aren't at least a hundred things I'd like to do differently. But what kind of fantasy is that? You can't put it at the bottom of a picture frame. At best it may keep me from making the same mistakes twice.

Q: Was it experiencing Hollywood that made you want to make changes in your films?
NR: Not experiencing Hollywood, but gaining more technique, learning more in the editing room. Hollywood is not the most advanced place in the world. It's remarkable that with all its money and talent not one new style or fashion has come from there.

Q: How did you get your first job directing movies?

NR: Through an awful lot of hard work and a lot of luck. It came to me through Dore Schary through John Houseman through Elia Kazan, through two directing jobs on Broadway, through three years of acting, two years of stage managing, writing, producing, directing for radio and television, through traveling the country on behalf of community theatres, through collecting folk music, and so on and lots more.

Q: You said you wanted to find out if film was for you. I assume that you did decide that.

NR: I did, I fell in love.

Q: I know you've had a lot of frustrations. Did they ever outweigh the love?

NR: No. I've come to believe there are no bad days, there are just bad moments. Or if there's a totally bad day, it isn't quite totally bad, it will have some good moments. I've learned to respect my films. I've learned to put aside all the sorrow and anguish that went into making them and see it all as just part of the experience, not anything for me to feel piqued or resentful about.

Q: Did some actors pose unusual difficulties to you?

NR: If I were to say yes to that, I'm sure the actors would say the same about me. Instead I propose to honor that as a serious question about the communication between directors and actors, and not as a gossip item. Difficulties between director and actor are a part of the interchange that happens in the course of making a film, which is always an arduous, however glorious, experience. They are among the many tensions, each and every day and night. I don't think any actor has ever deliberately imposed a difficulty on me, nor have I deliberately imposed a difficulty on an actor, except in the professional sense of providing an obstacle whose challenge could improve his performance. That is the way I believe people in film and theatre should behave, and that is the way most of those I've worked with have behaved.

Q: What kind of film are you making now?

NR: Right now I'm trying to become a good teacher. And I'm making about three films a day, with students.

Q: How do you feel about the direction cinema seems to be taking?

NR: I think it's at about the lowest ebb in history, I don't know why, it's bewildering to me. It kills me, the lack of knowledge of the medium that I see. They're not translating the medium from what is happening on the set into the cutting room. There's an immense fluidity and flexibility in film, but this abundance of possibility seems to inhibit the inexperienced director from getting the stuff on film that he needs.

Also, the leadership of Hollywood is always looking for a formula, you know? They say, "Ah, somebody made a hit film for $700,000, so all films have to cost $700,000." So 20 producers make 20 films at $700,000 each, and they all fall on their asses. In my opinion the reason that *Rocky* won the Academy Award is because people were relieved that a personal film had been made that was good and could get attention, a film that didn't cost $20 million, a film about relationships, ambitions, goals, struggles, hardships.

Of course there have to be the assembly line filmmakers to permit the art to flourish. On the other hand, you have to get impatient, willful, in a good sense. Get a little luck, make a film of your own. Don't be satisfied with this stuff.

I would like to help create a new concept of film as a living, continuously breathing thing, so you see the molecules of thought and emotion and experience working all the time, and in a kind of wonderful disorder that permits the audience to participate in creating its own order and drawing their own conclusions from what they experience. That is what I think we will finally come to. *Sesame Street* on television at times approaches this quality. Do you ever watch it?

I long for the day when I can be certain there's a filmmaker in every family, when the form of communication is not limited to the word or the page, when each kid can have a crack at giving a full expression to something of himself. How much richer the neighborhood would be, just one square block. We should be equipped and surrounded with the materials that creative activity calls for. Imagine a newly organized society in which some neighbors build a common kiln for their ceramics, some others build looms for handweaving to try and recapture some of the colors, textures, and pure relationships with materials that the American Indians had, another group builds a child day-care center, and another, a chamber music orchestra. What a city that could be. It could be, if some of us took parts in setting the foundations for such communities in a government which is a bit more of the people. That's what could be, as opposed to the evidences we have now of a police state.

Q: I wonder, having had the strength and wherewithal to produce and direct films as you did in Hollywood, why did you decide to do what you are doing now?

NR: Well, that's a fair question. I hope I can give it a fair answer. I would love to shoot films wherever they don't shoot at me. I take shots at Hollywood, but Hollywood's taken more effective ones at me. I went to Europe from Hollywood because for years I wanted to combine the adventure of living with the adventure of filmmaking, and I was led to believe that I would be able to do that in Europe. Instead I found that 90 percent of European production was financed by American capital and that the European producer has the same mentality as the American producer, which is the equivalent of the mentality of the man who ships herring out in tin cans. I made a lot of money, and I thought I could buck the system. I believed my own publicity. I was arrogant. I rejected film after film, I bought films, I ran into terrible luck. And I stayed away. If you don't play the game, if you're not present at the proper places at the proper times, they tell me it ain't good.

But just as we create our own disasters, we also create our own freedoms. I retired to an island in the North Sea and went on to my own self-destructive beat with some anguish and some ribaldry and, thankfully, some learning.

I'm very happy teaching. I love the process of discovery in other people, and when it happens to me I feel I've had a great big gift. And I want to make films, desperately. But not any film. I don't want to make a film that looks like all-weather paint splashed against a barn wall.

I have felt bitterness—and I know it has shown through at times—that I've not been able to make more films, whether because of the contradictions within myself or the nature of the stakes in this business. I've felt a lot of people, those who liked what I did up until '63, have been deprived of the further extension of my experience. It may sound terrible for me to say it, but I have felt that way. And yet there are all kinds of reasons why I shouldn't be bitter, because I've made some pretty lousy movies, and I've nearly always had a second chance, and there are no second chances, not in film nor in the very brief lives that we live.

In *Bitter Victory* Burton speaks a line in which I take refuge from time to time, a line from Walt Whitman: "Do I contradict myself? / Very well then I contradict myself."[53] It is a right I reserve for myself at all times. Burton does it consistently. He gave an interview a couple of years ago for *Playboy* in which he stated he had never learned anything from any film that he had ever been in. Then he went on to talk

---

53. The verse continues: "(I am large, I contain multitudes)." Walt Whitman, "Song of Myself," stanza 51, in *Leaves of Grass* (New York: Bantam Books, 1983).

about the size of Miss Taylor's derriere and to end the article by saying, " 'Do I contradict myself? / Very well then I contradict myself.' "
Perhaps he has not yet resolved the anguish of his instinct for self-
destruction. I hope I have. If I have it's probably only recently. I think
it's an active process, one which so many artists in all media have to
resolve.

The attitude toward today . . .

8 December 1977

The attitude toward today was balanced and calm. After Susan left the loft for work I went to sleep for two hours, then bathed, dressed, bought a book, two pair of socks, and looked for a flower shop. That wasn't entirely typical morning behavior. It's not so unusual for me to buy flowers, but to buy them this morning, to leave them behind instead of me, or a note, now seems sadistic, self-centered. A rose? Spring flowers or cactus plants? I couldn't find the shop. Perhaps not so balanced and calm.

In the taxi I looked up from the paper to scowl at the driver in the rearview mirror. Why should he have had his eyes there? To see what I was thinking of him? I thought I should take a look around at the world I was leaving. The thought returned that if I should reenter this hospital I'd never leave it alive. Not so balanced. Perhaps not. But it was a stale thought. One year old.[54]

Two books by Jerzy Koszinsky, two by Stanislavsky, *12 Steps and 12 Traditions*, *The Twenty-four Hour Book*, Auden's *A Certain World*, and an empty notebook, the only excuse for writing.

It might be good to start by relating the experiences and recalls to

---

54. Nick had been spitting up blood a year before and had checked into hospital for tests. X-rays showed a shadow on his lung that at that time was diagnosed as a fungus.

acting problems. But now there are other matters to think of. The doctors should be checked out. By whom? How?

I'd like the "folding chair,"[55] regardless. Along with the sense of resignation—more that than doom—has been the excitement of a new life beginning.

9 December 1977

A long talk with Susan and Caroline[56] about meditation. Attempts at it were interrupted by X-ray picture-taking and pulmonary testing, sleep and distraction. Gerry [Bamman] arrived and we played backgammon. I thought maybe my recall of the game by moves would help me during the bronchoscopy, which soon followed after showering. I indulged in different attitudes. Arrogance and self-importance (helped by a beautiful long robe Susan brought me, which I wore like a Russian Barrymore with sleighs and wolfhounds and Garbo awaiting me) switched with timorousness.

The tube reached the gag area and the doctor's arm dropped, withdrawing tube. I was reanaesthetized, the examining doctor was given a stool on which to stand, and the tube was reinserted. An assisting doctor said he couldn't see the light attached to the tube. The examining doctor said I had swallowed it. Hunh? The tube went through the larynx, the vocal chords (a visual sensation), and the light reappeared on the approach to the trachea. The doctors donned their lead aprons and called for suction, anaesthetic and fluoroscope. It wasn't much of a team, as teams are thought of—somewhat like my student directors. Brushes and more anaesthetic were inserted and injected into the apparatus, and after some gagging, sneezing, coughing, and spasming, it was finished, and the doctor wheeled me to the 18th floor, personally.

Susan arrived, looking gray and wan but beautiful. I fell asleep. She tidied up and left a loving note. These are days of deep anxiety for her and she controls it better than I. She is a wonderful unknown lady who sucks her finger. Jud arrived with cheesecake, coffee, and ice cream. I listened to the Wall Street and Washington reports. Read a paper, thanked the H[igher] P[ower], and went back to sleep. Now

---

55. A guest teaching position was created and funded specifically for Nick at New York University, largely through the efforts of Michael Miller, dean of the school's film and theatre department. Because of its provisional nature, Michael and Nick referred to the endowment as a "folding chair."
56. Caroline Cox Simon, aka C. C. Loveheart: actress and neighbor.

the nurse offers me a sleeping pill or hot milk. I settle for a back rub. So to it.

11 December 1977

Bogart and I shared levels of experiences in common with each other, but there must have been something else. We were both married to younger women, he to Bacall, I to Grahame,[57] and they were near to each other in age and pregnancy (Steven is two months younger than Tim). Both were talented actresses who worried about the same wrinkles, the twenties wrinkles. Each was promiscuous, Gloria by far the more offensively so. Each had her own style, but Bacall's was elegant, and she was the more intelligent of the two. Grahame schemed better and on a lower level.

We shared another, perhaps more devastating experience: booze. And as Betty was more elegant than Gloria in all ways, so was Bogie more elegant than I, especially with booze. At certain times when I would not drink—when filming, particularly, or in the period of preparation before filming—our relationship would alter. In some ways it became deeper, and in others only more formal. It is the abstinence factor that causes me to talk of Bogie at this time, 11 December, 4:30 A.M., in the tenth floor lounge of the Roosevelt Hospital, on 59th Street, New York City.

Bogie knew he had cancer, but wouldn't stop smoking—or drinking. I am smoking now. I haven't had a drink for fifteen months. If I had, I would be dead now, and that would make me furious. I loved Bogie so much I even bothered to convert him from Ike to Adlai, but I couldn't take the damned Chesterfield from his mouth, and Adlai became Betty's adventure. Reforms with Bogie had little longevity, but what the hell, he knew he was going to die. After the first operation one could hear the Romanoff sandab hit the bottom of Bogie's stomach, so he softened the creature's fall with a pool of scotch and beer, and settled a haze of Chesterfield smoke around it.

I want to live. I know I want to live. But I just can't stop smoking. I guess I don't have any style, the lack of which is certainly another middle class disease. (More about Bogie. Much more.)

Susan here early and late. Ricardo. Gerry. And Connie: "In hospital, organize your day." Good. So to it.

---

57. Gloria Grahame, Nick's second wife.

12 December 1977

Today Susan asked Dr. D., "How does one overcome fear?" Was she asking for her or for me? Dr. D. looked at me. Why did I feel I had to say something? I said, "By confrontation." Vague enough, but implying, I suppose, confronting that which you fear head on. That's okay for an implication, but hardly a remedy for the wound (pain). How about love? Dedicated love of life. Love of—for—God. "God grant me the serenity to accept the things I cannot change, the courage *to change* the things I can, and the wisdom *to know* the difference." All doing. All living. Must battle fear with love. Even the *want to love* will help.

Connie recommended William W. Long talk with Dr. D. re: procedure if I want a surgeon other than staff at Roosevelt. Central, spinal attitudes are involved. Why all the fuss? I'm just a very little one. Okay, so I'm a very big one. So what. Is my tissue any different than those before me, or those waiting, or those to come? Are the stakes any higher for me than they are for another? Do I stand up and claim all is mine, for I am more important to me than any other? I'm not. If I show that I am it's an act and it's forced. It's bloat. It isn't the central me. I accept or grab survival things—not important ones that would match an important person. Should I act as if I were important? No. Perhaps I could act as if I loved God—Susan—living—enough for the love to be important to them, or to me? I want to live because I'll miss breathing. It must be very uncomfortable. It makes me angry if I can't breathe, taste, and say hello. I want those things. Selfishly. They are important to me for simple reasons. So why do I continue to smoke? Fight sleep? (I know.) If I stop breathing I won't be able to smoke. And the thought of that is enough to make me furious. But it isn't enough to live. To live for the love there is and has been isn't enough. To live for the love to come and to give, is. So to it.

I pray that I may be shown the right way to live today, and I pray that I may pray that prayer each remaining day of my life. Somehow it seems inadequate and surface to pray with words and not feelings. God understands our needs most certainly, in any idiom, for He was not born in Wisconsin of German-Norwegian Americans with a limited knowledge of the meanings of sounds. An Eskimo, a Bedouin, and a Samoan are making the same prayer, asking the same guidance, and attention is being paid. What a wonderful thing for which to be thankful. The grain of prayer must stir in a stream of feeling, and that right there may be the whereabouts of the bottom line of truth.

That I want to have my cake and eat it is a truth of me, deeply rooted and hourly practiced, as if it were a basic need for peaceful coexistence. I pray for the strength and intelligence to uproot it. That I do this is a matter of continuing survival which must be measured in days, a day at a time.

And yet, I wish to light a cigarette—and what's more, smoke it. Not right away, perhaps. Not yet.

13 December 1977

Doctor D. arrived as I was changing my position on the X-ray table. Of course we all seriously knew there was to be an operation, and the operation's flight plan was at that moment being charted. The doctor brought new information, gleaned from the brushings made during the bronchoscope reconnaissance on Friday—unexpected flack in the air zones. It was time for a decision, or an expression of a preference in the direction of the surgeon-to-be. Aren't the first two words following surgeon always hyphenated? And if only one word, capitalized? Surgeon General, Surgeon Absurd, etc.? The name of Dr. W. has come to my attention. He was recommended by Connie Bessie, daughter of Morris Ernst and lifelong love who has had two operations for cancer, and who has a generally healthy attitude. Dr. W.'s name also came through an associate of Susan's father. I mentioned this to Dr. D. He accepted it and left a warm smile and a sad tone behind him. Not sad. More compassionate, I suppose, a tone with which I have no genuine familiarity.

By the time I was released from the picture machine I had experienced some clarity in my reasoning, or so it seemed to me. I revised my decision about the Surgeon-to-be. It is a decision for which I must take the responsibility. Suppose something untoward happens on the operating table. How will the recommender, in this case Susan's father, escape a feeling of remorse, or chagrin, or guilt, or anger with his daughter for having put him in that position? Later in the day I told Dr. D. I had changed my decision. In speaking the words I felt the rush of vain nobleness within me, and what had been a pure and simple thought and action was suddenly distorted by my own awareness of my tone. However, I know the truth of that thought, and that's the way it stands.

Visits from Ricardo, Gerry, Pierre, and Susan. I had such a desire to go home with her, as if to a secret garden. Instead I gave her the news in the corridor, and we hugged between games of gin rummy.

14 December 1977

After Susan left I began reading Margaret Drabble's *The Realms of Gold*, with Jerzy Koszinsky's *Cockpit* by my side in reserve. I fell asleep without having to resort to Koszinsky, but awakened an hour-and-a-half later, and went to the lounge to read. The night before last I'd fallen asleep with the TV set on and was awakened by my roommate, a Chinese man who owns a prepared food-to-take-out establishment, very noisily yanking the curtains surrounding his bed to screen the light from the screen. It does give off a nasty illumination—limited but intense. He is leaving in the morning. He had ringworm on one leg and "something wrong inside my cock." It would be needless for him to leave our acquaintanceship with bad feeling and no rest. He's a nice, middle-class fellow who wishes he could learn backgammon, and I believe him. He talks with excited high-voiced lyricism about Chinese poker, which I wish I could learn to play. His voice lowers when he talks of the graft, "plenty money," the police drag off their games.

I went to the lounge to read again in *12 Steps and 12 Traditions*, which sounds Oriental in origin. It could be the title for the introduction to a Japanese burying ground. At 2:00 a nurse informed me it was time to go to bed. At 3:30 a resident doctor sat down and we rapped about motivations for such a career. His evaluation: 15% to get rich, the balance to make a better-than-average living and enjoy prestige and power. He showed much appreciation for power. "Don't forget, you have something to say about your case. Don't let us push you around. If there's any rule you want to break, like staying up late, reading in the lounge, or having your wife stay after hours, just ask a doctor. Ask me. No problem."

I switched, with some malevolence, to the dedication of Vesalius, da Vinci's companion in grave-robbing, who became Pope and had to give up his practice. The good Dr. Resident was more a realist than I. He switched on me to Somerset Maugham, Lesley Howard and Bette Davis, and hailed *Of Human Bondage* for having solved some of his sex problems. Denying the absence of artistic creativity in medicine, he announced that his quarters were well laced with examples of his work in needlepoint, which I understand is very big this year. Perhaps it is a compensation for the internist who had hoped of becoming a surgeon.

When I next awakened it was elephant grey dawn and I was being blessed with a pleasant as opposed to an aching erection. I fondled myself lightly, and was suddenly set down by the realization that my cock, which had nothing wrong and lots of good inside, would never arrive at that depletion of stores, and that the possible joys of incest would never be reached in experience. Today the brain, liver, and bones come in for scannings. So shower, shave, breakfast, and to it.

The scannings did not take place. Kazan called. Houseman came by after rehearsal. The visit was warming and full. We talked of our wives, our children, and our friends, each reporting to the other as if these were matters of casual interest. We are somewhat wonderfully amusing characters together. We don't try to say or even stumble into saying things which can't be said.

High risk heart. Tim called twice.

15 December 1977

Liver scan; brain scan. Anxiety. Projection. (Intense. But it's getting to be less prominent.)

I love my four children sometimes one more than the other, and that's only natural, and also it's natural that it is always a beginning and an unending love. There is no qualification about it that doesn't resolve itself with "I love you" at the beginning, and each of you I love, and so do I love you, and all times and unendingly. I almost said "at the end." This may be the end, but also it may be that in the end is my beginning. If that is true, it is with you. I love each and all of you so much.

Well, from here on out, Mr. Ray, it's all form. Whatever content you have will now determine the form.

16 December 1977[58]

Operation. 3 hrs. They left the tumor inside and clamped me up again.

23 December 1977

What a beautiful day. I don't quite know when it began. It's been a little like an emotional recall going into a monologue, but I don't know where the emotional recall begins and ends, and the monologue begins and ends. It hasn't ended, obviously.

Dawn must have been coming up when it looked like the whole big window was brown burlap with soft light coming through. There was pain. I thought I'd slept for four hours. I'd slept for forty minutes. I wandered the corridors, I talked with nurses, I had an injection. At 6:00 I had a sleeping pill. It worked for about an hour-and-a-half. The nurse came in. An intern came in, a jolly student, who seemed like a complete apprentice, trying everything, doing everything. The other

58. Dated 16 December, but written 23 December.

day he cleaned my bandage, this morning he clipped the staples out
of my incision.

We talked of qualities of doctors. He reminded me of one of my
students, the one who's gotten more from the class than anyone else.
I had the chance to talk of one of the young doctor's heroes and say
nice things about him. In talking of him he exposed the lie that's
implied when I say, "If you're in this business to be loved, then you're
in the wrong profession." The surgeon we spoke of, who has a great
reputation as a surgeon, is also a man who has a reputation for being
very well loved. All day till now there has been evidence of so many
manifestations of love for me: a nurse who loaned me 50 cents, another who loaned me a dime, the surprise visit of Kazan, the phone
call from Susan, the right-on-the-nose visit of Mike Miller who arrived
just at the end of Kazan's visit with a pair of bedroom slippers. And
Bob, who should not smoke, shared his last cigarette with me, who
also should not smoke. I know I should not smoke, and I know also
I will resolve what that defiant attitude is within me that could be
my undoing.

I otherwise feel quite happy with myself and very happy about the
lack of self-pity. I feel very happy when Susan says she respects the
bravery with which I live, and I don't know what she's talking about.
I am not aware of any conscious act of bravery.

I related the question to Kazan: what have been our definitions of
courage? I find it difficult to hold my voice down. I should be singing
the body electric. Kazan and I must have covered forty-five years in
twenty-five minutes, and we were liking each other, and it was nice
to be able to play back to him how many things I'd learned from him,
how specifically I'd learned from him. Kazan and I talked technically,
we talked romantically, we talked professionally, we talked personalities, we talked events, we talked of Houseman. We showed each other
we loved each other.

Gerry called from the airport. His engine had just blown out, and
yet it was so nice and ludicrous to hear from him. Talked to Gerry
for a while and then said goodnight to Gerry. And then after saying
goodnight to Gerry, Jack R. came in, thought he wanted to take me
to a meeting. And now the phone is ringing . . .

24 December 1977

I must try to listen to my own reasoning. Very properly, it seems to
me, I selected Dr. Joe P. to be the surgeon.

One reason I almost instinctually veered away from Dr. W. was not the altruistic one, but the experiential one of having been closely involved with several doctors whose reputations were made because they had been successful in varying degrees in the diagnosis of celebrities. With one of those doctors I shared a mews house in London. He was personal physician to MPs, a number of directors, and the most glamourous of stars and musicians. But he also stole $50,000 from me and was indirectly responsible for my loss of $200,000. I believe he has since been indicted for malpractice.

Had I really wanted to draw on other professional acquaintances rather than my own independent judgment, there is a group of doctors and surgeons with whom I play poker once a month. They all have fine standing in the community. We could have taken a poll before cutting for deal.

The decision was made, the operation performed. The results were disappointing, but disappointing for strictly organic reasons, and not, in my opinion, as any reflection of the capabilities of the people who were responsible for the operation. Even assuming that the most negative of my many character defects, the willingness to self-destruct, was in full play, would it account for the lack of hesitation with which I accepted the results? I accepted the results with hope, and so with confidence in Dr. P. and Dr. D.

Then entered a wave of good feeling in the persons of Bill and Beverly Pepper and their genuine desire to be of some help to me if they possibly could. Bill has written a lot about scientists and scientific matters, including a biography of Dr. Barnard, and his current project is a study of survivors of cancer through Sloane-Kettering Hospital.

Bill said, "Look, don't you think you ought to have a second opinion, just as a matter of course?" When he suggested a second opinion would certainly not be unethical or unheard of, I accepted it, and said, "Well, okay," to Susan, "but Dr. P. is going to have to be happy with it." I called Connie. Connie was happy about it. Other people seemed to be happy about it. I was neither confused nor elated by it. And Dr. P. had not yet been consulted, nor had Dr. D. I deliberately was perasked Susan if she would be the one to discuss it with Dr. P., because in no way did I want to have any shadow on my confidence in him.

Then, before Susan and I had thoroughly discussed it, another element entered the scene. An interview that had been delayed for 48 hours with Dr. Young finally took place, and in the course of that interview he referred to a statistic[59] that I had no reason to doubt. It

---

59. Possibly concerning the chances of survival of those with metastasized lung cancer.

seemed a categorical answer, an easy point of reference. So I left the matter in D.'s hands. I said I didn't care for a second opinion. If he wished to have one, it was up to him. He said he wanted to go for another evaluation. He made the decision. I feel much relief.

Perhaps my hang-up in not being able to get down to anything really concrete in ordering the rest of my life, if that is possible, is resistance to setting down for myself the facts as I know them, and they are simply: On Friday the 16th they opened up my right lung, found it to be inoperable, closed it up again, and we are now awaiting the decision on what the next treatment should be. I hope that it is positive and direct, cobalt rather than medicinal, and I don't see much difference. In one case it is as inoperable as the other. I hope in some way they will help me function. I certainly intend to try to get myself into a position of being able to function for as long as Hubert Humphrey—whose case is currently gathering the most attention—has evidently been able to function since he received word of his cancer being inoperable. The difference is only in the two personalities and the amount of money and resources at our respective commands. I hope I rise to the occasion of myself as he has risen to the occasion of himself. There are many reasons for me to do this, not the least of which is Susan, who has made it impossible and possible for eight years. I cannot express the depth of my feeling about that, and I don't think an expression of the depth is important. I think only my actions, only what I do and the way I do those things I do do is what will matter. And now I should try to set about trying to do the things I can do within the limitations under which I must work. Within several days we should know more about those limitations. Until that time I think it will be difficult for her.

9 January 1978

A part of my body has grown cells that have become cancerous. I have cancer and am willing to give it away, get rid of it. That is not an unreal statement, since there is a possibility that I am not entirely willing to give it up. It tends to make me feel unique, separate from an immediate or general community. It automatically and relatively painlessly brings the acknowledgment of death to the foremost point of encounter. I am both confused and pleased there is as yet no evidence of fright. I say this from an intimate knowledge of myself which needs no more defense than fear itself would need defending. That I have no fear must be a great gift from a source unknown to me. It was unpredictable. It is, knowing my character somewhat, so far inexplicable. Perhaps the event of a few moments ago will bring a clue to insight:

I had been asleep. I awakened as my right arm reached the crest of an arc and I felt—experienced as real—a one-fingered cloth-and-leather mitten being quickly, deftly, snatched off my hand with one precise movement. I felt it, physically. Real. My arm was stretched upwards. I lowered it and immediately reviewed what had happened. That moment was so mentally centered that I was almost equally startled to feel my right arm rising upwards once more.

I was about to dismiss it as a dream to be considered in the morning. Instead I got out of bed to note it down, or certainly it would join the horde of other lost dreamings. I thought I would find such a half-dream interesting if somebody told me it had happened to him. Half-dream because the sensation was real. I can reproduce the feeling.

Earlier Susan and I had talked about being frightened, and I could say to her with absolute honesty at the time that being frightened was not an aspect of my state-of-being, however confusing that seems to be—my state-of-being, that is. It still has no convincing reality to me, all X-rays, feelings from surgery, cautions from doctors, analyses of malignancy, etc., notwithstanding. I find hope in that. Confusion too. And questions.

Why was it a snub-nosed mitten which covered my right hand? Was it the covering of fear which I deny? Was I being warned that it is not appropriate to be unafraid? Why am I not frightened? Why can't I pretend to be frightened? Because I am? Why do I find that I rebel against permitting fear to invade me? Do I want to have the encounter, and have all problems, all future anguish, if any, resolved for me? Must I now learn to fear the God with whom I am just learning to make contact and pray to with faith? Why was it a mitten? And why did I raise my arm a second time?

10 January 1978 A.M.

Could it mean the right hand knows what the left hand doeth? Could it have been a successful operation? In after-effect it is a hopeful experience.

[January 1978]

I like to act occasionally. That I would say condescendingly, I suppose. Yeah, I like to act once in a while. It kind of keeps me on track.

When I got on stage the first day of shooting for *The American Friend*

with Wim Wenders, I found that I was just terrible. Although I had
helped Wim write the part, I still found myself doing all the things
I scream at other actors for doing. When people would comment, "Oh,
you're acting," I'd say, "Yeah, I like to take a look at myself and see
if the stuff I'm telling actors still applies." That's partly true. But shit,
I also like to act. Why not? And I'm not as bad an actor as a lot of
those I've hired . . .

An actor must speak each line as if it were the very first or the very
last time it will ever be said by him. He knows this intuitively, or
else he has learned it as part of his training. Having learned it, he
devotes a large part of the rest of his life learning how to create the
illusion that he is saying this line, at this time, for the first or last
time. It must be one or the other, there is no exception. Whether the
line is "What time is it?" "I love you," or "Begin," whether he has
said that same line sixty times in shooting and reshooting one scene
in a film, or 405 times in repeat performances of the same role in the
same play, there is no exception.

I have, in my profession, dealt with this problem for fifty years.
Now I am dying of cancer (date and hour of death is not on the calen-
dar), and in three weeks I will be playing the part of a general in the
movie version of *Hair*.

THE FORGER

I want to leave you tonight with the character of the Forger. I think I'll leave it with four or five people to discuss, sift out.

Who is the Forger? The Forger is not to us in this moment one who manipulates metals into forms through heat and beating. He is a manipulator. The first object he began manipulating was himself. He manipulated himself into believing he had the right to enjoy the fruits and the products earned and made by humans other than himself, and that he had a magic gift which enabled him to gain those fruits and products of others, whether they be food, clothing, lodging, transportation, perfumes, station in society, mistresses, good will and companionship, attention and service, respect, and even love.

That gift was the ability to deceive. To deceive in order to steal, one must steal in order to deceive, if one is a Forger. A Forger must steal another's identity. Having stolen it, he must act it out, until the deed is done, the goal achieved. Like an actor. When that identity is worn out, he must steal another and continue the process until he is a body so filled with scars and plastic surgery, he cannot touch or recognize himself or any precedence in his desires, for he has wanted and tasted everything of others.

He dies unjudged, not knowing who he is. He never learned his gift was given him on loan for a few years, and that with fearless sharing it would have grown. He dies unjudged because he is no different than his fellows. Unless he is caught.

As all the plastic images used and worn are stripped away, what is left? Nothing identifiable. And didn't it take one to catch one? So who sits in the guilty chair for judgment? Who wants to sit there? Who can? No one. Then nothing is on trial. Not even a vapor sits in the chair, unless it be innocence.

Do you still want to be an actor?

We are about to begin preparation on a scenario that will involve exercises, improvisations, and characterizations we have done, scenes we shall write, and more, and that will give us the chance to integrate all our work. I was working on a scenario about a month ago. It was based on a ballad of Willy Nelson's, "The Red-Headed Stranger." I was trying to find the inner meaning of the character, or an aspect of him, so I put down a working title: *Macho Gazpacho*. We will call our scenario *Macho Gazpacho*. The Macho Gazpacho is a fellow who has a great deal of trouble finding himself.

The first scene will be the start of a day of training, your entrances in the first hours of the morning, your preparations, and then the first exercise, which will have to be selected, orchestrated, directed, and choreographed. It would be interesting for this to be directed by someone with documentary experience, because the director will have to find a style within the content of the people who participate. It's got to be something more than just setting up a camera and getting a photoelectric cell recording of people coming and going, the way they do in a bank.

The second scene will be a warm-up, which will end on the touching exercise.

Then we will come to the third sequence, the mirror exercise, which we will do today and tomorrow. At one point there will be a voice, just one single expression: "Something strange has just happened." Jake will direct.

Scene four will be an improvisation that will evolve out of what we do here today, but within that improvisation an incident will happen, either a prank or a theft.

There will be, in scene five, another improvisation, in which there will be a manipulation of people, which they find foreign and distasteful. They want to get away from the manipulation, and so at the phrase, "Pick up on Lennie, pick up on Lennie," they will pick up on his tempo, his speed.

That is immediately broken off when, in scene six, also an improvisation, an act of violence takes place, violence to one or two particular characters within the improvisation. The violence will be interrupted, and the people wanting to escape the violence will pick up again on the frantic movement of the group, carried to as high a climax as possible.

From there we will segue into a mood movement, scene seven, an escape from panic into joy, serenity, privacy.

Out of which will come scene eight. "Who is doing this to the group?" "Or is it just a feeling?" There will be spot scenes, a collage or montage of five or six expressions. Then curiosity turns to suspicion. Everybody is suspect, nobody takes anybody for granted anymore. We will find an overall group event for that.

Motivated by suspicion, the group unifies once again to set a trap. The trap is set and fallen into, and the identity of the one who has committed the thievery, the manipulation, and the violence is revealed.

The capture is followed by the punishment.

The punishment is followed by the epilogue, which is a question, or lots of different questions. There will be questions of judgment, and also a lyric kind of question: "I looked in my heart . . . / And what did I see I have not seen before? / Only a question less or a question more."

Our central character, whom we may see in scene seven or eight, is a man who lives in a society whose faults he condemns, but it is the only society available to him. He neither accepts nor adjusts to any situation; he rejects everybody. He needs this society, he wants to belong to it, to be accepted and recognized by it, as much as he wants to violate it. I say "he," but it could be a man or a woman. He is facile, skilled, imaginative. He reacts. Schemes. Manipulates. Steals. Lies. Violates. Paints. Sings. Dances. Mimes (mocks).

The group is the hero. The Forger is the disease which threatens to destroy it, the great American disease.

From here on, take a little, give a little . . .

Backgammon. Alarm rings. . . .

9 February 1978, 7 A.M.

Backgammon. Alarm rings. Susan pees; I think a thought about immortality. Shouldn't I be writing profound and loving letters for post-mortem publication? Scathing letters fraught with insight and prediction? What's to lose with prediction? Predictions would only be published if they were right. I don't seem to care as much as I should care. What has happened to my vanity, for heaven's sake?

Kazan on a Sunday morning. Houseman on a Sunday afternoon. A.A. on Monday. NYU on Tuesday, day. A.A. on Tuesday, night. Susan, Ivens, Lomax, Leyda, Bentley, Wednesday night. Thursday morning Susan on the telephone for a taxi. Susan at the doorway.

She has been an endowment funded by spirit, intelligence, and love. And the need of love in her churns as a positive force most of the time. I hope it does. (I can only sense her inner anguish, but) I hope it does.

I am spitting blood and it panics me this morning, with sadness. How, when can I let her know how very deep is my love for her. It is a gut and head panic I've never had before. Time hasn't been important until this morning—and I couldn't hold her close enough to let her know. In bed and at the doorway, Susan, I wanted to absorb you.

In the cab, en route to the airport on Long Island, I posed me a question: Since what early age have I wanted to die? Perhaps not die,

172

but experience death. To experience death without dying seems like a natural goal for me.

[15?] February 1978

My contract for the picture *Hair* specified a weekly salary, and if I should go a half-day or a day into the second week, I'd get the full second week's salary. Well, that's the way the shooting spread itself out, so I got a week's salary for a half a day's work.

So I had some extra money, and Las Vegas was only a three-hour bus ride away, and I hadn't been there to visit my money for a long long time—but I don't want to use that cliché, "to visit my money." With great deliberation and concentration and relaxation I got to Vegas and went directly to one casino with which I was quite familiar. I didn't like it at all this time. It made me nervous, so I walked out.

I went over to the Hilton, and on the way to the chemin de fer table I came to rest at the side of a roulette wheel that was about ready to spin. I called as much as I could cover of $3,000 on 32. It was the only number being played. It was quite early in the morning, late players were sleeping, and I thought, "Well, we'll see if I'm in tune. Why not? It's not going to cost me anything." Before I could change my mind, the ball was spinning. Sure as hell, the ball came up 32.

It's happened that I've won like that lots and lots of times, not only at the tables, but when I've bet on whether someone's going to default at tennis, or whether someone's going to make an impossible faux pas at a party, or whether something's going to happen before noon the next day. I usually win if the event has that peculiar feeling.

And I think it was basically a lack of courage—shit word, courage—that I stayed on and lost, because we've been living on very little, and we could have used the extra money. But right now money is like a tube from an oxygen tank going up my nose.

When I got back to Barstow I couldn't tell anybody about the incident. I just had to say I won. Then they found out I lost anyway because I had to go to the cashier to get money the next day. Stupid, stupid macho. Stupid pride.

What surprises me most about the venture was that when I lost the $3,000 I didn't go to one of the casino executives and borrow some money on credit, which I assumed I still had. I probably could have gone back $30,000 hooked. Once I'm hooked I want to go all the way. For a change, I didn't do that. I wonder why not.

I got married in Las Vegas once. To Gloria Grahame. I didn't like her very much. I was infatuated with her, but I didn't like her very much.

There was something vindictive about me that made me stay at the crap tables while she was waiting out the last few days before her divorce became final. I wanted to be absolutely broke. I didn't want this dame, who later proved to be as shrewd as she had begun to threaten to be, to have anything of mine. I didn't want her to have any money at all. I was in the middle of making *In a Lonely Place*. I lost a bundle.

I was at the crap tables when my best man, J. C. Flippen, came to tell me it was time to go to church. It was a cute little church on the grounds of the El Rancho Vegas. Here we were, two people, refreshingly starting out fresh—no dough. I went ahead with the marriage because she was pregnant and I had promised I would marry her. I'm that nice mid-western boy who goes on the credo that my word is better than my bond.

The joys of working on *In a Lonely Place* with Bogart took away some of the pain of the loss of the money when reality had to be faced. Gloria and I had a couple of pretty bad battles, making it imperative for us both to behave as professionally as possible on the set, which I'm glad to say we did, causing no extra anxiety to Bogart or my producer, Bobby Lord.

■ ■ ■

No day could have begun worse than this one. Ex-wife—daughter—socks—food—suitcase—letter from Tom—my class at NYU. How can they do without me. I'm losing money coming out here. My vanity doesn't need it. But—I went to the laundry, boiled a couple of eggs. The suit and jacket are out of season. Material satisfactions are not the purpose of living, and it's good to have to exercise that belief. But not every day, I scream inside. In your case, every day, say I to me.

I find my angers or resentments are largely bound in fear.

18 February 1978. Mid-pre-dawn at Houseman's, Malibu.

Upon my arrival John came to the door opening on Old Malibu Road. The house, searched out by Joan two years ago, cannot, to my taste, be surpassed by any other house on the beach, and in it are the two dearest, most elegant people known to me.

John's gait now has the trace of a slight shuffle, not present a year ago. Perhaps it was accented today by the baggy blue cotton trousers he wore and a hangover of the flu. A year ago, at 75, he ran a full block in pursuit of an open door on a NYC subway train. And Joan, at 61, is thinner, and unquestionably at the most beautiful in her life. After Ron Colby, who had driven me in from the *Hair* location at Barstow, had gone, John settled down to talk and complete the sorting of cancelled checks and other receipts for his income tax. (The man has never been able to be totally occupied by any one thing during the entire time I have known him.) When Joan leaned over to identify one scrap of paper or another—with joy, not irritation—, they were royal. I was transfixed. I love them so very much.

John, knowing I would sooner or later inquire of his mother, Mae (but it was hard for me to introduce the subject, not knowing if she had died during the past months; she is 99), said that recently her direct communications with him had been two: one, she accused him of having stolen money from her (When, I wondered, out of a tea cup when he was ten?); and the other: "You are not witty. But then, you never were witty, were you?" Dimpled, petite Mae would never accept, among many other things, the notion that a glass of wine could be anything but healthful. She always, especially on Doheny Street in the late '40s, made me ashamed of any attempt at abstinence.

Another previously invited guest, Jack O'Brien, arrived. He is the director of the latest revival of *Porgy and Bess* and of the Houston opera and theatre season, as well as a Neil Simon grabbag for TV. It is assumed he is talented as well as personable in a kind of "midwest" Broadway style.

Dinner of artichoke and broiled salmon. Joan's cooking has never in my recollection had a mark of imperfection. I learn Judd Kinberg is in California, and then Tim arrives to take me to a meeting in Winter Canyon, where I reencounter an old friend from Garden of Allah and RKO days. An excellent meeting, but I am unable to conceal several shots of pain, and become temporarily distracted.

An hour ago, I, bare-assed, went searching for some cheese and a bottle opener in the bar area, having already searched the kitchen, and was surprised by a flash of light and the dim figure of Joan watching me at the bar. Certainly she has every right to believe that my sobriety is a pose, that I was searching for booze, etc. Sometimes, a lot of times, alcoholism is a ghostly presence. And since I do not care much for myself these days, I permit the ghost to enter and cause dismay.

All my life, from earliest poem, I have shouted and espoused exultations and joys. It seems appropriate that I should phase out as a recovering alcoholic dying of cancer. I cannot sleep.

IN CLASS XIII

THE FORGER (CONT'D.)

[The work begins with sequence three, as discussed in Class XII, an improvisation directed by JAKE around the "mirror exercise." The results are screened for discussion.]

NR: The exercise was to choose a specific movement that is expressive of a character, so it becomes movement with a purpose. For a scripted scene the preparation behind your choice would be exhaustive, exhausting; but in improvisation the choice must be of the moment and instinctual.

Each movement introduces a new element, so one camera should follow the movement. Forget about the close-up camera at this point. Everybody is involved in the movement, whether as initiator or reactor. As the initiator of the movement makes his decision, picks his goal, goes towards it, another camera must pick up reactions—a shift of the eyes, turn of the head, slight wave of the body. Someone gives the movement, someone takes it. The camera's got to record who's giving and who's taking. That is the mirror.

You begin with a movement, and from that you evolve a character. If to that character you add an action, a very simple action, you'll find surprising things happen. Movement takes on a style, and provides tension and atmosphere.

Content determines form and form conditions content. A walk from here to there seems extended in time by the number of reactions to it, but the walk is induced by the character's inner action: "I want to do. To get what I want, I must do this." It is an inner action that takes him from here to there, not just a piece of business.

176

You don't have to get loaded down with plot. There is a group action, to do the exercise, and a number of different people involved in the event. Depending on the individual actions the actors develop within themselves, and the reactions to those actions, conflicts will develop between individuals, between groups, and between individuals in groups. Suppose, for example, in response to your movement and action there is a combustion, and you are impelled to change either an action or a relationship in a way that does not accord with the scenario you have in your head. Let it happen, because you may be about to be given a free gift. Conflict and climax are going to happen if you allow them.

In what we just saw the high camera did not honor the group in composition. The shot should have had the sense of an unfolding, like a flower's. The master shot must serve the purpose of conveying a sense of the spirit of the group, of the energy level of the group.

JAKE: I felt lost in the shooting, not in terms of the concept, but in terms of being able to communicate with the technicians, and at the same time to develop and maintain rapport with the actors. To go right into this scene out of continuity created confusion for the actors. But what hung me up the most was feeling the time pressure. I had to get through the scene because it was almost time for class to end. How do you deal with that?

NR: You cannot force it. You can't do anything about it, so you just have to let it go. Take it one moment at a time and use each moment fully within the given limitation. Do what you can. That's where your relaxation should come in.

TANDO: It's easy to work with a character when you have a script in front of you, but here there were no words, there was nothing already written. All we were given was an action. How do I create a backstory, a future, or a present when I don't know who I am? If the scene is that you're just coming into this class, who are you coming into this class—yourself, your character, your monologue character? There has to be one unifying theme. I understand shooting out of sequence, but somewhere there should be an overview of where each segment fits into the others.

JAKE: We have an outline of scenes, and we have a short synopsis of the overall concept. We're taking the basics of acting and the basics of camera setups and we're developing these different scenes. You as the whole group represent the abstraction of society. There's one person in here who's off in that abstraction, and we're calling him the Forger.

You were actors portraying actors doing the exercise. Your overall action as a group was to do the exercise. That's really all there was to it, until the presence was felt.

BETTY: Have you identified the Forger?

JAKE: I shot an introduction, an exterior. From there five latecomers come into the group. The group is already performing. The latecomers enter, and fit right into the group. I didn't take it as my purpose to have the Forger in the introduction, or to identify him.

JET: Who is the Forger?

NR: Nobody knows who the Forger is.

PETE: Does the Forger know?

NR: Nobody knows.

SAM: How are we going to choose the Forger?

NR: I don't know, Sam. I don't know who the Forger is yet. I don't know what he is yet, except that he is a manipulator. A falsifier of any kind usually has a great imagination, and will get trapped when it runs dry, or when he repeats himself once too often.

MARA: But the Forger is identified as a mysterious force that has entered the room. Leonard said, "Something strange is happening here." That's probably where the confusion began, since nobody had a clear idea who or what that something strange was.

CHARLOTTE: Can I ask whether we have a defined super-objective for the whole scenario?

NR: It has been read to you. Nat, read the statement again.

[NAT rereads the description of the Forger as read at the beginning of Class XII.]

The situation and the event is the class. Each of you as you are comes into the class within this circumstance.

BETTY: Through our improvisations you're hoping to turn it from an abstraction into something concrete.

NR: That's right. In society, very often you will find the individual gets the group. A bank cashier in Patterson, New Jersey, goes home for lunch every day, reads the Bible with his mother, then goes back to the bank where he handles other people's money, day after day: "Good morning, Mr. Octopus, good morning, Mrs. Jones." He gives them their money, cashes their checks. One day at noontime, instead of going home, he reaches under his cashier's shelf, takes out an M-22, goes into the street, and kills thirteen people.

Or there's the sniper isolated on top of a building in Ohio. Or the rapist in Central Park. Or the bomber.

In some scenes you will be playing not only your own character, but the character in a scene being rehearsed. The demands on you will be compounded when, as you are rehearsing, the Forger appears and threatens that scene. Now how do you respond—as yourself being threatened, your own character, or as the character in the scene?

I was knocked over when Glenda Jackson, the night after dress rehearsal of *Marat/Sade*, presented me with her script. She was playing the part of Charlotte Corday. In looking through her notations and her breakdown of the script I saw she was playing on several levels of reality throughout the entire performance: the reality of insanity, the reality of the moment, the reality of everyday wash-and-scrub, et cetera.

We can work for that intensity here. This is an exercise. You've got to stretch a little bit. The preaching is over, the lesson's begun. Let it tap you. Extend from yourselves using your imaginations, all the accoutrements around you, people, props, wardrobe. Some scenes should be costumed. Go all the way.

You can, by the way, take a characterization or a monologue or a scene that you've already done here and adapt it into the scenario. Suppose the theft of scene four happens within the context of the manicure scene we saw the other day, and you have to interrupt the scene because there's been a theft.

PETE: A real theft, you mean?

NR: Right.

PETE: So it's multileveled.

NR: That's what I'm trying to tell you. Do you play the characters, or do you play yourselves? There's an interesting problem for an actor in my book.

I've invited John Houseman to visit our class tomorrow. Principally I want him to see what we're doing.

You'll be unlikely in your lifetimes to be in the company of anyone more influential, experienced, or renowned in as many different aspects of the media as John Houseman. If you do not believe me, act as if you did. Perhaps many of you know him only as an actor, an Academy Award winner for his role in *Paper Chase*. Houseman is also one of the great producers in theatre, radio, movies, and TV. He was the man behind Orson Welles and the Mercury Theatre. He reorganized the Juilliard School and formed the Actor's Company, sits on the board of directors of the Martha Graham Dance Company, and is now writing an autobiography.

LEONARD: What do you look for in a producer?

NR: The producer has one function, to service the director. The minute he violates that, the director is in trouble and usually so is the film.

A good producer knows the value of an argument, and how to argue accordingly.

NAT: Argue with whom?

NR: With me. He's a man who has some humility toward the material being made into a film, so I can call him at four in the morning to thrash things around. I was very fortunate in having Houseman as my first producer, although we argued violently. I kicked him off the stage once, about the second or third week of shooting, I don't remember why. I'm sure it was a perfectly honorable argument, but he was furious with me, and I refused to have anybody furious on the stage except me.

JAKE: How does the producer know where to draw the line between servicing the director and interfering?

NR: It helps if he has more than a bowing acquaintance with the budget forms of a production, if he knows the stink and feel and grip and sweat and hours of making a film. It helps if he can subjugate his own desires to be a director. This ability was particularly enviable and noble in Houseman, because he did want to direct, and had done very well directing in the theatre. There are very few good producers. Houseman was the best producer I ever had. For a while I believed that Houseman and I together could take the phone book and turn it into a Delacroix omelette.

I would like to photograph him, if he does not object, but without being at all obtrusive. I'd like to try to do it without making him self-conscious. Pete, would you handle that?

I have not bragged to him about the methodology of our class, but I have bragged about the manageability we have obtained, and I hope we are able to keep that going for the balance of the day and week. Instead of all this psychologizing, rationalizing, and yum yum yumming, remember you have something very concrete to work with. What is your action? What are you doing? What are you really doing?

Death and Children

My opening for *Doctor and the Devils*[60] was a little bit ahead of its time. Since then others, the Swedes and a couple of Americans imitating the Swedes, have taken up where Buster Keaton left off, beginning a story with the director, assistant director, and script clerk at the burial site of the man whose story they're about to tell. For this scene I played myself, Lucie Lichtig, the scriptclerk, played herself, my assistant played herself; and as we explored the cemetery, I kept watching the kids that came there day after day. Five of them were the children of the cemetery's caretaker, and they lived on the cemetery grounds. The others, aged from three to ten, were the children of neighbors.

Somebody expressed horror at kids playing in a cemetery, but I couldn't help but feel how healthy this could be: here were kids who were going to grow up without any illusions about death. These children would not believe all the fairy tales, or create importances for themselves beyond their abilities. They would know they could not win enduring life by whatever great deeds they accomplished, that they were going to die as surely as a criminal would die. Several times I had the inclination to write to the University of Zagreb to ask if somebody in their sociology department could check on those kids to see how they fared into their teens. What happens when you expose kids to one of the fundamental realities of life, instead of covering it over with petticoats and handkerchiefs?

---

60. From the Dylan Thomas scenario with the same title. NR oversaw extensive preparations for shooting the film in Yugoslavia, but the production fell through.

THE FORGER (CONT'D.)

[Sequence four of Macho Gazpacho, *"The Theft," is presented. The improvisation is based on a scene set in a beauty
parlor, the "manicure scene" NR cites in the previous class.]*

NR: This was a disaster, absolutely shameful. Nobody functioned.

The scene is a beauty parlor. Pete is the hairdresser; Molly, the
cleaning-up woman and ex-con; Mara, the manicurist; Jet, the pedicurist; and Charlotte, the Contessa.

What is the action of the pedicurist?

JET/Pedicurist: I want to go home with the Contessa, to get what I can
from her.

CHARLOTTE/Contessa: She wants to be my lover.

NR: All you had to do for this scene was establish the atmosphere, the
elements, the characters and actions of the employees of the beauty
parlor, into which the Contessa makes her entrance. What happened?
It all just fell apart. You went on for hours of nothing before the
Contessa arrived, and when she did arrive, she arrived into nothing,
she had no entrance. You lost your actions, your backstories. Molly,
you lost your adjustment, your sensitivity to being the ex-con and
charwoman; the cameraman lost the shot; the director lost the mise-
en-scène; and Pete, you were unbelievably bad. Everything went to
hell. It was wonderful. What was your action, Mara?

MARA/Manicurist: To wait for the Contessa.

NR: You chose as a backstory something to do with the cancer of your
mother, didn't you?

MARA: Yes, that she couldn't pay her hospital bill.

NR: So you wanted to get money from the Contessa through a gratuity or miracle of some kind to pay your mother's hospital bill. May I suggest to you that it is not for the scene or sequence a very usable action. To go after money for your dying mother's hospital bill may be legitimate, but not in these circumstances, unless everyone knows you're using the ploy on behalf of the group. The action you chose weighed you down and inhibited your contribution to the scene. Play the game; try to choose your action within the environment of the story in which you all are involved.

There is a group action, a conspiracy, to strip the Contessa, to expose the Contessa, to get rid of the Contessa, or to get as much from the Contessa as possible. The group may even have written and signed a contract in explicit recognition of the conspiracy. The group action is made up of individual actions. Why do I, Nick Ray, want to expose her? I have my own reason. It is the variety of individual reasons within the group action that gives color to the scene. There are so many ways to get rid of her.

We've seen evidence that the scene could work. It has a beginning, a middle, and an end. But Mara's choice of the wrong action caused a great big hole, and immobilized her to the point of tremendous discomfort. She was fighting the given circumstance. Sometimes that's very good, the circumstance can become a character: a flooded river becomes an obstacle that you have to cross. In this case, however, the scene just flattened out and became monotonous and repetitive. The scene should come to a climax with the arrival of the Contessa, when all the knifing in the back among the beauty parlor employees turns into obsequious geniality.

MOLLY/Cleaning-up Woman and Ex-con: I'm very confused about this ex-con character. I've got so many images and possibilities to draw on, it's hard to choose which will be the strongest.

NR: May I suggest something? Get the autobiography of Frances Farmer.[61] She spent eight years in state institutions for the insane, and admitted to every kind of crime, every kind of personal character difficulty—frigidity, ravings, tantrums, violence—everything except alcoholism. She experienced every kind of indignity. You may find something in there you can relate to.

Pete, where was your sense memory? You were massaging her hair without having wet it down. Where was the shampoo? Everything disappeared. Why did that happen?

---

61. Frances Farmer, *Will There Really Be a Morning?* (New York: Dell Publishing Company, Incorporated, 1973).

Come up here, Pete, and swing a golf club.

[PETER swings an imaginary club.]

Are you putting? Are you chipping? Let's see.

PETER: I'm not playing golf here.

NR: Not at all. You're indicating that you are.

PETER: I don't know how to play golf.

NR: The choice of an activity is terribly important, because through the activity you may arrive at the emotion. The emotion may go dry on you, because of an interruption in your preparation, for example. You may be so prepared that you are bursting with laughter, or bursting with tears, and then somebody comes up to you and asks, "Hey, you got a token for the subway?" But it's time to shoot the scene. Thank God you have an activity to help you pull things together. The selection of an activity is as important as the selection of an action.

Try the swing again, Pete.

[PETER swings.]

This time you're a little more credible because you followed through and kept your eye on the ball. When you putt, do you putt off the left foot, or from both feet? As a director you have to know. There's nothing a director must not know. And when as an actor you choose an activity, you better choose one you know something about. I have to believe you up there.

In my early training as an actor it was absolutely imperative, if you were going to play the part of a cabdriver, to get a job as a cabdriver. In making *They Live By Night*, instead of having two weeks of rehearsal, I put Cathy O'Donnell to work as a filling station attendant for two weeks, and rehearsed for five days. Your work as actors is not complete until you have researched the part you're going to play. Pete's biggest sin as an actor, as the hairdresser, was showing. He was acting at being a hairdresser. He perhaps could not conceive in his mind that he could be a homosexual, but if he had worked hard enough at it, investigated himself enough, I think he would have found some springboard into it. If not, he has the IF: *"If* I were a homosexual—"* What are the influences you would come under? Would you automatically be isolated from normal life?

Not too long ago I was shocked to be asked about an actor playing an unattractive role on T.V.: "But how could he play that part? Wouldn't he be embarrassed?" The person who asked that question was holding some image of the actor as just a glamourpuss affair; she had no idea of what acting is about. Pete, your assignment is to play a homosexual hairdre␣␣er. How can you play such a part? Mara, you've been asked to play a haughty, nymphomaniac, pretentious, horrid Contessa. What is your answer?

MARA: There are things about playing that part that I enjoy a lot.

NR: Molly, you're an ex-con who wipes her nose on her sleeve, picks between her toes. Your hair is filthy, you look like you slept in a doorway the night before. How can you possibly face playing that part every night?

MOLLY: It's my privilege to do that. I'm an actress.

NR: You're an actress.

BETTY: It's scary, but it's fun.

NR: Of course it is.

CHARLOTTE: I wouldn't always want to do something simple, something close to me. I'd want to have to stretch.

NR: But of course. There's only one caution, however, and this is why I recommend reading the section on the actor in *Myth of Sisyphus*.[62] When on your deathbed someone asks, "Who are you?" don't confuse yourself with Blanche, Nora, Julie, Frank, Marlon. Know you're Charlotte, Jake, Harry, Pete. How are you going to do that? By getting to know who you are.

This morning was wonderful, there were five rehearsals going on at the same time. For the balance of the day I want to see you very well organized, and everybody at work.

Let's do this scene again. Now perhaps the Ex-con/Cleaning-up Woman will steal the Contessa's purse and hide it in her mop bucket.

■ ■ ■

[The scene is set up, played, and shot again, and then screened for discussion.]

NR: Tell me, Harry, in your opinion, what happened during the improv?

HARRY: I felt the actors hadn't quite found their characters yet. I felt if we continued with the shooting, the actors' attitudes would intensify and their actions would solidify. But their actions kept changing, and got a little obscured. Somebody stole something and no one saw it, not even the victim. I was ducking under cameras, giving other cameras directions, giving cues to actors, and somebody stole some-

---

62. Albert Camus, *The Myth of Sisyphus and Other Essays* (New York: Random House, Incorporated, Vintage International, 1991).

thing and I missed it. I was the director, and I was watching the whole thing, and I missed it. I realize what I need to do is edit like crazy.

NR: The idea behind the scene was that a real theft would take place, right? How are you going to edit something when you don't even know if you've got it on film?

Here we had a perfect example of the director coming on the set and not knowing what's happening, either to him or to the scene. Harry, you must have a very clear and specific image of what you want before you come on the set so that once the scene is shot you can answer the questions: Has the content of the scene been realized? Does it satisfy you? Just as the actor has only himself to work with, so does the director have only himself, his own responses. You have to train your instrument and keep it in tune day by day, just like the actor.

Through improvisation this scene has taken on the structure of a short play. Various attitudes were developed among the characters, but those attitudes disintegrated to pointlessness because the actors' and director's actions were unclear, amorphous. Now I would like this scene done once more with the audience all around and participating, just as you did a while back with monologues—the director always holds some sinister trap in mind. The audience should see the ex-con steal the purse, no matter how she does it. And over here, paying the bill with a phony check and buying a wig for his wife, is the Forger, whom we don't yet know as the Forger. He sees the ex-con ripping off the Contessa, and blackmails her.

MOLLY: What does the Forger want from her?

NR: I don't know. I don't know if it'll work, but it's a possibility around which the group can take on an action.

What kind of action can we have for the group? What kind of image can we have?

LEONARD: We're the gods.

NR: The gods? You are the gods. Not bad. I had thought of baby vultures. Have you ever seen the baby vultures along the Tamiyami Trail? There's a big stretch of highway in Florida, and at a certain time of year the trees alongside it are loaded with baby vultures. At first they look kind of endearing, but within them is infinite corruption. The Contessa is good prey for baby vultures. The audience shall be baby vultures out to get the Contessa. If you have some particular evil thought in mind, tell the hairdresser, the pedicurist, or the manicurist. Put your thoughts into their inner monologues. Stick like an evil conscience to the characters in the improv. Try to understand what they are really playing, what they are really saying, what they are really hiding, what you think they are really feeling, and make them say it. Speak any observation, any feeling you may have. A couple of you could align with the Contessa, but it would be more interesting if you were evil against her, and told her exactly the wrong thing to say.

■   ■   ■

[The actors run through the scene once more—with some additional and unexpected adjustments.]

NR: Come up here for a moment, will you, Charlotte? I want to try to illustrate what I mean by a beat.

[NR guides her in a clockwise circle around some chairs facing the audience.]

Pete comes and rescues you from the fray, right? And as he does, he takes you around to join Molly, who's seated and waiting for comments from the class. Here [at two o'clock] there has to be something, a specific memory or sensation, that pulls you out of the role of the Contessa. It changes your rhythm, and so the transition is made from one level, at which you play the Contessa under attack in a beauty shop, to another that's completely different, at which there is receptivity, curiosity—and you're back in the classroom. Then something else will happen which can bring you to yet another level. In order to make these transitions, actions and beats are very important for you to understand.

In constructing an improvisation it is very often necessary and advisable for the person directing to have a surprise that he can inject into the scene as a catalyst to bring the individual actions and the conflict together. When the Contessa was flattening out, I pulled Tando and Paolo aside and told them, "Go on in, strip her, destroy her." In fulfilling that action they helped bring about the hysteria, the popping of Charlotte's contact lens, and the climax of the scene. It was a very cruel way of doing it, but I chose people with whom I had worked previously, whom I knew to have some experience in control, and who would understand this as an acting adjustment, and not just the opportunity to vent loose aggressions.

It's your obligation as director to help the actors contribute, to maintain their energies. You must be prepared and remain in control. This does not mean scarring the people working with you. Your authority generally is best maintained through your ability to stimulate the imaginations and respective interests of the people involved, all of which gain focus through you, so in this way you are, at worst, a benevolent dictator.

In this case a lucky accident of reality intruded: Charlotte lost her contact lens. A moment of energy came into the scene, a moment of life. I didn't know she wore contact lenses, and even if I had, I would not have counted on her being able to pop one on cue.

The accident was an experience within the improvisation, and so it becomes a beat for Charlotte to work for in performance. The value and purpose of the improvisation, to develop a performance and help the actor contribute, has been realized. Now she must confront the same problem she had when she made her late entrance to class: how does she re-create that accident of reality? The popping of the lens must become a part of her equipment, her sense and affective memories. In her preparation she must work to get that moment back, beginning with the specifics, the feeling, the fear.

SAM: It seems to me in this instance the power of reality can't be reconstructed because it owes so much to the event not having been planned. She could do something similar, but not the same.

NR: But that's the actress's problem, Sam.

SAM: Is it her problem, or the director's?

NR: It is the director's problem in that he must know the actor's techniques, having practiced them himself as an actor, in order to help her recapture that moment and use it.

I Hate a Script[63]

I hate a script. I resent a script. It's inevitable that I'm going to fight with the script, no matter how I choose it. The script represents authority, and I resent authority, it's a flaw in my character. So what do I do? I tell myself, I have to live with it. But I don't have to live with it. I have to confront it, I have to work on it. In choosing a script I work on it if I don't like it to see if I like it, or I work on it if I like it to see if I'm crazy and should reject it instead. I select a script from instinct, from intuition, from a combination of some knowledge and experience, and because it interests me. I've had very few good scripts, although for the period during which I worked in Hollywood I was lucky that one out of every four films I did was a film I wanted to do.

Sometimes a good script seems very important, despite the relatively minor role words play in a film. The script provides a foundation for improvisation. The script allows me to know and have on paper what I want, so I can communicate it with facility to the other people with whom I'm working. Sometimes I feel lazy and would like to have it all there in front of me, but the tightest scripts I've worked with have not turned into my best films. The celluloid strip is not made in the writer's studio.

The first major script I wrote all by myself was called *Savage Innocents*, a film about Eskimos. When I finished that script I thought I

---

63. Revised from the piece, "Story into Script," *Sight and Sound*, August 1956.

had about as good a piece of film writing as I'd had so far in my career. But I'd written two climaxes without realizing it, and had to shoot both about 700 miles south of the North Pole, at around 50 to 60 degrees below zero. It's very expensive to make a mistake like that. I have had to change every script I've written myself wherever I've not anticipated in my study the things that happen on a set. I'd have fired myself a half-dozen times if I'd really expected to do what I had written out so carefully. It's an entirely different world when you get away from the typewriter, when you get out into the atmosphere where there are a hundred people putting everything together, from accountants to truck drivers to camera loaders to late actors—not to mention the weather. As fertile and multifaceted as my imagination may or may not be, I cannot control the elements. On *Johnny Guitar*, which I was producing as well as directing, I spent half a day balancing my will as producer to get on with it against the appearances of the sun. Because there are certain times when the sun becomes the director, when I'm not the director at all.

And new ideas come up all the time. Actors bring you ideas. Who are you working with, after all? You are working with people. You have to find out who they are so you can use them, the materials within them, their experiences, so you don't have somebody up there just saying lines. But these are factors most screenwriters find difficult to accept or understand.

So there is a traditional writer-director hostility in Hollywood, and it is a unique kind of hostility. Basically, each resents his dependence on the other. The writer needs the director for his story to be realized; the director needs the writer to give him a story in a form he can realize.

From this situation springs a good deal of misunderstanding and bitterness. The writer claims that his creative contribution is underestimated—the director and stars nearly always receive more publicity and acclaim than he, and yet hasn't he created the characters and the story, written the dialogue and evolved the structure?

If the writer's case were as simple as this, he would be the most ill-treated professional in the film industry. Unfortunately for him, it is not. First, there are perhaps a half-dozen first-rate writers in Hollywood. Most outstanding creative writers will prefer literature or the drama, to which their contribution creates no ambiguity. The famous novelists who come to Hollywood and write scripts seldom arrive with an open mind about the new medium they are exploring, and seldom learn very much about it. Nearly all of them return with an ironic, rueful image of the monstrous director or producer. The writer, they claim, is not *understood*.

In the same way, a few writers who have attained fame and influence in Hollywood will turn to direction in order, they claim, to preserve the integrity of their scripts. This is an admirable theory, but on the whole a deplorable practice. To bring it off requires the exceptional talent of a John Huston or a Preston Sturges at their best. There are many writers-directors whose films are unsatisfactory precisely because they overestimate the writer and underestimate the director. The writer-director is much too indulgent to the writer, reluctant to cut a word of that brilliant dialogue, a sentence of that verbose scene; but the too specific setting down of patterns or talk can thwart the freedom which the director must feel. This kind of freedom I've never heard anybody talk about.

The most talented Hollywood writers are those who recognize the special nature of writing for the movies and acknowledge the creative claims of the director. ("One of the functions of the director," says Gilbert Seldes in *The Movies Come from America*,[64] "is to save us from the writer enamored of his own wit; another is to save us from the players enamored of their own personality; and a third is to save us from the producers . . .") This involves, sometimes, a difficult kind of abnegation for the writer, who is working in a medium in which the image, and not the word, has the final impact. "It was all in the script," a disillusioned writer will tell you. But it was never all in the script. If it were, why make the movie?

There is a revealing story told in this connection by the German director Fritz Lang. When he made his first Hollywood film, *Fury*, in 1935, he knew about thirty words of English. The brilliant picture that emerged was considered too controversial and disturbing by a distinguished front office executive. Irately he summoned Lang to his office and accused him of having changed the script. Lang replied that his lack of English made this impossible; comparing the script with the finished film, he showed that not a line of dialogue nor a situation had been changed. All the same, the executive complained, the film was entirely different from the script.

I can't start a piece of work unless I know what I want to say. I keep that in mind as long as I can, and then something comes along to change it. In relation to the reality of making a film the script is

64. Gilbert Seldes, *The Movies Come from America*, ed. Garth S. Jowett (Salem, New Hampshire: Ayer Company Publishers, Incorporated, 1978).

nothing more than a theory, a theory which will be modified in the making and execution of the blueprint that comes from the theory and embraces all the logistics, finances, and other practicalities. The theory will be further modified by the editing and lab work—in its adequacy or inadequacy, or in the imaginative application of technical facilities. Then the theory will be expressed in perhaps an entirely different way in the advertising campaign and the film's distribution, and then still further modified, or maybe heightened, by the audience reception in the theatres, where for the first time the theory becomes a living entity.

The elements of a film or story will have formed a pattern before the director or scriptwriter begins to interrupt it. The director of a film or the author of a script finds the story already in progress, either in his imagination or when he goes home to dare face an empty sheet of paper for the first time. At that moment he interrupts the flow of history, he interrupts his characters in their given circumstances. A more productive, less shattering, way of looking at it is that the dynamics of a script in preparation or in production are such that at a certain point it takes on a life of its own, and the director or writer had better just follow that, forget his own rigid line, and let life grow and breathe—and kids grow up in spite of us. I recommend one chapter in a book by John Howard Lawson, *The Theory and Technique of Playwriting*.[65] It's a short chapter: "Unity in Terms of Climax."

Starting from an original idea, the tendency of most writers is to make it "literary," to present a situation primarily in terms of dialogue. The theatre is literary; film is not. So the director has to fight against this, and the result is often to make the writer accuse him of being illiterate. There may be a scene in which a writer is especially proud of his dialogue, it may be good dialogue; but what is really needed for the scene is not good dialogue but a visual conception, and the dialogue just has to go. What replaces it may seem, to the writer, banal—and here another misunderstanding can arise.

Someone remarked that a fundamental tenet of Stanislavsky's system is to help an actor say "What time is it?" and mean one of maybe twenty different things: "I want to leave" or "I want to stay," "I love you" or "I hate you," "I'm worried" or "I don't care," and so on. In this sense even the most apparently banal line of dialogue can achieve dramatic meaning through the inner moment, the state of being and

---

65. John Howard Lawson, *Theory and Technique of Playwriting* (New York: G.P. Putnam's, 1936).

the urgent need. Only the director is in a position to help the actor create this effect.

If writers were able to work more closely with directors from the beginning of a film's conception, the results and the mutual understanding would improve. The director must reinforce the writer, provide visually that which the writer doesn't give him in content. Writers as a rule are afraid of writing head-on conflict and climax; they're afraid of blowing the works, that they won't have enough imagination to create a new complex or conflict once the elements of the old one are fully played out. Every scene of tension, or every scene of comedy, has a given circumstance from which conflict grows. But at this point most writers tend to dribble off, rattle on with meaningless stuff, take up space so they can turn in their five pages a day. Very few writers have ever been on a set. They don't know the demands of the camera, they don't know the demands of the overall situation. It is the director who has to find all the properties of camera, relations to space, time and people, to create a given circumstance that is vital enough that the audience can sense it, and know there's a tension or relaxation—even if they come in in the middle of a scene. That's the only way the director can really help the author, and he doesn't necessarily do it politely. The whole process of film is catching the essence of a moment, and keeping that alive.

WRAP-UP

[For their last session together, NICK has had the students pre-pare and screen an assemblage of short clips from film shot during the previous weeks of class.]

NR: I certainly don't have any organized recapitulation of the experience we've had these past weeks.

The nature of our work together has been fairly experimental, and so some people necessarily have suffered some falls, but in this profession people are always going to have to suffer some falls. I'd hoped by having you put together those bits of film you enjoyed, without explanation, apology, or discussion, you'd see a collage of rather intensive work and growth within this group.

We learned something about the eyes: that you talk with your eyes, you talk with thought. We discussed the fact that a person can be seated in a chair, completely immobile, and command more attention than if he were running all over the set. You picked up any number of little devices just by being together on the hot stage, bumping into each other, with four rehearsals going on at one time. Once during a major political demonstration I walked into the organizers' office, and there were seven televisions televising three different speeches, while people were at their desks doing artwork, making phone calls, writing news releases. The concentration in each person there was total, because each person knew what he wanted to do. It didn't bother me at all that a group of you had to rehearse upstage, another downstage, and another on the stairwell—I thought it was beautiful.

There was no need for complaint about lack of space: when you've got something to do, you can do it.

We learned quite a bit about containment, about the choice and importance of objects and activities. We explored the difference between doing a monologue on stage and on film.

I'd say we almost achieved real manageability. There's a little ways to go yet, but to the extent that you each experienced working as crew, director, and actor, you gradually began to appreciate one another. And there's been a minimum of gossip, that element so destructive in groups.

I found the experience to be ultimately exciting, depressing, despairing, prideful, hopeful, hopeless—I don't care that we never finished the scenario as long as each of you took part in a sequence.

How do you feel?

CHARLOTTE: I felt in a state of limbo through the whole *Macho Gazpacho* exercise. There was so much intellectual stuff going on in terms of the concept of the piece, I felt it a waste of time.

NR: It is true that we improvised scenes out of continuity that eventually would have to relate to one another, and that made for some confusion. But the confusion has to be dealt with. On a soundstage it will be a thousand times worse. You will be in the dark constantly. It is a problem for the director; but your irritation with it as an actor makes it a problem for you as well.

CHARLOTTE: But *no* one seemed to know what was going on.

NR: Does anyone else feel the same way?

MOLLY: I felt extremely confused without a story to follow, shooting the exercises, and doing so much of the work in improvisation. I felt very frustrated at the lack of structure.

NR: It showed in the acting, but that's still no excuse for your not finding an action.

MOLLY: I'm not excusing that—

NR: Nor for your not being able to carry through on your action.

Suppose you are working on a documentary, how do you handle that? Do you suppose you will be given lines? You won't see a scenario, you won't even see an outline, but you still will have to find your actions. I think this exercise was badly needed.

Don't believe for a moment that if you get on a Hollywood set it will be all honeypie and roses, that you'll be in a situation of continuity, control, and daily satisfaction. In my career I've had maybe four scripts completed before I began shooting. On *55 Days to Peking* the writers worked at night to come up with the scenes we'd shoot the next morning. Ava Gardner, David Niven, and Charlton Heston, pretty high-priced actors, had to wander their way through. I began *Lusty Men* with seventeen pages of script, with Mitchum, Susan Hayward, and Arthur Kennedy.

Whether this scenario was realized with any perfection at all is not important. We were not working for perfection. The scenario was a resource for the daily problems directors and actors face on a set. That the directors were overtalking came from insecurity, but that insecurity diminished as their experience increased.

We are in a learning process. It is not to be measured by the satisfaction you derive from an individual scene according to traditional drama school techniques established largely for the convenience of their teachers. It would be a breeze, believe me, to keep giving you monologues and scenes, and let you regurgitate that old hash day after day, one script after another, but you wouldn't stretch a single muscle. If it was too uncomfortable for you this way, you had an option, but I'd have done you no favor by conceding to your discomfort. You've got to learn how to wing it, not only as directors, but as actors as well.

ERICA: Especially in the beginning when we were told this wasn't a documentary, we were not to be ourselves, we were to play ourselves, I was very confused as to where life and the story merged, and where they separated.

NR: Would anyone like to answer that? . . .

It may be a question of wording. What was meant was that you start with yourself. Whether you're playing Caligula, or a member of the cabinet of Caligari, you start with yourself.

Michael Redgrave told me that Noel Coward, certainly one of the finest playwrights of comedies of manners in this century, always insisted his actors come to their first rehearsal with all their lines letter-perfect. Why? He wanted to get the lines out of the way so he could begin creating. Now it was he who had written those lines, yet he took them as only an outline. The real life of the play had to come through the people who were playing it.

In Wim Wenders's film I played the part of a quasi-forger, not in the strictest sense of forger as one who signs another's name, but forger as one who manipulates anonymity. I played a painter whose early works were found by an entrepreneur to resemble those of the English artist, Turner. The entrepreneur found a market where, under a cloak of mystery and anonymity, he could sell a couple of the paintings for five thousand dollars and ten thousand dollars. He came back for two more and sold those for twenty thousand dollars and twenty-five thousand dollars. In writing a letter to Wim this past weekend I found myself relating an experience I'd had with an actor, and so upon writing the letter I looked again at a book one of you got for me from the library, *The Criminal Mind*.

I want to read you a sampling from two or three letters from a forger. He says: "The more you give of yourself and the more you really reveal, the less people know about you. Maybe that's why some people call me mysterious." Then: "Please forgive me, no one has ever done anything to me that I didn't let them. My problem is what I do to myself." Familiar ring?

And then: "I've been a preacher, a millionaire, a teacher, a bum, a musician, an actor, an addict, a convict, and a prick, and if I haven't learned to fight by now, I'm also a pile of shit. We have exercise equipment in here"—that's federal prison—"and I rode the bicycle twelve miles today, jogged five miles on the treadmill, did sit-ups on the slant board, and lifted some weights. I'm training like a fighter, because no one is going to dust me without one helluva fight."

From an earlier letter:

Out of all the people I have known, worked with and helped in my lifetime, I can't get five thousand dollars to save my life. I have not told you everything about my life, so you think what I say is all fantasy. Let me tell you what is not fantasy. If I do not bail out this week, I am dead, and I mean literally. If you get me out, I will get you five thousand immediately. I will pay you ten thousand dollars for your help above and beyond that. I would have done this anyway if I had known you needed it. Call me a prick, a con man, anything you wish to believe, but I have never let a friend down . . .

In God's name, help. I'm in the twilight zone. I'm telling the truth. I have only conned where I have had to for survival . . . I've had to con some people who eventually became my friends, but never after they became my friends.

The fellow was sprung from the federal penitentiary a few weeks later. And he who never let a friend down was loaned some cash during his few days out, and while he was going to pay five thousand dollars, and ten thousand dollars, et cetera, et cetera, he did not pay back even a small amount of get-around money.

These are the facts of the forger. Preacher? Absolutely. Musician? Absolutely. Actor? Absolutely. And lots more. So many facades, credit cards, names of other people. He didn't know or own his own. As an actor he had great potential, but not a chance in the world, for he could never get in touch with himself. I think it's important for us now, on the last day of class and our work with *Macho Gazpacho*, to know that it was based on some reality. Don't forget the reality of the Forger.

The choices you make in living your lives are the realities of building a character. Evasions of reality and the taking on of high-blown theories can only lead to nonrealization of function and purpose in your daily lives, and they can only lead to emasculation of your scenes and ideas in your professional lives as directors. You don't have a chance unless you do the nitty-gritty. It would be beautiful if it were otherwise. It would be beautiful if we could all just sit and wait for that divine moment of inspiration, but most of us poor suckers can't get away with that. At least we're not running for our lives. At least we have a chance—to breathe, walk freely, and learn those ABC tools that can liberate us and make us available for those wonderful moments of exultation in living and in acting.

There is not much separation between an action in life and an action in the theatre.

Written but not sent to Wim Wenders

7 May 1977

My dear Wim:

... Not long ago a male actor, aged 35, with whom I had great difficulty in stripping him down to his essential reality, was arrested by the FBI and put in prison for forgery. He was from the Midwest, his father was a lawyer. He was graduated from university with degrees in psychology and theology. He had been the pastor of a midwestern church, a musician (trumpet), owned two jazz and soul nightclubs, formed and owned an advertising agency, and already spent one-and-a-half years in a California prison on an earlier conviction of forgery.

At this moment he is again a fugitive, having jumped bail, and I receive phone calls from unknown places as if from a miscreant son. When he told me he was afraid the FBI was closing in on him, and for what reason, I began doing research on the criminal mind, the forger's mind in particular. It is work I should have done as preparation for your film, which I now wish I could do all over again.

No wonder I had difficulty getting him to work from himself outwards. Like most actors he can't recognize who he is. But now, a strange contradiction: once again a fugitive, he seems to be continuing the work we were doing together, and some of his communications have the ferocity of a man clawing at himself. Or has he added a new front? How fateful! I have become the forged father of a forger. ...

199

Written but not sent to a forger

Jeff:

If you recall, I tried to make a serious point of the difference between the actor's (teacher's, director's) use of the word *intention* and the word *action*. Unhappily, my position in relation to you reflects the merit in that observation. God knows my intention to help you has been (and is) strong, honorable, and sincere. My action has been halting, interrupted, and confused. The most likely reason for this? The backstory never came together! Contradictions could not and still cannot be resolved. Self-interest is threatened. You are the center of your universe. It cannot be a surprise to you that you are not the center of mine, even though your interests have been central to me many of the past two hundred hours.

You say you have read much about me. It is possible that in one of the articles you learned that I was one of those people whom H. Hughes (whom I admired, respected, may even have loved) could not buy. The people Howard manipulated with money finally didn't even provide him with the kidney machine that he helped invent.

I don't want to see you go to prison. It didn't help you very much the last time, and I'm convinced that our penal system stinks, and our judiciary is sorely wanting. But I cannot change them. I cannot change a fact—or a fantasy.

In transmitting information to me, or to anyone else trying to help you, please try to make it pull together, now and in the future. I am confused, frustrated, and without any possible avenue into "I want to _____, because _____, etc.," and am therefore unhelpful, but still hopeful that the image and the reality will come together for you. A very big and talented part of you is sure as hell capable of moving in that direction. And I remain yrs.

P.S. "Forgive me, I grovel before your talent, I'd gladly give you ten years of my life, but I cannot let you have the horses."

—Shamraev, *The Sea Gull*, Act II[66]

---

66. Anton Chekhov, *The Sea Gull*, trans. Ann Jellicoe, ed. Henry Popkin (New York: Avon Books, 1975).

We Can't Go Home Again

*[The following was written by NR around a photographic
plate of Pablo Picasso's painting, "*Minotaur Moving His
House," *as it appeared in* Picasso's Picassos, *by David Douglas Duncan.*[67]*]*

   Upon this soiled and dampened, snow-salt-sprinkled page, lit by a
500-watt and a 300-watt lamp, the old man trained a Bolex at eight
inches in order to produce a scene of death and resurrection in positive terms of symphonic resolution which would, if ever resolved into
cinematic frames, proclaim to hell with death, and life is change, do
not fear the fog, the certain fog, nor the fog within and around you.
The young priest stood to the left behind the heaviest wattage, unpho-
tographable unless the lamps and camera, which were pointed downwards onto this minotaur of self in turmoil, were suddenly, miracu-
lously, dexterously, turned in an opposite direction. And the young
priest exploded, threw a mug of brew against the wall, scattering
shattered remnants, and said, "Why don't you learn to shut up once
in a while?" And the old man, whose turmoil continues as he writes
and brushes the snow-salt off the drying page, watched his favored
student with astonishment because he had not yet learned that a
camera pointing downwards on this printed page could not simul-

---

67. (New York and Evanston: Harper & Row, Production Edita).

taneously point upwards to accommodate his declaiming, "I don't want to be photographed or think about this film any longer. I want to go!" —"So go, you fool, why don't you! Go!"

The young priest stumbled left and stumbled right and mumbled, "Where's my coat?" And the old man said, "There!" And so the young priest left as the girl who had been in capricious mood and overt loving with his closest friend came giggling into the shattered, scattered, slammed-upon room with her stupefied lover at her side.

The old turbulent character who was frantically sponging spray from the flying mug off these cherished pages had set his camera down, and using his born-with eye said, "Until now nobody had a monopoly on insensitivity. I congratulate you! Get out of here! Now! Split!" And the young lady said, "You are right." The garage door slammed. She again said, "You are right!" The stupefied one left with her, and the garage door slammed again, and the minotaur heard echoes of the priest's name being called. But in seconds the door of the VW was slammed shut, the motor started, gears shifted. Tires sounded their rubber on the black dead-ending circle of a road, and the old one looked at his companion of the page and wrote this to Susan; and then went out and put a bright light above the slammed door of the garage and waited—but only for a moment, perhaps a moment more or less—before calling his love for comfort. He called but could not call. His guts and churning hope for life with purpose lay with the crockery that shattered around his feet when the young priest could no longer stand the sound of young lovers loving.

But why did you negate, fail to express, your own identity at this moment of the film?

■　■　■

A film director long discontent with life in the capitol of the dream merchants had retired from the scene to find refuge in the dunes of an island in the North Sea. But his escape was interrupted by two young attractive con artists who brought him back to the scenes of conflict in the streets and federal court of Chicago.

He fell in love, and since by this time his fortunes had lapsed (collapsed), he had to make some money. His lady took a job in New York, and they sloshed through the sleety streets of the city trying to put the Chicago film and sound together on nothing but energy. There was no recourse for the director except to take a job as professor of cinema in an upstate college, to which he traveled with full intention of growing a goatee, buying a crooked cane, walking a crooked mile, and impressing his students with his rhetoric and ponderosity, meanwhile completing his autobiography.

Something had changed, however. The students had also retired from the conflicts of the late '60s, and submerged themselves in what they thought a safe and serene womb, where no outside voices could be heard, least of all that of a Hollywood director.

One night, as school was just beginning, three students tumbled into the quarters of the new professor. The professor-director concentrated on de-imagizing himself as a Hollywood director successfully enough to gain the confidence of his students. They began to bring him their thoughts and problems, and he transposed them into scenes, asking their approval to film them, and they agreed.

The result is a documentation, not a documentary, a feature-length color film of the history of our youth during the past few years.

The lead actors are Tom Farrell, Leslie Levinson, Richard Bock, and myself, with a number of supporting roles. Typical of my generation, I play the part of a betrayer.

It is a film of large scope, in terms of people and spectacle, shot at a 166/1 ratio with very primitive equipment, student camerawork, grip work, gaffers, and everything else.

It is a departure in filmmaking, a multiple-image show, making use of Nam June Paik's video synthesizer and resting on the concept that we don't think in straight lines, and that the celluloid strip recognizes neither time nor space, only the limit's of man's imagination.

1973

Lightning Over Water[68]

[An exchange between Nick, Wim Wenders, Gerry Bamman, and Susan a few days after shooting on Lightning Over Water *had begun in March 1979.]*

NR: Refresh my memory of the time around the first operation. Was I expecting to die?

GB: I don't have any real strong recollection of our talking about dying, but in the period before that first operation I remember your being very, very aggressive about exploring and exploiting every possibility that existed for survival. You sent me to research your doctor, because he had blue eyes and red hair. Do you remember sending me to research the possibility that people with blue eyes and red hair would be prone to panic in moments of crisis? I actually did it, and

---

68. Taken from the *I Ching*, "WEI CHI/Before Completion":

Fire over water:
The image of the condition before transition . . .

. . . The task is great and full of responsibility. . . . At first . . . one must move warily, like an old fox walking over ice. The caution of a fox walking over ice is proverbial in China. His ears are constantly alert to the cracking of the ice, as he carefully and circumspectly searches out the safest spots. A young fox who as yet has not acquired this caution goes ahead boldly, and it may happen that he falls in and gets his tail wet when he is almost across the water. (Richard Wilhelm, trans., *I Ching* [Princeton: Princeton University Press, 1983], p. 248).

was assured that there was no known correlation between psychological weakness and those physical characteristics.

WW: But can you trust these sources?

GB: They were the best I could find.

WW: They weren't blue-eyed themselves?

GB: And then I remember the conversation you had with that doctor about everybody liking him. Do you remember that?

SR: You asked the doctor, "Everybody likes you, but are you bold? Will you take chances?"

NR: Yeah, I made a big thing of that.

GB: I remember you let me read a page in the journal, and I remember something in there about how on the way to the hospital the taxi driver caught your eye in the mirror, and you said to yourself, "What the fuck is he looking at me like that for? Does he think I'm going to die?" That was written, but you never talked about that.

[Susan reads from Nick's journal.]

WW: Do you remember having written that?

NR: Parts of it.

WW: I've reread diaries from the time when I was really in trouble. I didn't remember a single word. It wasn't me that had written them.

NR: I didn't remember a word of this until Susan began reading it. Strange.

WW: It is almost as if the very act of writing it was what it was all about, and not even what it meant, just writing it down.

SR: Writing like breathing.

WW: I think there's nothing more calming than writing something down, writing one's thoughts about it. I think it's the best cure for anything, for any kind of fear.

How close were you to Bogart? Did you see him until the very end, when he died?

NR: No. I went to Europe. I called Betty [Lauren Bacall] and asked how he was, and she said, "You were the first one he asked about. He asked, 'Where the hell is Nick?' I told him you were here when they brought him from the hospital." And she said, "When are you going to Africa?" I said, "Day after tomorrow." She said, "When are you coming back?" I said, "I don't know, five, six months." She said, "Oh Christ, all of us will be dead by then." And that was it.

Gerry, what other stuff do you remember now?

WW: Why do you want to remember this especially, this first operation?

NR: Well, I feel it was a kind of important event in my life.

WW: More than the second or the third one were?
NR: No. Maybe. I don't know. Values like that have disappeared.
SR: The second operation was described to you by Dr. W. as "a great adventure."
WW: It was the implantation,[69] yeah? I remember, Nick, that you asked me whether you should have this operation done or not, because it was such an adventure, and I didn't know how to answer. Then you said yourself you had been an adventurer all your life, which answered it. And you still are, I think.
NR: Still am what?
WW: An adventurer.
NR: On the adventure?
SR: That too.
WW: That too, yeah.
SR: It was pretty intense around the time of the brain tumor, because the pressure of it created a kind of dislocation in your thinking, but instead of being really dislocated you were just a lot purer. I remember one night when I called you to say goodnight you were very upset, and I came up to the hospital around midnight. You said you had been seeing the face of your mother. You wrote about it.
WW: When did your mother die? How old were you?
NR: 51, I think.

[Susan reads the section from Nick's journal.]

NR: Go on.
SR: That was all. Would you like a piece of that steak? You said you wanted a steak, and Wim's got a steak.

[Wim gives Nick some steak.]

GB: Then there was the time later on when you were very depressed. It was the only other time that I can remember our specifically talking about dying. You were very worried about not being lucid, and you were asking me how your thinking compared to the time after the first operation. I asked you if you were thinking about dying, and the only thing you said to me was, "How can you think about *nothing?*"
     Of course backgammon was also a measure of your health.
WW: Yeah?
GB: When you were back into competitive fettle you were obviously

---

69. Nick endured three major surgeries, two on the lung, in December 1977 and April 1978, and one on the brain, in May 1978. The second procedure entailed implanting radioactive seeds to shrink the lung tumor.

in better health than when you were unable to concentrate long enough to make a move.

WW: Actually, Nick has been having a strain of bad luck lately, he lost a couple of games in a row.

WW: When's the last time you played poker?

SR: Right before the second operation. I happen to remember because he lost all the grocery money.

WW: Did I tell you I spent three days and three nights in Reno in order to learn how to play? It cost me two thousand bucks, but I do play some good six-card stud now.

SR: Do they play six-card stud?

WW: Seven is too much cards, and five-card is just too heavy. Five-card, you've gotta be rich.

GB: You know that's how Nick and I met, don't you?

WW: No.

GB: Poker. A friend of ours brought Nick into a game that I held every once in a while, and he said, "Listen there's this friend of mine who wants to play, and he doesn't have any money, but he really wants to play, but we can't be too tough on him." And he came in and won almost a thousand dollars and walked away, this poor old man that we were supposed to feel sorry for.

WW: That's what happened to me in Reno. I was playing at this table, it wasn't big stakes. I was playing at this table with seven guys, I had eighty bucks, but I was good. I started at twenty, that was the minimum stakes. I won eighty, slowly, and these two old ladies came in, with these fancy hats and all this makeup, making some silly jokes, asking, "What kind of a game is that?" and asking what the rules were. They only had the minimum entry together, so the dealer asked, "Is it okay with you gentlemen if these ladies play?" And everyone said yes. They had these little stakes in front of them, and everybody else had ten times more. And so one of them, the funny one who kept talking and making jokes about baseball and football, won the first pot, and everybody was happy, so she had a little bit higher stakes in front of her, and then she won ten in a row. She ripped everybody off. Everybody. I sat until the very end. I had three hands where I was up against her, and she always had a better hand. Three times. I must have lost two hundred. I learned a lot about the game.

Do you feel, Nick, as if we should try a scene today, or should we do it tomorrow and talk about it some more?

NR: Well, because you phrase the question the way you do, you make me think that you know less about acting than you think you do. And

I don't think that's true, but it is not fortunate phrasing. I cannot approach answering this question without—

WW: In a way I thought I would end this scene just by your asking the question,[70] and then we would cut to some words, either outside or maybe sitting somewhere, and talk about that. I didn't mean for you to answer it right in this scene.

NR: Right. And I don't want to answer it right here in this scene, and—

WW: Maybe I shouldn't ask you then, at all.

NR: This is why I'm trying to twist it around. I'm learning primary things about acting every day that we're working. I have talked about the importance of the inner meaning of the word *action* for some two months among some people, two years among other people. I ask them to play their action and they don't know what the hell I'm talking about. When I said after the second day of working on this film that once again I'd learned something, what I had learned again was that action is the most helpful, most meaningful tool I can find in the vocabulary of this profession. And every time I hear Pat[71] or you or the cameraman saying, "Put your arm a little more that way, your head a little more that way," I want to ask you, "What is the scene about?" No one ever starts off by saying what the hell the scene is about.

Now I don't think everybody has to work my way, I think it would be disastrous if everybody worked my way. But I know that when they do by mistake employ this method, they immediately become about five times better.

The reason I was better in the last take tonight than in any other take today was for that reason alone. It gave me my footing, it gave me my comfort.

We are working under tremendous pressure. Or everybody else is. I think I am working under less pressure than anybody else, because, in spite of all these verbotens that you have verbote, I can find your method absolutely acceptable.

WW: There is something, you know, that is not acceptable for me in my own method, and I'm kind of helpless about it. And you were talking about it a little bit earlier when you said that the important thing is what the scene is about.

NR: Right.

---

70. "Why did you come here, Wim?"
71. Pat Kirk, assistant to the directors.

WW: I find myself more and more at a dead end where I realize that I'm more interested in what the scene looks like, and whether the light is right and the frame is right, and I don't know what to do against this.

NR: Well, try answering all the questions: What is the scene about? down to, What is the character about? What does the character want? But first try to answer, What are *you* about in this? What do *you* want in this? It'll take you a little more time, but you're going to find it gives you solid ground to step on. And if things don't go right, you change them, or help the character change them. And don't be afraid of making a mistake with them, or of others making a mistake. The moment I feel that you know what the scene is about, you know, I can move freely. I've never known that so clearly before.

You've heard me say that if you find a natural among actors, fuck acting. If you find a natural among directors, fuck directing. So many directors direct in order to impress others that they are directing—

WW: Sure, yeah. So many with the experience of it lose being naturals, and I feel right now that I'm not a natural anymore. I'm not as comfortable with myself, and you, and any other actor, as I was when we were shooting *The American Friend*. Obviously it's something you can lose.

SR: I don't know that being comfortable has so much to do with how well you are functioning.

GB: I certainly don't know Wim that well, but I've seen it in other directors, and I've certainly seen it in actors. The temptation is always there to deal with something that's more secure, more tangible than the most central question. In acting, almost always the first tendency is to try to find the easy answer, and if you allow yourself to do that you can get lost.

WW: In filmmaking, making images instead of people work is an easy way out. I'm doing that. So obviously the ideal is the image works and the people inside it.

NR: And they both work together, and they both work separately.

WW: That's what I learned from looking at *We Can't Go Home Again*, because the image doesn't count at all in there, or it counts on a different, totally different level, with all that split-screen and everything. It's like the opposite of what I am doing with framing and lighting. And there are some things, like Tom shaving his beard, that I could never get on screen with my kind of work. And the relations between those images you had is something I could never get on film. Well, not with my way.

NR: Not with your way. You know, I reluctantly quote Kazan very often, reluctantly because I now think I'm a better director than he is, but I think he's a more alert and ruthless mind than I am. I remember the first time he said to a group of us, "Use whatever works, for chrissake!" And to that extent I'm a pragmatist.

I learned something recently from Gerry. It used to be unthinkable to me that any aspect of a character or a scene applied from the outside in could be of any creative worth or have any spark of genius to it. Then in one of his body movement classes I heard Gerry talk about the movement and the gesture of the body giving a thought to the mind, and then the thought being given back to the body. Now why should it have taken me so long to see that?

Use whatever works! Well, but I was deeply offended at that at first.

WW: I would be too. If you would say that to me in a scene, with my little acting experience of two days now, I would feel I was not being treated properly.

NR: And in your case you wouldn't be. And you may disappreciate equally my saying, after giving you an action, or after you've already found your action, "Well, let's not talk about it, go ahead and do it!" I hadn't acted for quite a while when I found myself on your set two years ago, and I was terrible, and I didn't know which way to turn my left foot rightwards till you and Dennis came up to me and said, "Hey Nick, stop showing it! Do it!"

WW: It worked immediately.

NR: Yeah. And so it has worked with you. Now you're not always going to be able to use the same vocabulary with each actor. In no way.

WW: And sometimes you can't even use it twice.

NR: Sometimes you can't. I couldn't use it twice with you today at one point, I forget what it was, do you remember?

WW: Yeah, I think it was when I was in the other bed, and you had only heard me, you hadn't watched me, because you were in this bed and I was over there, and just hearing me you knew what I had done wrong. Remember that?

NR: Yeah, yeah.

WW: And that too is kind of opposite to the dead end as I define where I am.

NR: Yeah, but this doesn't all come as a gift, it isn't all a happy swim down the river. We don't even know how it accumulates. How many times have you started off a sentence with two or three words and some vague idea in your mind, but not knowing its conclusion, and before long you have a sentence there, and it's right, and people are responding to it. Know what I mean?

WW: Yeah. That only happens, for me, if I'm asked something, or if I'm telling somebody something. Right now that's the case, but it hasn't taken place for me once in these two or three days I've been in front of the camera. Maybe I was too scared, but I always knew the end of the lines, and that would make me feel like not doing a good job as an actor. So I don't have the means to start a line while camera's rolling and not be aware of the end of it.

NR: I was talking about in conversation or discussion when sometimes you're just filling up air space.

WW: At Vassar, with the audience discussion, when you were answering questions after *The Lusty Men*, I saw you thinking and talking, and that was what was moving everybody, and there wasn't a single line that wasn't the truth, or that was prepared to impress in any way. That's why I'm really very, very proud that we went there and that we recorded it.

I don't know what you think about the film that we're doing right now in relation to that and whether we shouldn't turn it around once more and create situations and discussions like this with a lot of people—

SR: Or with you, since that's where the story seems to be.

WW: So maybe we should consider writing something, or prepare for something, a talk about acting, for instance. We should just set ourselves into a situation where we can talk like right now, to each other.

NR: I want to talk to you about so many things, about everything you know about acting, for example. I feel I have to start from scratch.

WW: We could give it a try, for instance. We could just set up a situation at the sofa at the back, and talk about *We Can't Go Home Again*. I have some very, very urgent questions about that. But if I asked them now, and then afterwards we said, "Well now let's make a scene like this," I'm afraid I couldn't function anymore.

For instance, in the scene we shot yesterday and today, we prepared the situation that you were going to show me *We Can't Go Home Again* in the evening. So why don't we do that? Let's look at the film again. I'd like to see it again. And then we can record a talk about it with all the means we have—camera, video.

We should have a look at *We Can't Go Home Again* together, and then sit in the corner, Tom, you, me—in a way I'd like to include Gerry, and Bernard, too, because he had a talk about *We Can't Go*

Home Again that was for me very, very interesting. What do you think?

NR: Fine. I am at a remarkable stage in my life. I've seldom been so receptive of other people, and I think this is the way we'll get to find out what the film is about. I think I know what the film would like to be about, and I think it would like to be about dying.

WW: Yeah.

SR: Yeah, but do you approach from the front door or the back door.

WW: Yeah, but do we let it be what it would like to be, or do we oppose it, make it a film about living.

NR: Approach it, ask it a polite question or two.

GB: It seems to me that this scene that Nick was just looking at in which you ask him the question is leading towards that as well, isn't it?

NR: I think it is, even though it's a question about acting.

GB: It's leading towards that, and also towards a fairly natural conclusion, after that scene between the two of you.

WW: Well, this scene between the two of us isn't done yet. But in a way I feel more urgent about trying to talk about *We Can't Go Home Again*. So why don't we make the film more obey to urgent needs? Do you agree that we should all see the film together, then go on?

NR: Yeah.

WW: So maybe we should prepare the sofa in the back . . .

And when the time comes
Once more, and when the time comes,
And once again, when men will say this is the way and that is not,
I hope I will be long forgotten and then revived
In the exaltation of the youthful knowledge of immortality,
By a flicker of film and a flash of hope,
And only once again
I'd find the question in my heart forever living and dying,
But only one more time.

"He realized he was witnessing . . ."

He realized he was witnessing a potential of the human mind to save itself. It lay deep within the brain, untouched and un-known until it was needed. Eventually it appeared and took con-trol, as it did of him now, creating and insulating space between his body and the dangers before it—allowing him the time and the clarity to best decide on how to save himself. With this calm he began his first day.[72]

To take an inventory of one's body, one's self-portrait, one's self-es-teem, one's intentions, one's acts, one's inner character and its traces of cowardice, spontaneous bravery, melancholia and elation, depen-dence and acts of faith, one's love of fathers, mothers, sisters, brothers, a stranger's handshake, one's prejudices and fancies, fantasies and adulations, loves in art and history and back seats of cars, love of objects and conflicts and self-debasements, one's resentments of un-known sacrifices and those recognized, one's delusions, vanities, memories, the fun and commonplaces, common people, the figure-heads on boats or on the shore . . .

---

72. From *Kidnapped!* by Curtis Bill Pepper (New York: Harmony, 1978). Pepper had just published this book about the kidnapping of the heir to the Lazzaroni biscuit business by the Italian Red Brigade. NR optioned the film rights to the story, and SR began writing the screenplay.

■ ■ ■

Friday [5/78]

Morning. The Spring Street Bar is still open. In Covent Garden, London, some bars opened at five. I cannot recall a moment of joy there except my first, second, and third discoveries of the flower market. The third discovery was in the company of Alan Lomax. It was a good morning. Rare. Moments of joy seem to have been rare.

Does confusion cause paralysis? Yes, it does. Does paralysis cause confusion? Yes, I suppose so. Perhaps it's a matter of selection. To perform an act of selection would put a temporary end to paralysis and give momentary relief from confusion. Another act might follow, and the paralysis would become limbered. We are once more back to action.

What do I want to do? Make amends. Begin. Make a list. Then write the letters, make the phone calls. I will. But first I will go back to bed while I still have the power to move my legs and mind enough to direct them. And what will I do in bed? Think. And fall asleep, paralyzed by more confusion. I have too little information with which to think. Better to make a list.

■ ■ ■

"I am willing to give up my cancer." With these words the meditation begins. Do I say these words as a benediction? Is it possible I cherish my two-and-a-half degrees of cancer as a Shriner cherishes his 33rd? Does that mean that, like a juvenile delinquent, I would threaten a life for the sake of attention, and that that life is mine? It is possible. It is shocking, unnerving. The thought is nauseating. I am, at the moment, tight from my stomach's pit to the back of my jaws. I am sick. Not from the disease. The disease is a symptom, of want and frustration, achievement. Success without effort has suffocated my white cells in a last desperate demand that success be paid for, by death, the most common of all experiences. Hey look, Ma! I'm dancing!!! Can you believe that a human being who has managed to have more than ordinary success, who has lived for 66 years, knows right from wrong, and has 2½-degree cancer, would continue to smoke? Can you? What shattering sense of unworthiness and guilt could possess such a person? That's enough time on this for now. Whew!

■ ■ ■

[1978?]

Susan:
    Shape Up.

Unless you take a healthy turn in your direction for the purpose of a "fearless inventory," you are in danger of having even the most positive aspects of your personality disintegrate. Your situation, domestic, of living with a particular type of invalid, tends to feed those character defects such as arrogance, of which you are aware, and severely test your high quality instincts and impulses so they too are endangered by threat of stunting (as in growth).

■ ■ ■

[February 1979]

People don't seem able to successfully conspire. Tim capped what I've known for six months or more. Too bad.

Tim back to California after a gratifying reunion. A dear friend.

■ ■ ■

[The following entries from Nick's journal were undated, but written in Spring 1979.]

> I looked into my face and what did I see
> No granite rock of identity — faded blue
> Drawn skin and wrinkled lips and sadness
> And a wildest urge to recognize and accept the face of my mother
> And the will to find all the places to word down the love
> for my wife, chambers to hold and protect her silent thoughts.
>
> N/?

■ ■ ■

If any decision is to be made, the central disposer is health.

■ ■ ■

You have observed in me a mammoth will to live.

■ ■ ■

Soon the time will come to reach for pen and make a note that the time has come to select a place for burying.

Mr. Inside Out

I am a sensible object in physical space.

No matter the circumstance, no person is close to me except me. I am close to me. I am inside out, so outside rests within. Outside wasn't always comfortable there. It took terrible agitation to get there in the first place, and once there, peace had to be made with anonymity. The squirming and squeezing brought some attrition, and wounds stayed open longer than a cut on the nose or a scraped knee, but the scars formed the new comfortable quarters in which Mr. Outside now resides. The walls are red and brown washed with watered van Gogh yellows. The heating pipes are blue; the windows, one-way black. One chair is straw not yet amber, its rockers, red.

In a valley of chameleons a chameleon goes unnoticed. So does a white panther on a sea of ice and snow. Until it moves.

I move and go unnoticed. I enter an invisible door.

When you move you are in danger. And I imagine you are dangerous.

You come to me to collect what I have done inside. I do not go to you. There is coffee on the stove, cream in the icebox, sugar on the barrell, and a cup on the hook. Help yourself. In there are two new paintings. My best. Take them. Pay as much for them as you can. Leave the money on the barrel. Goodbye.

So. I am an artist. If you call me an artist I am an artist. It's better you say it than I. Am I also a crook? I think not.

218

FILMOGRAPHY
Bernard Eisenschitz

Titles are listed chronologically as Ray worked on them. The date given at the start of each entry is the release date, or the date of completion if release was delayed.

Films Directed by or Contributed to by Ray

1945   A TREE GROWS IN BROOKLYN

20th Century-Fox. Director: Elia Kazan, Screenplay: Tess Slesinger, Frank Davis (with contributions by Anita Loos). From the novel *A Tree Grows in Brooklyn* by Betty Smith. Director of photography: Leon Shamroy. Music: Alfred Newman. *Second assistant director:* Nicholas Ray. Producer: Louis D. Lighton.

   Cast: Dorothy McGuire, Joan Blondell, James Dunn, Lloyd Nolan, Peggy Ann Garner, Ted Donaldson, James Gleason, Ruth Nelson, John Alexander, J. Farrell McDonald, B. S. Pully, Charles Halton, Art Smith.

   Release: February 1945.
   Running time: 128 min.

1945   CARIBBEAN MYSTERY

20th Century-Fox. Director: Robert D. Webb. Screenplay: Jack Andrews, Leonard Praskins (*dialogue revisions* by Nicholas Ray). Adaptation by W. Scott Darling, from the novel *Murder in Trinidad* by John Vandercook. *Dialogue director:* Nicholas Ray. Producer: William Girard.

Cast: James Dunn, Sheila Ryan, Edward Ryan, Jackie Paley, Reed Hadley, Roy Roberts.

Release: June 1945.

Running time: 65 min.

1945 TUESDAY IN NOVEMBER

Office of War Information Overseas Branch. *The American Scene* series no. 13. Director (staged scenes): John Berry. Screenplay: Howard Koch, for The Hollywood Mobilization. Animation: United Films, Inc. (John Hubley). Director of photography (staged scenes): Ernest Laszlo. Editor: Harvey Johnston. Music: Virgil Thomson. Production manager: Irving Lerner. *Associate producer:* Nicholas Ray. Producer: John Houseman.

Running time: 18 min.

1946 SWING PARADE OF 1946

Monogram. Director: Phil Karlson. *Screenplay:* Tim Ryan. From an original story by Edmund Kelso (in collaboration with Nicholas Ray). Producers: Lindley Parsons, Harry A. Romm.

Cast: Gale Storm, Connee Boswell, The Three Stooges, Ed Brophy, Russell Hicks, John Eldredge.

Release: January 28, 1946. Running time: 74 min.

1948 THEY LIVE BY NIGHT

RKO Radio. *Director:* Nicholas Ray. Screenplay: Charles Schnee. *Adaptation* by Nicholas Ray, from the novel *Thieves Like Us* by Edward Anderson. Director of photography: George E. Diskant. Camera operator: Edward Bergholz. Art directors: Albert S. D'Agostino, Al Herman. Editor: Sherman Todd. Music: Leigh Harline. Bakaleinikoff. Producer: John Houseman.

Cast: Cathy O'Donnell (Keechie), Farley Granger (Bowie), Howard Da Silva (Chickamaw), Jay C. Flippen (T-Dub) Helen Craig (Mattie) Will Wright (Mobley), Marie Bryant (Singer), Ian Wolfe (Hawkins), William Phipps (Young Farmer), Harry Harvey (Hagenheimer), Will Lee (Jeweller),

Produced 1947. Release: Spring, 1949 (London). Running time: 96 min.

1949 **A WOMAN'S SECRET**

RKO Radio. A Dore Schary Presentation. *Director:* Nicholas Ray. Screenplay: Herman J. Mankiewicz. From the novel *Mortgage on Life* by Vicki Baum. Director of photography: George E. Diskant. Art directors: Albert S. D'Agostino, Carroll Clark. Editor: Sherman Todd. Music: Frederick Hollander. Producer: Herman J. Mankiewicz.

Cast: Maureen O'Hara (Marian Washburn), Melvyn Douglas (Luke Jordan), Gloria Grahame (Susan Caldwell), Bill Williams (Lee), Victory Jory (Brook Matthews), Mary Philips (Mrs Fowler), Jay C. Flippen (Fowler), Robert Warwick (Roberts), Curt Conway (Doctor), Ann Shoemaker (Mrs. Matthews)

Produced 1948. Release: March 5, 1949. Running time: 84 min.

1949 **KNOCK ON ANY DOOR**

Columbia Pictures. A Santana Production. *Director:* Nicholas Ray. Screenplay: Daniel Taradash, John Monks, Jr. From the novel *Knock on Any Door* by Willard Motley. Director of photography: Burnett Guffey. Art director: Robert Peterson. Editor: Viola Lawrence. Music: George Antheil. Producer: Robert Lord.

Cast: Humphrey Bogart (Andrew Morton), John Derek (Nick Romano), George Macready (District Attorney Kerman), Arlene Roberts (Emma), Susan Perry (Adele), Mickey Knox (Vito), Barry Kelley (Judge Drake), Dooley Wilson (Piano Player), Cara Williams (Nelly), Jimmy Conlin (Kid Fingers), Sumner Williams (Jimmy), Sid Melton (Squint), Pepe Hern (Juan), Dewey Martin (Butch), Robert A. Davis (Sunshine), Houseley Stevenson (Junior), Vince Barnett (Bartender), Thomas Sully (Officer Hawkins), Florence Auer (Aunt Lena), Pierre Watkin (Purcell), Gordon Nelson (Corey), Argentina Brunetti (Ma Romano), Dick Sinatra (Julian Romano), Carol Coombs (Ang Romano), Joan Baxter (Maria Romano),

Release: February 22, 1949.
Running time: 100 min.

1949 **ROSEANNA McCOY**

A Samuel Goldwyn production distributed by RKO Radio. *Director:* Irving Reis (and Nicholas Ray). Screenplay: John Collier (and Ben Hecht). From the novel by Alberta Hannum. Director of photography: Lee Garmes. Producer: Samuel Goldwyn.

Cast: Farley Granger, Joan Evans, Charles Bickford, Raymond Massey, Richard Basehart, Gigi Perreau, Aline MacMahon, Marshall Thompson, Lloyd Gough.

Release: October 12, 1949. Running time: 100 min.

1950 **BORN TO BE BAD**

RKO Radio. *Director:* Nicholas Ray. Screenplay: Edith Sommers. Adaptation by Charles Schnee, from the novel *All Kneeling* by Ann Parrish. Additional dialogue by Robert Soderberg, George Oppenheimer. Director of photography: Nicholas Musuraca. Art directors: Albert S. D'Agostino, Jack Okey. Editor: Frederick Knudtson. Music: Frederick Hollander. Producer: Robert Sparks.

Cast: Joan Fontaine (Christabel Caine), Robert Ryan (Nick), Zachary Scott (Curtis), Joan Leslie (Donna), Mel Ferrer (Gobby), Harold Vermilyea (John Caine), Virginia Farmer (Aunt Clara), Kathleen Howard (Mrs Bolton), Dick Ryan (Arthur), Bess Flowers (Mrs. Worthington), Joy Hallward (Mrs Porter), Hazel Boyne (Committee Woman), Irving Bacon (Jewelry Salesman), Gordon Oliver (The Lawyer).

Produced 1949. Release: August 27, 1950. Running time: 94 min.

1950 **IN A LONELY PLACE**

Columbia Pictures. A Santana Production. *Director:* Nicholas Ray. Screenplay: Andrew Solt. Adaptation by Edmund H. North, from the novel *In a Lonely Place* by Dorothy B. Hughes. Director of photography: Burnett Guffey. Camera operator: Gert Anderson. Art director: Robert Peterson. Editor: Viola Lawrence. Music: George Antheil. Producer: Robert Lord.

Cast: Humphrey Bogart (Dixon Steele), Gloria Grahame (Laurel Gray), Frank Lovejoy (Brub Nicolai), Carl Benton Reid (Captain Lochner), Art Smith (Mel Lippman), Jeff Donnell (Sylvia Nicolai), Martha Stewart (Mildred Atkinson), Robert Warwick (Charlie Waterman), Morris Ankrum (Lloyd Barnes), William Ching (Ted Barton), Steven Geray (Paul), Hadda Brooks (Singer), Alice Talton (Frances Randolph), Jack Reynolds (Henry Kesler), Ruth Warren (Effie), Ruth Gillette (Martha), Guy L. Beach (Mr. Swan), Lewis Howard (Junior).

Release: May 17, 1950. Running time: 94 min.

1951 **ON DANGEROUS GROUND**

RKO Radio. *Director:* Nicholas Ray. *Screenplay:* A. I. Bezzerides. Adaptation by A. I. Bezzerides and Nicholas Ray, from the novel *Mad With Much Heart* by Gerald Butler. Director of photography: George E. Diskant. Art directors: Albert S. D'Agostino, Ralph Berger. Editor: Roland Gross. Music: Bernard Herrmann, conducted by the composer. Producer: John Houseman.

Cast: Robert Ryan (Jim Wilson), Ida Lupino (Mary Malden), Ward Bond (Walter Brent), Charles Kemper (Bill Daly), Anthony Ross (Pete Santos), Ed Begley (Captain Brawley), Ian Wolfe (Carey), Sumner Williams (Danny Malden), Gus Schilling (Lucky), Frank Ferguson (Willows), Cleo Moore (Myrna), Olive Carey (Mrs. Brent), Richard Irving (Bernie).

Produced 1950. Release: February 12, 1952. Running time: 82 min.

1951 FLYING LEATHERNECKS

RKO Radio. Howard Hughes presents an Edmund Grainger production. *Director:* Nicholas Ray. Screenplay: James Edward Grant. From a story by Kenneth Gamet. Director of photography: William E. Snyder. Technicolor. Art directors: Albert S. D'Agostino, James W. Sullivan. Editor: Sherman Todd. Music: Roy Webb. Producer: Edmund Grainger.

Cast: John Wayne (Major Dan Kirby), Robert Ryan (Capt. Carl "Griff" Griffith), Don Taylor (Lieut. Vern "Cowboy" Blythe), Janis Carter (Joan Kirby), Jay C. Flippen (Master Sgt. Clancy), William Harrigan (Dr. Curan), James Bell (Colonel), Barry Kelley (General), Maurice Jara (Lieut. Shorty Vegay), Adam Williams (Lieut. Malotke), James Dobson (Lieut. Pudge McCabe), Carleton Young (Capt. McAllister), Steve Flagg (Lieut. Jorgenson), Brett King (Lieut. Ernie Stark), Gordon Gebert (Tommy Kirby).

Release: September 19, 1951. Running time: 102 min.

1951 THE RACKET

RKO Radio. *Director:* John Cromwell (and Nicholas Ray). Screenplay: William Wister Haines, W. R. Burnett. From the play by Bartlett Cormack. Director of photography: George E. Diskant. Editor: Sherman Todd. Sound: Frank McWhorter, Clem Portman. Producer: Edmund Grainger.

Cast (actors directed by Ray italicized): *Robert Mitchum* (Captain McQuigg), *Lizabeth Scott* (Irene), *Robert Ryan* (Nick Scanlon), *William Talman* (Johnson), *Ray Collins* (Welch), Joyce MacKenzie (Mary McQuigg), *Robert Hutton* (Ames), Virginia Huston (Lucy Johnson), William Conrad (Turck), *Walter Sande* (Delaney), *Les Tremayne* (Chief Craig), *Don Porter* (Connolly), *Ralph Peters* (Davis), *Howard Joslyn* (Sgt. Werker), *Steve Roberts* (Schmidt), *Pat Flaherty* (Clerk), *Johnny Day* (Menig).

Release: December 12, 1951. Running time: 88 min.

1952 **MACAO**

RKO Radio. *Director:* Josef von Sternberg (and Nicholas Ray). Screenplay: Bernard C. Schoenfeld, Stanley Rubin. From a story by Bob Williams. Director of photography: Harry J. Wild. Editors: Samuel Beetley, Robert Golden. Producer: Alex Gottlieb.

Cast (actors directed by Ray italicized): *Robert Mitchum* (Nick Cochran), *Jane Russell* (Julie Benson), *William Bendix* (Lawrence Trumble), *Thomas Gomez* (Lieut. Sebastian), Gloria Grahame (Margie), *Brad Dexter* (Halloran), *Edward Ashley* (Martin Stewart), *Philip Ahn* (Itzumi), *Vladimir Sokoloff* (Kwan Sum Tang), Don Zelayo (Gimpy), Emory Parnell (Ship Captain), Nacho Galindo (Bus Driver), *Philip Van Zandt* (Customs Official), *George Chan* (Chinese Photographer).

Release: April 30, 1952. Running time: 80 min.

1952 **THE LUSTY MEN**

RKO Radio. A Wald-Krasna Production. *Director:* Nicholas Ray. Screenplay: Horace McCoy, David Dortort. Suggested by a story by Claude Stanush. Director of photography: Lee Garmes. Art directors: Albert S. D'Agostino, Alfred Herman. Editor: Ralph Dawson. Music: Roy Webb. Producers: Jerry Wald, Norman Krasna.

Cast: Susan Hayward (Louise Merritt), Robert Mitchum (Jeff McCloud), Arthur Kennedy (Wes Merritt), Arthur Hunnicutt (Booker Davis), Frank Faylen (Al Dawson), Walter Coy (Buster Burgess), Carol Nugent (Rusty), Maria Hart (Rosemary Maddox), Lorna Thayer (Grace Burgess), Burt Mustin (Jeremiah Watrous), Karen King (Ginny Logan), Jimmy Dodd (Red Logan), Eleanor Todd (Babs).

Release: October 1952. Running time: 113 min.

1953 **ANDROCLES AND THE LION**

RKO Radio. G. P. Productions. *Director:* Chester Erskine (additional scenes: Nicholas Ray). Screen adaptation: Chester Erskine, Noel Langley, Ken Englund, from the play *Androcles and the Lion* by Bernard Shaw. Director of photography: Harry Stradling. Editor: Roland Gross. Producer: Gabriel Pascal.

Cast (actors directed by Ray italicized): Jean Simmons (Lavinia), Alan Young (Androcles), Victor Mature (Captain), *Robert Newton* (Ferrovius), Maurice Evans (Caesar), Elsa Lanchester (Megaera), Reginald Gardiner (Lentulus), Gene Lockhart (Menagerie Keeper), Alan Mowbray (Editor), Noel Willman (Spintho), John Hoyt (Cato), Jim Backus (Centurion), Lowell Gilmore (Metellus).

Release: January 3, 1953. Running time: 95 min.

1954 JOHNNY GUITAR

Republic Pictures. *Director:* Nicholas Ray. Screenplay: Philip Yordan. From the novel *Johnny Guitar* by Roy Chanslor. Director of photography: Harry Stradling. Trucolor. Art director: James Sullivan. Editor: Richard L. Van Enger. Music: Victor Young. *Associate producer:* (uncredited) Nicholas Ray. Producer: Herbert J. Yates.

Cast: Joan Crawford (Vienna), Sterling Hayden (Johnny Guitar), Mercedes McCambridge (Emma Small), Scott Brady (Dancing Kid), Ward Bond (John McIvers), Ben Cooper (Turkey Ralston), Ernest Borgnine (Bart Lonergan), John Carradine (Old Tom), Royal Dano (Corey), Frank Ferguson (Marshal Williams), Paul Fix (Eddie), Rhys Williams (Mr. Andrews), Ian MacDonald (Pete).

Release: May 27, 1954. Running time: 110 min.

1955 RUN FOR COVER

Paramount. *Director:* Nicholas Ray. Screenplay: Winston Miller. From a story by Harriet Frank, Jr. and Irving Ravetch. Director of photography: Daniel Fapp. VistaVision. Technicolor. Art directors: Hal Pereira, Henry Bumstead. Editor: Howard Smith. Music: Howard Jackson. Producers: William H. Pine, William C. Thomas.

Cast: James Cagney (Matt Dow), Viveca Lindfors (Helga Swenson), John Derek (Davey Bishop), Jean Hersholt (Mr. Swenson), Grant Withers (Gentry), Jack Lambert (Larsen), Ernest Borgnine (Morgan), Ray Teal (Sheriff), Irving Bacon (Scotty), Trevor Bardette (Paulsen), John Miljan (Mayor Walsh), Gus Schilling (Doc Ridgeway), Emerson Treacy (Bank Clerk), Denver Pyle (Harvey), Henry Wills (Citizen), Phil Chambers, Harold Kennedy, Joe Haworth.

Release: April 29, 1955. Running time: 93 min.

1954 HIGH GREEN WALL

Revue Productions. *General Electric Theater* series. *Director:* Nicholas Ray. Teleplay: Charles Jackson. From a short story, *The Man Who Liked Dickens*, by Evelyn Waugh. Director of photography: Franz Planer. Art director: Martin Obzina. Editor: Michael R. McAdam. Producer: Leon Gordon.

Cast: Joseph Cotten (Henty), Thomas Gomez (McMaster), Maurice Marsac (Aubert), Marshall Bradford, Ward Wood (Search Party).

Broadcast: October 3, 1954, CBS. Running time: 26 min.

1955   **REBEL WITHOUT A CAUSE**

Warner Bros. *Director:* Nicholas Ray. *Screenplay:* Stewart Stern. Adaptation by Irving Shulman from a story by Nicholas Ray. Director of photography: Ernest Haller. CinemaScope. WarnerColor. Art director: Malcolm Bert. Editor: William Ziegler. Music: Leonard Rosenman. Producer: David Weisbart.

Cast: James Dean (Jim Stark), Natalie Wood (Judy), Sal Mineo (Plato), Jim Backus (Jim's Father), Ann Doran (Jim's Mother), Corey Allen (Buzz Gunderson), William Hopper (Judy's Father), Rochelle Hudson (Judy's Mother), Dennis Hopper (Goon), Edward Platt (Ray), Steffi Sidney (Mil), Marietta Canty (Plato's Nurse), Virginia Brissac (Jim's Grandmother), Beverly Long (Helen), Ian Wolfe (Professor), Frank Mazzola (Crunch), Robert Foulk (Gene), Jack Simmons (Cookie), Tom Bernard (Harry), Nick Adams (Moose), Jack Grinnage (Chick), Clifford Morris (Cliff), Robert B. Williams (Ed, Moose's Father), Louise Lane (Policewoman), Jimmy Baird (Beau), Dick Wessel (Guide), Nelson Leigh (Sergeant), Dorothy Abbott (Nurse), House Peters (Officer), Gus Schilling (Attendant), Bruce Noonan (Monitor), Almira Sessions (Old lady Teacher), Peter Miller (Hoodlum), Paul Bryar (Desk Sergeant), Paul Birch (Police Chief), David McMahon (Crunch's Father).

Release: October 27, 1955. Running time: 111 min.

1956   **HOT BLOOD**

Columbia Pictures. A Howard Welsch Production. *Director:* Nicholas Ray. Screenplay: Jesse Lasky, Jr. From a story by Jean Evans. Director of photography: Ray June. CinemaScope. Technicolor. Art director: Robert Peterson. Editor: Otto Ludwig. Music: Les Baxter. Songs: Ross Bagdasarian. Choreography: Matt Mattox, Sylvia Lewis. Producer: Harry Tatelman.

Cast: Jane Russell (Annie Caldash), Cornel Wilde (Stephan Torino), Luther Adler (Marco Torino), Joseph Calleia (Papa Theodore), Mikhail Rasumny (Old Johnny), Nina Koshetz (Nita Johnny), Helen Westcott (Velma), Jamie Russell (Xano), Wally Russell (Bimbo), Nick Dennis (Korka), Richard Deacon (Mr. Swift), Robert Foulk (Sergeant McGrossin).

Release: March 23, 1956. Running time: 85 min.

1956   **BIGGER THAN LIFE**

20th Century-Fox. *Director:* Nicholas Ray. *Screenplay:* Cyril Hume, Richard Maibaum (with contributions by Ray, James Mason, Gavin

Lambert, Clifford Odets). Based on an article, *Ten Feet Tall*, by Berton Roueché. Director of photography: Joe MacDonald. CinemaScope. De Luxe. Art directors: Lyle R. Wheeler, Jack Martin Smith. Editor: Louis Loeffler. Music: David Raksin. Producer: James Mason.

Cast: James Mason (Ed Avery), Barbara Rush (Lou), Walter Matthau (Wally), Robert Simon (Dr. Norton), Christopher Olsen (Richie Avery), Roland Winters (Dr. Ruric), Rusty Lane (La Porte), Rachel Stephens (Nurse), Kipp Hamilton (Pat Wade), Betty Caulfield (Mrs. La Porte), Virginia Carroll (Mrs. Jones), Renny McEvoy (Mr Jones).

Premiere: August 2, 1956. Running time: 95 min.

1957 THE STORY OF JESSE JAMES
(GB title: THE JAMES BROTHERS)

20th Century-Fox. *Director:* Nicholas Ray. Screenplay: Walter Newman. Based on the screenplay by Nunnally Johnson for the film *Jesse James* (director Henry King, 1938). Director of photography: Joe MacDonald. CinemaScope. De Luxe. Art directors: Lyle R. Wheeler, Addison Hehr. Editor: Robert Simpson. Music: Leigh Harline. Producer: Herbert B. Swope Jr.

Cast: Robert Wagner (Jesse James), Jeffrey Hunter (Frank James), Hope Lange (Zee), Agnes Moorehead (Mrs. Samuel), Alan Hale (Cole Younger), Alan Baxter (Remington), John Carradine (Reverend Jethro Bailey), Rachel Stephens (Anne James), Barney Phillips (Dr. Samuel), Biff Elliot (Jim Younger), John Doucette (Sheriff Hillstrom), Frank Overton (Major Rufus Cobb), Barry Atwater (Attorney Walker), Marian Seldes (Rowena Cobb), Chubby Johnson (Askew), Frank Gorshin (Charley Ford), Carl Thayer (Bob Ford), Robert Adler (Sheriff Trump), Clancy Cooper (Sheriff Joe), Sumner Williams (Sam Wells), Tom Greenway (Deputy Leo), Mike Steen (Deputy Ed), Aaron Saxon (Wiley), Anthony Ray (Bob Younger), Tom Pittman (Hughie), Jason Wingreen (Tucker Bassham), Louis Zito (Clell Miller), Mark Hickman (Bill Stiles), Adam Marshall (Dick Liddell), Joseph Di Reda (Bill Ryan), J. Frederick Albeck (Jorgensen), Kellog Junge, Jr. (Archie, age 4).

Release: March 22, 1957. Running time: 93 min.

1957 BITTER VICTORY
(French title: AMÈRE VICTOIRE)

Transcontinental Films S.A./Robert Laffont Productions/Columbia. *Director:* Nicholas Ray. *Screenplay:* René Hardy, Nicholas Ray, Gavin Lambert. From the novel *Amère Victoire* by René Hardy. Additional dialogue: Paul Gallico. Director of photography: Michel Kelber. Cine-maScope. Art director: Jean d'Eaubonne. Editor: Léonide Azar. Sound editor: Renée Lichtig. Continuity: Lucie Lichtig. Music: Maurice Le Roux, conducted by the composer. Producer: Paul Graetz.

Cast: Richard Burton (Captain Leith), Curd Jürgens (Major Brand), Ruth Roman (Jane Brand), Raymond Pellegrin (Mokrane), Sean Kelly (Lt. Barton), Anthony Bushell (General Paterson), Alfred Burke (Lt. Col. Callander), Andrew Crawford (Pte. Roberts), Nigel Green (Pte. Wilkins), Ronan O'Casey (Sgt. Dunnigan), Christopher Lee (Sgt. Barney), Fred Matter (Oberst Lutze), Raoul Delfosse (Lt. Kassel), Harry Landis (Pte. Browning), Ramon de Larrocha (Lt. Sanders), Christian Melsen (Pte. Abbot), Sumner Williams (Pte. Anderson), Joe Davray (Pte. Spicer), Lt. Harris (Evans).

Premiere: September 1957 (Venice Festival). Running time: 103 min. In the US: release, March 1958; running time: 82 min.

1958 **WIND ACROSS THE EVERGLADES**

Warner Bros. A Schulberg Production. *Director:* Nicholas Ray. Screenplay: Budd Schulberg. Director of photography: Joseph Brun. Technicolor. Art director: Richard Sylbert. Editors: George Klotz, Joseph Zigman. Music: Warners' Music Library. Producer: Stuart Schulberg.

Cast: Burl Ives (Cottonmouth), Christopher Plummer (Walt Murdock), Gypsy Rose Lee (Mrs. Bradford), George Voskovec (Aaron Nathanson), Tony Galento (Beef), Howard I. Smith (George), Emmett Kelly (Bigamy Bob), Pat Henning (Sawdust), Chana Eden (Naomi), MacKinlay Kantor (Judge Harris), Curt Conway (Perfesser), Peter Falk (Writer), Fred Grossinger (Slow Boy), Sammy Renick (Loser), Toch Brown (One-Note), Frank Rothe (Howard Ross Morgan), Cory Osceola (Billy One-Arm), Mary Osceola (Suzy Billy), Sumner Williams (Windy), Toby Bruce (Joe Bottles), Mary Pennington (Mrs. George Leggett), Hugh Parker (Lord Harry), Brad Bradford (Thumbs).

Release: August 20, 1958 (Florida). Running time: 93 min.

1958 **PARTY GIRL**

Metro-Goldwyn-Mayer. A Euterpe Production. *Director:* Nicholas Ray. Screenplay: George Wells. From a story by Leo Katcher. Director of photography: Robert Bronner. CinemaScope. Metrocolor. Art directors: William A. Horning, Randall Duell. Editor: John McSweeney, Jr. Music: Jeff Alexander. Choreographer: Robert Sidney. Producer: Joe Pasternak.

Cast: Robert Taylor (Thomas Farrell), Cyd Charisse (Vicki Gaye), Lee J. Cobb (Rico Angelo), John Ireland (Louis Canetto), Kent Smith (Jeffrey Stewart), Claire Kelly (Genevieve), Corey Allen (Cookie La Motte), Lewis Charles (Danny Rimett), David Opatoshu (Lou Forbes), Ken Dibbs (Joey Vulner), Patrick McVey (O'Malley), Barbara Lang (Tall Blonde Party Girl), Myrna Hansen (Joy Hampton), Betty Utey (Party Girl).

Release: October 28, 1958. Running time: 99 min.

1960 THE SAVAGE INNOCENTS
(Italian title: OMBRE BIANCHE; French title: LES DENTS DU DIABLE)

An Italian/British/French co-production: Magic Film (Rome)/Joseph Janni, Appia Films (London)/Gray Film-Pathé (Paris). Released by Rank (UK), Paramount (US). *Director:* Nicholas Ray. *Screenplay:* Nicholas Ray. Adaptation by Hans Ruesch and Franco Solinas, from the novel *Top of the World* by Hans Ruesch. Director of photography: Aldo Tonti, Peter Hennessy. Super-Technirama 70. Technicolor. Art directors: Don Ashton, Dario Cecchi. Editor: Ralph Kemplen, Eraldo Da Roma. Music: Angelo Francesco Lavagnino. Producer: Maleno Malenotti.

Cast: Anthony Quinn (Inuk), Yoko Tani (Asiak), Peter O'Toole (1st Trooper), Carlo Giustini (2nd Trooper), Marie Yang (Powtee), Andy Ho (Anarvik), Kaida Horiuchi (Imina), Yvonne Shima (Lulik), Lee Montague (Ittimangnerk), Francis De Wolff (Proprietor of Trading Post), Marco Guglielmi (Missionary), Anthony Chin (Kidok), Anna May Wong (Hiko), Michael Chow (Undik), Ed Devereau (Pilot). Narration spoken by Nicholas Stuart.

1. Several of these technical credits are dubious, given the co-production practice (in Britain as well as Italy) of doubling up on technicians to satisfy union requirements. This is why Baccio Bandini, for example, is credited as co-director in Italian sources.

2. In the English language version, Peter O'Toole is dubbed by Robert Rietty. O'Toole had his name removed from the credits before the film's British release. He *is* credited, third in the cast list, on American, French, and Italian versions.

Release: March 1960 (Rome). Running time: 107 min. In the US: release, May 24, 1961; running time: 89 min.

1961 KING OF KINGS

Metro-Goldwyn-Mayer. A Samuel Bronston Production. *Director:* Nicholas Ray. Screenplay: Philip Yordan. Directors of photography:

Franz F. Planer, Milton Krasner, Manuel Berenguer. Super-Technirama 70. Technicolor. Art director/costumes: Georges Wakhévitch. Editors: Harold F. Kress, Renée Lichtig. 2nd unit directors: Noel Howard, Sumner Williams. Music: Miklos Rosza. Producer: Samuel Bronston.

Cast: Jeffrey Hunter (Jesus Christ), Robert Ryan (John the Baptist), Siobhan McKenna (Mary, Mother of Jesus), Hurd Hatfield (Pontius Pilate), Ron Randell (Lucius, the Centurion), Viveca Lindfors (Claudia), Rita Gam (Herodias), Carmen Sevilla (Mary Magdalene), Brigid Bazlen (Salome), Harry Guardino (Barabbas), Rip Torn (Judas), Frank Thring (Herod Antipas), Guy Rolfe (Caiaphas), Maurice Marsac (Nicodemus), Grégoire Aslan (Herod), Royal Dano (Peter), Edric Connor (Balthazar), George Coulouris (The Camel Driver), Conrado San Martin (General Pompey), Gerard Tichy (Joseph), José Antonio (Young John), Luis Prendes (The Good Thief), David Davies (The Burly Man), José Nieto (Caspar), Ruben Rojo (Matthew), Fernando Sancho (The Madman), Michael Wager (Thomas), Felix de Pomes (Joseph of Arimathea), Adriano Rimoldi (Melchior), Barry Keegan (The Bad Thief), Rafael Luis Calvo (Simon of Cyrene), Tino Barrero (Andrew), Francisco Moran (The Blind Man). Uncredited: narration spoken by Orson Welles.

Release: October 30, 1961. Running time: 168 min.

1963   55 DAYS AT PEKING

Samuel Bronston Productions. Released by Rank (UK), Allied Artists (US). *Director:* Nicholas Ray (and Andrew Marton, Guy Green). Screenplay: Philip Yordan, Bernard Gordon. Additional dialogue: Robert Hamer. Director of photography: Jack Hildyard. Super-Technirama 70. Technicolor. Production design/costumes: Veniero Colasanti, John Moore. Editor: Robert Lawrence. Director 2nd unit operations: Andrew Marton. Second unit director: Noel Howard. Music: Dimitri Tiomkin, conducted by the composer. Producer: Samuel Bronston.

Cast: Charlton Heston (Major Matt Lewis), Ava Gardner (Baroness Natalie Ivanoff), David Niven (Sir Arthur Robertson), Flora Robson (Dowager Empress Tzu-Hsi), John Ireland (Sergeant Harry), Harry Andrews (Father de Bearn), Leo Genn (General Jung-Lu), Robert Helpmann (Prince Tuan), Ichizo Itami (Colonel Shiba), Kurt Kasznar (Baron Sergei Ivanoff), Philippe Leroy (Julliard), Paul Lukas (Dr Steinfeldt), Lynne Sue Moon (Teresa), Elizabeth Sellars (Lady Sarah Robertson), Massimo Serato (Garibaldi), Jacques Sernas (Major Bobrinski), Jerome Thor (Capt. Andy Marshall), Geoffrey Bayldon (Smythe), Joseph Furst (Capt. Hanselman), Walter Gotell (Capt. Hoffman), Alfred Lynch (Gerald), Alfredo Mayo (Spanish Minister), Martin Miller (Hugo Bergmann), Conchita Montes (Mme. Gaumaire), José Nieto (Italian Minister), Eric Pohlmann (Baron von Meck), Aram Stephan (Gaumaire), Robert Urquhart (Capt. Hanley), Nicholas Ray (US Minister).

Premiere: May 6, 1963 (London). Running time: 154 min.

1964 CIRCUS WORLD
(GB title: THE MAGNIFICENT SHOWMAN)

Samuel Bronston Productions. Director: Henry Hathaway. *Screenplay:* Ben Hecht, Julian Halevy, James Edward Grant. From a story by Philip Yordan, Nicholas Ray. Producer: Samuel Bronston.

Cast: John Wayne, Claudia Cardinale, Rita Hayworth, Lloyd Nolan, Richard Conte.

Release: June 25, 1964 (New York). Running time: 137 min.

1970 MARCH ON WASHINGTON. NOV. 15, 1969

Dome Films, Inc. A film by Grady Watts editing, and Claudia (Weill) cameras, Bill (Desloge) camera, Bob (Levis) sound, François (de Ménil), Sarah, Jim, Eli, Marty, Ellen (Ray), Nick (Ray) direction, Tom, Mike. 16 mm, colour.

Running time: 18 min.

1973–1976 WE CAN'T GO HOME AGAIN

(A film) By Us. *Producer/director/screenplay:* Nicholas Ray. Collaboration on screenplay: Susan Schwartz. Film crew: students from Harpur College, Binghamton (N.Y.). Among the successive technicians: Camera: Doug Cohn (35 mm), Stanley Liu (1st year), Danny Fisher (2nd year), Tim Ray (35 mm, summer 1972), Charles Bornstein (35 mm, 1973), Jerry Jones (San Francisco, 1974). Music: "Bless the Family" by Norman Zamcheck. Editing: Carol Lenoir (New York, summer 1972), Richie Bock (1973 version, then San Francisco, 1974), Charles Bornstein, Danny Fisher, Max Fischer (Amsterdam, summer 1973), Frank Ceverich (Sausalito, 1974), Tony Margo (Burbank, 1975). Production associates: Arthur Whithall, Susan Schwartz.

Cast (all the leading characters play themselves): Nicholas Ray, Tom Farrell, Leslie Levinson, Richie Bock, Danny Fisher, Jane Heymann, Jim North (Bum/Santa Claus), Steve Maurer, Stanley Liu, Jill,

Hallie, Phil Wiseman, Steve Anker, etc. Brief glimpses of: Jane Fonda, Tom Hayden, Rennie Davis, Bill Kunstler, Abbie Hoffman, Allen Ginsberg, Jon Voight.

Produced 1971-1976. Premiere screening: May 1973 (Cannes Festival). Running time: (Cannes) 90 min.

1974 THE JANITOR
(Episode no. 12 of *Wet Dreams*)

Film Group One, Amsterdam, with Cinereal Film, West Berlin. *A dream by* Nicholas Ray. Director of photography/Editor: Max Fischer. 16mm. colour, blown up to 35mm. Production co-ordinators: Max Fischer, Jim Haynes.

Cast: Nicholas Ray (The Preacher/The Janitor), Melvin Miracle, Anneke Spierenburg, Dawn Cumming, Marvelle Williams, Mary Moore, Kees Koedood, Falcon Stuart, Barbara, Burnie Taylor.

Start of filming (Ray's episode): May 1973. Other episodes directed by Jens Joergen Thorsen, Sam Rotterdam, Dusan Makavejev, Oscar Cigard, Falcon Stuart, Max Fischer, Heathcote Williams, Lee Kraft, Geert Koolman, Hans Kanters. Release: January 25, 1974. Running time of episode: 14 min.

1978 MARCO

Direction: Nicholas Ray. Based on the first chapter of the novel *Marco, A Novel of Love* by Curtis Bill Pepper. Directors of photography: Robert La Cativa, Danny Fisher. 16mm colour.

Cast: Claudio Mazzatenta (Dario), Jim Ballagh and Ned Motolo (Cops), Gerry Bamman (Booking Officer).

Running time: 11 min.

1980 LIGHTNING OVER WATER

Road Movies Filmproduktion GmbH, Berlin, Wim Wenders Produktion, Berlin, in association with Viking Film, Stockholm. *Directors/ Screenplay:* Nicholas Ray, Wim Wenders. Director of photography: Ed Lachman. In colour. Video: Tom Farrell. Editor: Peter Przygodda (first version); Wim Wenders (definitive version). Music: Ronee Blakeley. Producers: Chris Sievernich, Pierre Cottrell.

Cast: (all playing themselves): Gerry Bamman, Ronee Blakeley, Pierre Cottrell, Stephan Czapsky, Mitch Dubin, Tom Farrell, Becky Johnston, Tom Kaufman, Maryte Kavaliauskas, Pat Kirck, Edward

Lachman, Martin Müller, Craig Nelson, Timothy Ray, Susan Ray, Nicholas Ray, Martin Schäfer, Chris Sievernich, Wim Wenders.

Premiere (first version): May 1980 (Cannes Festival); definitive version, November 1, 1980 (Internationale Filmtage, Hof). Running time: 116 min. (first version), 91 min. (definitive version).

Acting Roles

1977 DER AMERIKANISCHE FREUND
(THE AMERICAN FRIEND)

Road Movies Filmproduktion GmbH, Berlin/Wim Wenders Produktion, Munich/Les Films du Losange, Paris. Director: Wim Wenders. Screenplay: Wim Wenders. From the novel *Ripley's Game* by Patricia Highsmith. Director of photography: Robby Müller. Producer: Wim Wenders.

Cast: Bruno Ganz, Dennis Hopper, Lisa Kreuzer, Gérard Blain. As guests, the directors Nicholas Ray (Derwatt/Pogash), Samuel Fuller, Peter Lilienthal, Daniel Schmid, Alexander Whitelaw, Jean Eustache.

Premiere: May 26, 1977 (Cannes Festival). Running time: 126 min.

1979 HAIR

A Lester Persky and Michael Butler Production. Director: Milos Forman. Screenplay: Michael Weller. From the stage musical *Hair* by Gerome Ragni and James Rado (book and lyrics) and Galt MacDermot (music). Director of photography: Miroslav Ondricek. Producers: Lester Persky, Michael Butler.

Cast: John Savage, Treat Williams, Beverly D'Angelo, Annie Golden, Dorsey Wright, Don Dacus, Cheryl Barnes, Melba Moore, Ronnie Dyson, Richard Bright, Charlotte Rae, Nicholas Ray (The General).

Running time: 122 min.

Appearances in, or Contributions to, Documentary Films

1974 I'M A STRANGER HERE MYSELF

October Films, Cambridge (Massachusetts). Directors: David Helpern, Jr., James C. Gutman. Screenplay/Commentary: Myron Meisel.

Director of photography: Austin De Besche. 16mm colour. Editors: Richie Bock, Frank Galvin. Sound: Richie Bock. Commentary spoken by Howard Da Silva. Contributions by Nicholas Ray, John Houseman, François Truffaut, Natalie Wood, Tom Farrell, Leslie Levinson and the group from *We Can't Go Home Again*. Running time: 58 min. Premiere: January 7, 1975.

Television

1945 CLIMAX (series)

CBS: *Sorry, Wrong Number*. Production: John Houseman. *Direction:* Nicholas Ray. *Teleplay:* John Houseman, Nicholas Ray. From the radio play by Lucille Fletcher. Cast: Mildred Natwick. Broadcast: Summer 1945.

Running time: 30 min.

INDEX

216–217; on *Lightning Over Water*,
xxxvi–xxxvii, 213; loss of sight, xix,
xlvii; mother of (Lena Toppen), xli, 9,
22, 122, 207, 217; premonition of, xxiv,
xxviii, xxxvii; recovery from alcoholism of, xxxii–xliii; research of doctors
by, 158, 205–206; screen credits of,
219–234; sisters of (Alice, Ruth, Helen),
xli, 10–11, 23; teaching techniques of,
xxviii, xxix, xxxviii–xl, xlvii, 4, 6–7,
196; vision of, 154. *See also* Directing;
Director; Naturals; and *names of individual films and the Filmography in this
volume*
Ray, Susan (née Schwartz), xv–xl, passim, xlviii, 4, 8–9, 56, 157, 158, 160,
161, 164, 165, 166, 167, 172, 203,
205–213 passim, 216–217, 233
Ray, Timothy, xix, xxxi, xxxvi, xlv, 83,
159, 163, 175, 217, 231, 233
Realms of Gold, The (Drabble), 161
Rebel Without a Cause, xxvi, xlvi, 9, 39,
57–58, 62, 79, 88, 108, 115, 116, 120,
131, 226
Redgrave, Michael, 196
Red-Headed Stranger, The (Nelson), 170
Relaxation, 76, 126, 177. *See also* Con-
centration
Resettlement Administration, xliii
Rhythm, 132, 133, 134–136, 187
Rhodes, "Doc," 22
Richard III, 12, 142
Richardson, Sir Ralph, 1–2
RKO, xliv, xlv
Robinson, Earl, xlii, xliii
Rocky (Stallone), 154
Rogell, Syd, 123
Rogers, Will, 130
Rohmer, Eric, xlvi
Rolling Stones, xlvii
Roosevelt, Franklin, xlii, xliii, xliv, 123
Roseanna McCoy (Reis), xlv, 221
Rossellini, Roberto, 25
Rosenman, Leonard, 108, 226
Royal Family, The (Ferber), 24
Rules, 3–4, 85
Rush, Barbara, 58, 227
Russell, Jane, xlvi, 224, 226
Russell, Lord Bertrand, 123, 124
Ryan, Robert, 58, 106, 222, 223

San Sebastian Film Festival, xv, xxviii
Savage Innocents, xxvi, xlvi, 65, 106n,
189, 229
Saxe, Alfred, xlii

Schary, Dore, xliv, 153, 221
School for Scandal (Sheridan), 24
Schulberg, Budd, xlvi, 228
Schulberg, Stuart, xlvi, 228
Schwartz, Susan. *See* Ray, Susan
Script, 25, 189–193; breakdown of, 70,
91–104; central idea of, 91, 93; read-
through of, 16–17, 196; sub-actions in,
93, 99; techniques for writing of, xvii
Sea Gull, The (Chekhov), 201, 201n
Seeger, Charles, xliii
Seeger, Pete, xliii
Seldes, George, 191, 191n
Self-image, 62, 199
Self-pity, 38, 67, 68, 128, 164
Sesame Street, 154
Set, environment of, 61–62, 126,
195–196
Shakespeare, William, 46, 90, 115, 116
Shame, 18, 77, 79, 80
Shamraev, 201
Shaw, George Bernard, 33, 110, 224
Shepard, Sam, xxv, 70, 90
Showing, 34, 49, 51, 129, 184, 211. *See
also* Anticipating; Forcing; Indicating;
Telegraphing
Shulman, Irving, xlvi, 226
Sight and Sound, 189n
Signature. *See* Auteur theory
Silvers, Phil, 127–128
Simmons, Jack, 109
Simms, Taffy, 123, 124
Simon, Neil, 175
"Sit on it," 38, 68
Smith, Patti, 90
Sokolov, Anna, 73, 140
"Song of Myself" (Whitman), 155
Sorry, Wong Number, xliv, 234
Spectator, 140, 141
Stage Group, The, 139
Stage Left! (Williams), xxvn, xlii
Stanislavsky, Konstantin, 3, 38, 38n,
48–49, 60, 60n, 73, 83, 112, 131, 140,
157
Stanislavsky Produces Othello (Stanlis-
lavsky), 60, 60n
Stanwyck, Barbara, lxiv
State University of New York at Bing-
hamton (Harpur College), xxvii,
xxix–xxx, xlvii, 203
Stern, Isaac, 83
Stern, Stewart, xlvi, 39, 59, 226
Steve Canyon, 40
Stevens, George, 108